AMONG
THE
UKRAINIANS

AMONG THE UKRAINIANS

Peter Shirt

Laundry Press

TABLE OF CONTENTS

Symbol of Hope – Limonov: A Young Scoundrel – Lysenko and the Manipulation of Science – Smuggling Animals

To my sons

A Note on Transliteration and Names

Place-names and people's names are a tricky subject, especially for those whose native language is not Ukrainian or Russian. As a result, I have used the transliteration that I believe the non-native reader will encounter most commonly, and/or that which is most easily pronounced by the reader. The soft sign usually marked with an apostrophe has been omitted. References in the notes at the end of the book, however, follow the style of the individual publications.

Traditional Ukrainian and Russian names come in three parts. These are the first name, the patronymic, and the family name. Patronymic names are derived from the first name of a child's father. So, a boy, Alexei, whose father is called Ivan will be called Alexei Ivanovich and the boy's sister, let's say her name is Natalia, will be called Natalia Ivanivna. The patronymic is an official part of the name, and the respectful way to refer to a person, particularly in a formal situation, is by their first name and patronymic. In the book, in the interest of readability, I do not include patronymics either during conversations or when referring to other characters.

Most first names have many of nicknames and diminutives. Natalia may be referred to by those close to her as Natasha. Alexei, particularly when he is a small boy, might be referred to as Alyosha, Alyoshka, Alyoshenko, and so on. My family can often understand my mood or how serious I am about something by the way I refer to them, and when I first met my wife I thought she had many friends. It turned out to be just a few with many endearing nicknames. In order not to confuse the reader, I generally avoid using nicknames in the book.

To those who believe that these concessions to easier reading are not faithful to the Ukrainian or Russian languages, inconsistent, or wrong, I apologise.

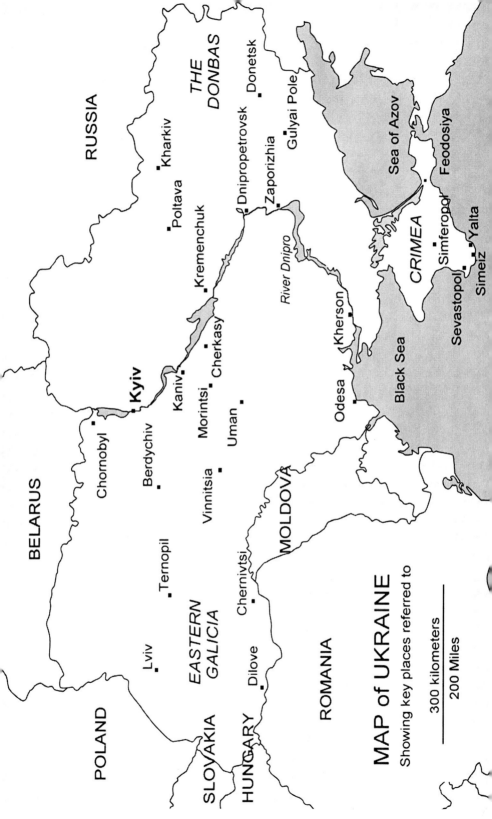

MAP of UKRAINE
Showing key places referred to

300 kilometers

200 Miles

BELARUS

POLAND

RUSSIA

SLOVAKIA

HUNGARY

ROMANIA

MOLDOVA

EASTERN GALICIA

THE DONBAS

CRIMEA

Lviv

Ternopil

Chernivtsi

Dilove

Vinnitsia

Berdychiv

Chornobyl

Kyiv

Kaniv

Morintsi

Uman

Cherkasy

Kremenchuk

Poltava

Kharkiv

Dnipropetrovsk

Donetsk

Zaporizhia

Gulyai Pole

Kherson

Odesa

Simferopol

Sevastopol

Simeiz

Yalta

Feodosiya

River Dnipro

Sea of Azov

Black Sea

INTRODUCTION

BEFORE EMBARKING ON THE STORY of the people of Ukraine, one of the first challenges I had to address was the question, "Who are Ukrainians?" And to do this I had to start with the geography of Ukraine.

Few realise just how big Ukraine is. If we exclude the Russian Federation, which is partly located in Asia, Ukraine is the largest country in Europe. Even fewer realise — and most are surprised to hear — that Ukraine sits at the geographical centre of Europe. In 1887, geographers from the Austro-Hungarian Empire set up a commemorating stone in the village of Dilove, in the Transcarpathian region. Though at least five other locations contest the honour (depending on what you measure), the point to note is that it's a cultural and political notion, rather than a geographical one, that Ukraine lies on Europe's eastern edge. European Union Commissioners please note: Ukrainians are Europeans, and not Eurasians.

Many people have suggested that the origin of the name "Ukraine" means "Borderland," which is the title of Anna Reid's book about Ukraine, published in 1999. Whilst this may be true, I believe it is incorrect to infer that Ukraine is located at the extremity "beyond which," in the words of the early mapmakers, "there be dragons." It is more appropriate to consider Ukraine as a crossing point where people trade and intermarry, and where ideas are exchanged.

Let's look at the evidence. If we look to history, parts or the whole of Ukraine has at one time or another been controlled by

Russians, Austrians, Frenchmen, Swedes, Poles, Greeks, Germans, Lithuanians, Bulgarians, Turks, Tatars, and Mongols. Today Ukraine shares an international border with seven other countries (Russia, Moldavia, Rumania, Hungary, Slovakia, Poland, and Belarus), and no country has a greater number of neighbours. And the latest census data (2001) shows that more than one hundred and thirty nationalities and ethnic groups call Ukraine "home." This exposure to diverse sources of people, culture, and arts has made for a long and colourful, but turbulent history.

Nowadays when foreigners think about ordinary Ukrainians — and I'm expressly excluding the rich elite here — or for that matter people from other former Soviet republics, the stereotype they invoke is invariably one of conformity; a drably dressed proletariat in outdated fashion. Despite what the census data says about diversity, we see a monolithic society populated by *Homo Sovieticus*.

After nearly three hundred years of Russian rule as part of the Empire, and then the Soviet Union, this conformity is hardly surprising. One of the goals of the Soviet system was the creation of a unified people with the single social identity of "Soviet." Nationality became secondary, delegated to indicating ancestry and leading to the odd consequence that siblings or even identical twins may hold passports of different nationalities. Often a boy would take his father's nationality, and a girl would take her mother's.

I first visited the Soviet Union in the winter of 1981, at the height of the Cold War. Travelling from Nahodka (near Vladivoskok) in the Russian Far East, to St. Petersburg on the shores of the Baltic Sea, I was overwhelmed by the size of the land and the diversity of people and places. If the journey was taken unbroken on the Trans-Siberian Express it was a journey of ten days, and, if I recall correctly, some ninety-six stops.

It is impossible for me not to have preconceptions, but that journey laid bare the idea of the Soviet Union as a monolith. Supervised constantly by an Intourist Guide, I was introduced to a dozen or so ethnic people during the journey who introduced themselves proudly.

"I'm a Yakut," said a man, hitting his breastbone with his fingers. He was just one of more than forty five indigenous peoples living in Russia. He was intrigued by my Polaroid camera, having never had his picture taken before.

"I'm Tatar," said another, shaking my hand vigorously.

Yet — and this is the reason I recount the anecdote — my guide referred to all of them as Russian or Soviet, using the two words interchangeably.

In post war period, it was common to believe that industrialisation, urbanisation, and the Soviet policies would erode ethnic or national characteristics, and Western historians, journalists, and writers also joined the party by incorrectly concluding that the nationality issue had been solved.

Many fell into this trap.

A few years after my journey, Colin Thubron wrote his now famous classic, *Among the Russians,* which is described as "A vivid account of a journey he made by car from St. Petersburg (then Leningrad) and the Baltic States south to Georgia and Armenia towards the end of the Brezhnev era."

Not many living in those countries, I suspect, would agree to the label "Russian."

And more commonplace examples abound. Following the Chornobyl explosion, *TIME* magazine published a photo of "Chornobyl, Russia." The first President of Ukraine, Leonid Kravchuk, was occasionally asked by Western diplomats, "In which part of Russia was Ukraine located?" and both the BBC and the New York Times often refer to writer Nikolai Gogol as "the Russian writer, Gogol."

The idea that the Ukrainians, as well as Georgians, Belarusians and so on, are first and foremost Russians and Soviets was firmly established.

"Does it really matter? We're all brothers," responded a Russian colleague in Moscow, after I had reeled off a list of names of famous Ukrainians claimed by Russia. He was implying the distinction was both tiresome and petty.

Perhaps he has a point. Perhaps the wound caused by the excise of

Ukraine from Russia is still not healed. But, on the other hand, being part of an independent nation means having heroes of whom you can be proud, and who embody the values and spirit of the people. I might get away with referring to Robert Burns as being a British poet, I thought in response to his challenge, but I wouldn't fancy my chances of leaving alive a Scottish New Year's party if I insisted that he was an English poet.

What happened in practice was that Ukrainians who achieved something significant were, and continue to be, referred to as Russian or Soviet. Worthy Ukrainians were either elevated to Russian or Soviet heroes or discredited. Scientists, doctors, and engineers were promoted to the Russian (later Soviet) Academy of Sciences in St. Petersburg, and distinguished men and women were awarded titles such as "Hero of the Soviet Union," "Pilot Cosmonaut of the Soviet Union," and "Inventor of the Soviet Union."

If we review this labelling in the context of Ukraine as an independent country with its own history — as this book tries to do — some of the greatest artists, scientists, engineers, and doctors should be referred to as Ukrainian first, and Soviet second, but not Russian.

This is not an attempt to claim that Ukrainians are very different from Russians. Of course, Ukrainians — particularly those who live or lived in the east of the country — are very close in terms of culture, language, behavior, and attitudes, and we mustn't forget that there are eight million ethnic Russians in Ukraine's population of nearly forty-six million people. Such similarities are to be expected when two peoples live together, side by side, for centuries. The differences, on the other hand, are subtle, and I've explored them further in the book. For now, let me sum it up with a joke that alludes to the distinctness:

A Russian and a Ukrainian find a US$100 note lying on the ground, and the Russian picks it up.

"Let's split it like brothers," he suggests.

"No," replies the Ukrainian, "let's split it 50-50."

So, the approach I have taken to defining "Who is a Ukrainian?" is a pragmatic one that follows the lead of the Ukrainian Constitution. It is a territorial approach that refers to the "People of Ukraine" as being those who live in the nation of Ukraine, as defined by its current boundaries. Those who were born in this territory, including historical characters, and those who have lived most of their life in Ukraine, were considered subject matter for this book. It is a compromise that will throw up some interesting questions and probably provoke disagreement, and you must decide whether or not it is successful.

Finally, a few words about what the book is, and what it is not. I feel myself neither qualified, nor desiring, to write a history. So, there is no chronology to the book, and I may have omitted whole periods of history. It is not a travel guide, but I do describe my experience of living in Ukrainian cities and of traveling to many of the regions of Ukraine.

I shine my torch beam on characters and events and try to illuminate things as seen through the eyes of contemporary Ukrainians. And the reader who is patient enough to finish the book will realise that this is not an erudite work, but an account of real lives, past, and present, sometimes based on incomplete information, or perhaps from a biased perspective.

It is a journey of discovery, and, like all journeys, the direction and speed of travel is never constant, the planning is occasionally inadequate or flexible (depending on your interpretation), and I or my companions may be unreliable. Some of the people you will encounter on the following pages are ordinary — but I hope that none of them are dull as a consequence — and many of them are extraordinary. All of them, I believe, have something to tell us.

For me, the idea that the Ukrainian people deserved to be more widely known for their contribution to history developed slowly, but insistently. Between plaster boarding and paying bribes to get work completed in my house, everything I read, or everyone I spoke to, gave me a snippet of a story or a nuance of the Ukrainian way of life that I felt had rarely been told before. And that was how this book came about. It is the story of my travels through contemporary Ukraine where I met ordinary people, shared with them the joys and endless challenges of daily life, and many of the remarkable, under-recognised people of Ukraine who contributed to her history.

PONDERING UKRAINE'S CONTROVERSIAL HISTORY

THE DRIVER'S WINDOW of the black Mercedes glided down silently as we approached the guard post. The interpreter, seated in the front passenger seat, broke the nervous silence of the passengers. "The Borovitsky Gate is the oldest entrance to the Moscow Kremlin which was built on the instructions of Grand Prince Yury Dolgoruky," he said.

"You know that means that the citadel of the all-Russian people was built by a man from Ukraine," I responded. "I'm increasingly of the view that Ukrainian people deserve to be more widely known for their contribution to history."

Yury Dolgoruky was the founder of Moscow and, in 1954, an imposing monument of him, mounted on a horse, was erected on Moscow's Tverskaya Street, the city's principal avenue that leads down to the Kremlin. He died during the first year of construction of the Kremlin, and his body was laid to rest in the Saviour Church in Berestovo in Kyiv.

"Perhaps Ukrainians should be more highly regarded in Moscow," I suggested.

"I wouldn't say that too loudly in this neighbourhood," retorted the interpreter. "President Putin recently questioned Ukraine's very existence as a sovereign state."

"But don't you agree it's true? Yury Dolgoruky was the great, great grandson of Vladimir I of Kyiv, the Grand Prince, who brought Christianity to this entire region in 987. I'd say that deserves some recognition."

I was then remembering the fact that President Putin considers the collapse of the Soviet Union to be the biggest geopolitical disaster of the twentieth century, and that Ukraine played a significant role in the collapse. Many in Russia hold the view that Ukraine is simply a political idea that was born in the nineteenth century and used by Austria and Germany, in particular, to undermine the unity of the Russian state.

Yury's father, Vladimir Monomakh, was also a Grand Prince of Kyiv and he is buried in Kyiv's Saint Sophia Cathedral. His head cap, nowadays called "Monomakh's Cap" or the "Golden Cap," was the crown of all the Muscovite Grand Princes and Tsars, from Dmitri Donskoi to Peter the Great. A symbol of Russian autocracy, it is the oldest crown displayed at the Kremlin Armoury.

The driver exchanged words with the security guard, and we proceeded through the Borovitsky Gate into the Kremlin. Now the interpreter, who had been pondering my comments, said, insistently, "Kyivan Rus was the start of Russian history, not Ukrainian history."

"But how can you deprive the Ukrainians of this history and call it Russian history when it took place in their capital city?"

I recalled that Edward I of England defeated the Scots and ceased the Coronation Stone which then resided in Westminster Cathedral for seven centuries. But that doesn't mean the Scottish people have no right to their history.

"Stop this nonsense," barked the businessman seated to my right in the back of the car.

He had been unusually quiet, perhaps pondering the tactics for the meeting with the Russian President, or still agitated by the refusal of the President's administrative staff to allow him to travel by helicopter into the Kremlin from his private jet at Vnukovo Airport. This was a privilege the Russian President had only allowed once before to a visiting US President.

His eyes bore down on me, and his Yorkshire accent roughed up the edges of his words as he said sternly, "If you mention Ukraine during this meeting, I'll have your guts for garters."

It was both the first and last time that I entered the Kremlin without paying.

Russian versus Ukrainian History

The idea that Russia's history, rather than Ukraine's, started with Kyivan Rus — the largest contemporary European state by area, dominated by the city of Kyiv from about 880 to around the middle of the twelfth century — strikes me as rather odd. Of the few histories I have read, they all seem to start with primitive indigenous people, or early agriculturalists, and not in the medieval period. And they never start in someone else's capital city.

And yet the idea is common.

The History of Russia, published in 1854 by Walter Kelly, starts the synopsis by saying "It was in the ninth century of our era that the first step was taken towards combining those loose elements under the sway of a conquering race, which imposed its own name on the vanquished. From that point, therefore, we date the rise of the Russian Empire."

More recently, *A History of Russia* by John Lawrence informs us that "the Kyivan era is the cradle of Russia," and in his history of Russia, Vladimir Volkoff advances the idea that "Russia begins with Vladimir the Baptist."

The statements are all the more surprising because they are written by Western historians who had the privilege of objective analysis. But in almost any book of Russian history that you care to pick up, you can find similar statements and a line of reasoning that has the transparency of borscht soup.

Why, for example, have historians described the Austro-Hungarian lands as a multinational empire, but referred to Russia (including Ukraine and Belarus) as a homogenous empire? In doing so they made Ukraine part of an empire before it could become a nation. How do they reconcile the fact that the term "Ukraine" came into use in the twelfth century, but the term "Russia" was only coined in the eighteenth century by Peter the Great? Did they not realise that tenth-century Kyiv, with a population of fifty thousand people, was probably two and a half times the size of London, and the largest city in Europe? Yet, not a single brick had been laid to build Moscow?

Indeed, if you follow the logic of some historians who say that the Princes of Vladimir, Suzdal, and Moscow claimed sovereignty over Kyiv because of dynastic links, the English could also have a claim. Vladimir Monomakh's first wife was Gytha of Wessex, the daughter of King Harold of England, who, according to tradition, was killed by an arrow in the eye at the Battle of Hastings.

What I am missing, of course, is the idea of survivor bias. The idea that Ukraine either has no separate history, or that its history is subordinate to and part of Russia's history, is because Ukrainian history has rarely been written by Ukrainians. History is written by the victor and the Russian view has always prevailed.

With the exception of a brief period following World War I, no independent Ukrainian state existed until the collapse of the Soviet Union in 1991, and those people — mostly a handful of Ukrainian historians who expressed views contrary to the Russian view — were dismissed in a cursory manner as "Nationalists" and were either marginalised, or worse, silenced.

In general, the strong-arm tactics employed by Russia are because the concept of "Russia" — which constitutes the huge land area — has always been made up of many diverse ethnic groups. The social contract has always been that these groups submit to the powerful leader in order to survive. Part of the glue that holds the fabric together — what Bernard Lewis would term "the foundation myth" — is the need for Russia to attach herself to something significant, in order to improve or conceal her humble origins. In Russia's case, the foundation myth states that the "Mother of Russian cities" is Kyiv, and that the Great Russians are the natural leaders of their east Slav brothers, the "Little Russians" (Ukrainians), and the "White Russians" (Belarusians).

I don't know why Western historians have not produced more objective histories of Ukraine, but it would appear to distil down to three excuses: they lacked objective source material, they have reworked old material, or they coveted their access to Russian and Soviet leading figures. Thankfully, recently written histories — and a few histories that until now have been suppressed for decades — are beginning to provide a more balanced view, and one that proposes that Kyivan history is a predecessor of Ukraine, Belarus, and Russia.

President Putin was not moved to accept our business proposition on that day in 2003, and the following year, after twenty-five years of corporate service and a few years of living in Moscow, I quit my job. Disillusioned with corporate life, and exhausted, I needed a change. I bought a run-down house in Ukraine that was sorrowed by decades of negligence, and set about breathing new life into it.

When I told people what I was doing, a common reply was, "Oh, that's where so-and-so comes from." The names included the President who was poisoned, the Prime Minister with the plaited hairstyle, the feisty brunette who won the Eurovision Song Contest, and the footballer bought by Chelsea. Chornobyl was commonly mentioned often, but, for the most part, people thought Ukraine lay somewhere beyond Germany, and had been part of the Soviet Union.

Older friends pointed out that "they fought on our side" during World War II. But no one realised their death toll was between five and eight million. Even the lower figure is greater than the military losses of the United States, the British Commonwealth, Canada, France, Germany, Japan, and Italy combined.

There was no awareness that Ukrainians had invented the antibiotic, the first parallel-processing computer, built the space ship that put the first man in space, discovered X-rays, won the Olympics on behalf of the Soviet Union, or provided the inspiration for the character of James Bond — just to name a handful of successes. Worldwide, these things made people's lives easier, led to breakthrough developments in science, or entertained millions.

If my friends had met a Ukrainian at all, the chances were that she worked in a bar, or he was working as a plumber using a false Polish visa.

More surprising to me was that Ukrainians didn't know their own history, and that people from different regions within Ukraine believed a different history. Some shrugged their shoulders. They had heard too many versions of their history to take it seriously, and anyway, it didn't put bread on the table.

As one man explained it, "The Soviet politicians told us what they wanted us to believe, and the Ukrainian politicians tell us what we want to hear." He recalled that the people had only heard about the 1930s man-made famine in the 1980s. It devoured, perhaps, ten million Ukrainian lives — the equivalent of a 9-11 terrorist attack every day for fifty years (for the United States to suffer a corresponding loss). Yet, it had remained a secret for fifty years.

A personal story, told to me by a young woman and poignant because of the story's setting and her age at the time, provides some insight into when the Soviets lost control of history.

History in Chaos

"Sit down, Maxim," the history examiner ordered the boy, the cleverest in the class. "Tell me everything you know about Mykhailo Hrushevsky's book, *An Illustrated History of Ukraine.*"[1]

Maxim thought for a few moments, and his classmate Irena, who recounted the tale to me, recalled how he shuffled uneasily in his chair. The Soviets prohibited the book because it offered a view of Ukrainian history that differed from the Russian view of Soviet historiography.

"I know nothing about the book," Maxim answered, suspecting it was some sort of trick, "but Hrushevsky was a historian who fought for an independent Ukrainian state and who later repented and became a Bolshevik."

Irena and eight other colleagues sat at the back of the room, waiting their turn to sit in the exam chair. They barely dared to look at the examiner.

"Is that it?" The examiner looked disappointed.

Normally the exam process would involve each of them randomly selecting a piece of paper from among many that lay on a table. On each was written a different question, and the students would spend a few minutes gathering their thoughts before taking turns to sit in the seat and answer it.

"I shall leave you for a few minutes so you can discuss if you all want to continue with the exam. If so, for each of you the price for grade 5 is twenty-five roubles, for grade 4, twenty roubles and so on."

Irena was a conscientious 14-year-old student then. "My nerves were on edge," she recalled. "It was the first time any of us had been asked directly for a bribe, but the discussion was brief."

"We'll choose option two," answered Maxim when the examiner returned, "and we'll talk to our parents this evening about how much each of us can pay."

Only later did it become apparent what had happened. The Central Examination Board for History was in chaos. As part of Perestroika, articles had recently appeared in journals, obviously with official sanction, stating unambiguously that Soviet history would need to be rewritten. Because of the confusion, neither pre-set exam questions nor independent examiners were being sent to the schools, and disillusioned history teachers had been told to muddle through as best they could.

The following year the history exam was scrapped completely throughout Soviet schools and a topical joke at the time was, "Who can tell what is going to happen yesterday!"

The Challenge of Independence

As I pondered the route that Ukraine has followed in the last twenty years, I was torn between disappointment that progress towards a better economy and social justice hasn't been greater, and awe at the size of the challenge Ukraine has faced since it gained independence — not least because of the determination of Russia to return Ukraine to its jurisdiction. These were issues I had discussed during a recent visit to the British Ambassador's residence in Moscow.

I was attending a breakfast meeting at the Embassy hosted by the Ambassador in honour of the visit of a Secretary of State, and as I and a group of about twenty businessmen waited for the Secretary to arrive, I recalled I had first visited the Embassy in the winter of 1981. Then, I found it to be an island of safety in a steely-grey sea of foreignness. A friend in England had told me to look at the snow-covered roof to decipher messages scrawled in the snow. Satellites passing overhead, he assured me, would transmit the top secret information to London. Now, such naivety is long gone.

The green-roofed British Ambassador's residence stands by the Moscow River on the Embankment of Saint Sophia. Opposite stands the indomitable Kremlin, its imposing brick red wall punctuated by watchtowers. In 1931, Stalin agreed to allow the British to use the building as its Embassy in the Soviet Union, but regretted it soon afterwards upon seeing the gaily coloured Union Jack flying on its roof.

The house was built by the Ukrainian Pavel Kharitonenko in the 1890s. Pavel inherited the most profitable sugar business in Ukraine (and the Russian Empire), but he preferred life in Moscow. He demolished the sugar storage depot that existed on the riverside site and built a traditional Muscovite-style house, one that would surprise guests with its gothic-style interior complete with an oak-panelled Scottish baronial hallway, carved ceiling, and a broad staircase defended by a majestic eagle. With an appropriately large white and gold ballroom, the magnificent mansion was designed for grand formal entertaining.

A few minutes after the Secretary arrived we took our seats at the large table where a traditional English breakfast was being served. A bald-headed businessman seated to my left asked me to pass the bread.

"Do you think the 'bread basket' of Ukraine will once again be controlled by Russia?" I asked, as he delicately lifted a croissant from the basket. I knew it was a common view that Russia cannot regain the status of world power without controlling Ukraine.

"I think it's likely, and if not overtly, then covertly," replied the experienced Russia-watcher. "The loss of Ukraine was deeply unsettling to Russia, and it's sobering to recall that Ukraine was a part of the Russian Empire before Texas or California was part of the

USA. Yet, imagine Washington's reaction to an independent California or Texas!"

According to this view, Ukraine is a pawn in the bigger game of power politics between Russia and others. The tension is heightened now that the goodwill that was generated towards Ukraine by the Orange Revolution has dissipated. Ukraine has failed to grasp the opportunity and remains mired in its own internal power struggles at the time when Europe and the USA may allow the Russians greater freedom in their own back yard, in exchange for cooperation in neutering Iran's nuclear ambitions.

"The size of the challenge facing Ukraine following independence cannot be overstated," he continued. "Most experts made the error of believing that Ukraine would be the first of the former Soviet states to stabilize because it was the most industrialized. But it wasn't a simple case of taking a scalpel and cutting it off from mother Russia."

As I learned later, Ukraine had almost none of the essentials for independent life: no banking system, no currency, no tax collection system, no foreign relations or embassies or border customs, no separate identification of its citizens, no property rights, and no experience of self-governance. Fully four-fifths of all industrial businesses had part of their process cycle (material sourcing, transport or sales, for example) outside of Ukrainian territory. Nearly all the networks that the Soviets had built converged on Moscow (rather than Kyiv), and ties between adjacent Ukrainian regions or cities were weak or nonexistent.

"A quick review of other countries facing the challenge of independence shows that they had it easier than Ukraine," added the businessman. Over the next few minutes he reeled off a list of countries. The Baltic States, for example, had been independent nations before being swallowed up into the Soviet Union. Latin American countries had the makings of a market economy when they embarked on their route towards democracy. And former colonies of Great Britain and France, such as India and Vietnam respectively, had an emerging middle class and a functioning civil service when they achieved independence.

The businesman's concluding comment was that most Ukrainians don't really know who they are; a point made strongly by those versed in the history of statehood who say that Ukrainians as a community of people should, at least, have been defined before they obtained their nation state. The wording of the first official post-Independence documents pandered to the nationalist voices by referring to "the Ukrainian people," but Ukraine's population aren't a heterogeneous group and millions of ethnic Russians in the east and in Crimea felt excluded. Five years later, the phrase had evolved subtly to "the people of Ukraine" but the fundamental issue of identity remains.

VIKINGS AND COSSACKS

"UKRAINE, YOU SAW, YOU CONQUERED," read the poster on the side of the gangplank as I boarded the cruise boat for a trip down the River Dnipro.

In the fourth century BC, when the river was called Boryshpen, Herodotus described it as "the most beautiful river of them all." Today, despite centuries on an unhealthy diet of sewerage and industrial chemicals, Europe's third largest river is still impressive. Also impressive is the Dnipro Princess. Longer than a football pitch, and with four decks, she seems somewhat out of place nearly a thousand kilometres from the sea.

A sudden judder signals that she had set sail, and slowly but steadily the night lights of the city and the illuminated pear-shaped gold domes of the Kyiv's churches — subtly different from the onion-shaped domes of Moscow and St. Petersburg — recede into the distance. Some thirty-six hours downstream lays the city of Zaporizhia whose region was the home to the Cossacks.

Of Ukraine's national symbols, the Cossack is perhaps the most enduring, endearing, and most caricatured, being used to sell anything from frozen pelmeni (a sort of Ukrainian gnocchi), to clothes and beer. The symbol is also special because it is not claimed by anyone else as a national hero. The Cossack was, and is, Ukraine's national hero.

For evidence, you need look no further than the nation's coat of arms. On the left it features a shield supported by a crowned lion from the Galician coat of arms, and on the right a Cossack in traditional dress wielding a musket, the symbol of the Cossack state. Sitting on top is the crown of Vladimir the Great, symbolizing Ukrainian sovereignty, and red fruits and wheat adorn the bottom of the coat of arms, symbolizing the country's agricultural heritage.

There are two overwhelming reasons why people of diverse origins have migrated to Ukraine over the millennia. The first was to exploit the abundance of natural resources. Quite simply, no nation in Europe has more abundant natural resources than Ukraine. Secondly, they were en route to somewhere else and Ukraine was merely an obstacle.

Natural Resources

Archaeological evidence has shown that it is a misconception that the steppe, the vast grassland of Ukraine, was uninhabited before the arrival of the Cossacks. Excavations have found some of the earliest evidence of grain cultivation in Europe, dating from seven thousand years ago. For more than two millennia before the birth of Christ, southern Ukraine functioned as a source of cereals for the towns and cities of the Black Sea that traded with the classical civilizations of the Aegean and Mediterranean seas.

Much later, people would learn that Ukraine has one-third of the world's most fertile black soils (called *Chernozerms*), and it would become the breadbasket of the Russian Empire and the Soviet Union. Hitler also recognised the fertility of Ukraine, once remarking that he needed Ukraine so Germany would never be hungry. In the late Soviet period, Ukraine produced a quarter of the Soviet Union's entire agricultural output. A favourable climate and a readily available water supply make it a veritable Garden of Eden.

By the eighteenth century it was also becoming apparent that Ukraine was blessed with magnificent mineral wealth, and this was to form the basis of Russia's industrial development. In Soviet times, Ukraine was one of the world's most important mineral producing countries, responsible for the production of nearly five percent of the world's mineral products. At the zenith of the Soviet Union's power, Ukraine supplied one-half of the iron ore, one-quarter of the coal, and one-third of the steel for Soviet industrial production. Whether these resources were used to make swords and canon, railway lines, or satellites, whoever controlled these resources controlled one of the key drivers of political and economic power.

The Tsars and the Soviets knew this only too well. The model that Moscow pursued was to use Ukraine as a source of primary raw materials and heavy industry processing, and to give them finished consumer goods in return. In practice, finished goods were scarce, and with nothing to buy, workers could be kept on subsistence wages. This was the unsustainable model of Communism.

Ukraine's Geo-Strategic Position

Defending Ukraine from those who came to exploit her resource wealth was particularly difficult. The great tablecloth of the steppes covers the whole central swathe of the country, with mountains serving as natural defences only in the southwest (the Carpathian range) and in the south (the Crimean range).

Some of the earliest invaders came from Scandinavia, and used the Dnipro as a commercial north-south trade route to Greece. As trade grew, Kyiv developed on the site of a defensible promontory overlooking the mighty river. The city's location was also on the tongue of land that extended from between the Caspian Sea and the Ural Mountains, and through which poured the savage and mysterious hordes of the eastern lands.

As Snowyd wrote eloquently in 1935, "By the very geographical position of their country, the Ukrainians were made into the vanguard of the western world against the hordes of white and yellow nomads rolling in waves through the 'gate of the people.'"[1]

Though it is barely recognized in the West, the Mongol hoards were stopped in their tracks in Ukraine, and the flowering arts and cultures of Western Europe were spared debasement.

Nowadays, we commonly refer to the aspect of a country's geographical location as its "geo-strategic position," and in this context Ukraine has played a historical role as a "buffer" state. It is a demeanour that has proved impossible to throw off. It was familiar to the armies of Napoleon or Hitler as they tried to march eastwards to Moscow, and it was familiar to the Russian Communists as they tried, but failed, to join forces with sympathizers in the Balkans in the 1920s.

This is pertinent because it may well be the predominant theme of Ukraine's history in the early decades of the twenty-first century. Ukraine is destined to remain a buffer zone unless it can find the right balance in its orientation to Western Europe and the USA on one hand, and Russia on the other. Since all will accept Ukraine only on their terms, this makes Ukraine a pawn that each of them will play in a grand political game.

I had been thinking about all of these things as the Dnipro Princess was making its way downstream toward the city of Zaporizhia. By 7 a.m. the next morning, industrious hands had set the breakfast tables in the dining room and cooked a meal. Outside, on deck, all the signs were that it would be a warm spring day. The air was still chilled and the sky was marred by a few isolated cumulous clouds. The ship cast a pale shadow on the plate-like river as we appeared to float effortlessly past rolling hills and forest groves.

During breakfast I met a small group of Scandinavians who were searching for evidence of their family histories. In 1781, one thousand Swedes left the community of Hiiumaa, in the eastern Baltic, for a new life on the fertile black soils of the steppe. After several months of trekking they made home just about a hundred kilometres from the mouth of the Dnipro, and established the town of Gammalsvenskby (which means "old Swedish town"). More than half perished during the trek, and by the end of the next winter less than one hundred and fifty people survived. But from this small core the community survived through wars and famines, and today some of the townsfolk still speak Swedish.

Arrival of the Vikings

The extent to which Norsemen (a tribe also known as "Varangians" who originated from the area of Roslagen County in Sweden) played a role in establishing Kyivan Rus, the region centred on Kyiv, is a subject of hot controversy. The earliest written history, *The Chronicle of Bygone Years*, dates from 1116, and was written by Sylvester, Prior of St. Michael's, during the reign of Price Vladimir in Kyiv. From a version of the text transcribed in 1377, Sylvester is clear about the invitation to the Varangians by the Slavic tribes who occupied the region. He wrote:

> There was no law among them, but tribe rose against tribe. Discord thus ensued among them, and they began to war one against another. They said to themselves, 'Let us seek a prince who may rule over us and judge us according to the law.' They accordingly went overseas to the Varangian Russes: these particular Varangians were known as Russes, just as some are called Swedes and others Normans, English, and Gotlanders, for they were thus named. The East-Slavic peoples said to the people of Rus, 'Our whole land is great and rich, but there is no order in it. Come to rule and reign over us.'

This text is problematic for many Russians because it implies that the Slavs were incapable of establishing their own state, and that Russia did not have a purely Slavic birth. As a result, many Russian historians have adopted a difficult position; they claim the heritage of Kyivan Rus for Russia, but they reject the evidence of how it came about.

Rus, Ruthenians, and Russia

Undoubtedly, the issue is clouded by the similarity of the words, Rus and Russia. This is a confusion created largely by Russian and Soviet politicians, as well as by historians for political purposes.

Kyivan Rus became the geographical term referring to the land around Kyiv, and it most probably derives from the name of the people of Roslagen, the Varangians. The people of Kyivan Rus were known as "Rusyny" or Ruthenians, but the people of the northeast, particularly those in the Vladimir-Moscow-Suzdal principalities in what is now Russia, did not adopt the term, preferring the name "Moscali" from the twelfth century onwards. This separate identity suggests that they have a weak claim to the Kyivan state.

The word "Russia," which people confuse as being the same as, or a modern variation of, the word Rus, only came into usage in the eighteenth century when Peter the Great used it to describe his realm. The word "Ukraine," on the other hand, was in use from the twelfth century onwards.

That the Varangians played a role is certain. Aside from my rudimentary observation that the colours of the national flags of Sweden and Ukraine are the same, archaeologists have uncovered an abundance of evidence. Coins excavated from the northern Russian city of Novgorod date precisely from the time of the invitation. Burial chambers contain the trademark circular shield of the Vikings. Hundreds of place names and names of rivers in Ukraine are of Scandinavian origin, and thousands of Ukrainian people are named Oleh, Olha, and Ihor from the names of the Viking gods Helge, Helga, and Ingvar. Newly discovered sources, including works written in Arabic, Latin, and Icelandic, all confirm the presence of the Varangians.

Adolf Hitler had his own crude way of phrasing it when he commented that, "Unless other peoples, beginning with the Vikings, had imported some rudiments of organization into Russian humanity, the Russians would be living like rabbits."[2]

From the evidence available, it seems highly probable that the Varangian Prince Riurik made the journey to Novgorod in the 850s, and that by the 870s the Varangians had taken control of cities such as Smolensk and Kyiv. Whether the Varangian's subjugated the Slavs and ruled by force, or had a more balanced relationship based on, say, commercial trade, we do not know. But the warring tribes were quelled, and over the next two centuries Kyivan Rus emerged as the largest state in Europe, and as a multi-ethnic, unified social and economic entity based on Christianity and the gradual emergence of the Slav languages.

The Bishop of Saxon Titmar of Merseburg, a German clergyman of the eleventh century, characterized Kyiv in his chronicles as "a big city with more than four hundred churches, eight marketplaces, and uncountable number of citizens."[3]

The ruler of Kyivan Rus, Yaroslav the Wise, did much to strengthen ties with Western Europe. No one knows how the marriage came about, but his daughter Anna married Henry I King of France, and became the regent, ruling the country in the name of her son. She took with her from Kyiv a missal – a book of prayers and rites — and all French monarchs, except the Bonapartes, were crowned after swearing their oaths on it. (In 2005, Ukrainian President Victor Yushchenko was among the guests of honour at an unveiling ceremony of a statue of Anna of Kyiv in France.)

Yaroslav also introduced a form of democracy called, a "Veche," a town council comprised of all free male citizens who would discuss such matters as war, law, and who would rule each town. But by establishing a system of princedoms in which succession moved from father to son, from elder to younger brother, and from uncle to nephew, he sowed the seeds for the state's demise. Hundreds of princes put forward succession claims, numerous disputes ensued, and the slow break-up of the eastern Slavs began.

The Mongol Influence

In the middle of the twelfth century the cities of Novgorod and Suzdal both rebelled against Kyiv's primacy, leaving the loose confederation of states severely weakened and vulnerable to attack. In 1240, the nomadic Mongols from the east, led by the grandson of Genghis Khan, conducted a series of bloody wars, defeating the Kyivan state and warring with the other main principalities.

Perhaps more than any other event, the Mongol invasion shaped the political, religious, and cultural history of the Vladimir-Moscow-Suzdal principalities, and what would later become "Russia."

The Mongols banished the free speech of the Veche, conducted censuses of citizens five hundred years before they became widespread in Western Europe, and implemented a strict process of conscription and tax collection. It was a foretaste of the strong central government that has come to characterise Russia until today.

The downfall of the princes allowed the Orthodox Church to rise as the embodiment of both religious and national identity, and in 1322 the centre of the Orthodox Church relocated from Kyiv to Moscow. Moscovy now became inward-looking and suppressed, a principality seeking solace in faith. It was clearly on a different development trajectory than Kyivan Rus.

Prince Danylo of Halych, grandson of Vladimir Monomakh and head of the Galicia-Volynia principality in what is now western Ukraine, checked the westward advance of the Mongols and managed to recapture Kyiv to become the king of Kyivan Rus. Though he eventually had to accept the Mongol dominion, he built a number of cities, such as Lviv, where he continued progressive policies that were not unlike the Veche. He protected the peasantry from exploitation and encouraged Armenian, Jewish, and German merchants to settle in the cities, thus creating a thriving community open to a wide range of cultural influences, including close contacts with the Roman Catholic Church. Danylo's rule — enlightened for the historical period — promoted values that would later come to characterise the Cossacks of the Ukrainian steppes.

The Dnipro Hydroelectric Dam

According to my guidebook:

> On November 8, 1927, on the tenth anniversary of the October Revolution in fulfilment of the legacies of V. I. Lenin, leader of the world's proletariat, and by the efforts of the working masses of the first Labor Government in the world — the Union of Soviet Socialist Republics — the governments of the USSR and the Ukrainian SSR laid the foundations of the Dnipro

hydroelectric station, with a capacity of 650,000 horsepower, a powerful level of socialistic construction of the USSR.[4]

So began the five-year construction of Europe's largest dam, which set a world record for poured concrete (1.2 million cubic metres) and heralded the period of construction of other Soviet showpieces such as the Moscow-Volga Canal, the industrial centres at Magnitogorsk and Novosibirsk east of the Urals, and the Moscow Underground.

Now, as I stood on the elevated platform of the Dnipro Princess' sun deck, it looked as though we had come to the edge of the world because the hand of man had stopped the flow of the river. The rolling, hilly landscape was long behind us, and the river now flowed across a flat plain covered with meadows and forests. From upstream the Dnipro dam is disappointing, naturally, but as you descend the sixty-metre lock, emerge downstream and then look back, you begin to contemplate the feat of engineering here.

The guidebook's purely technical description emphasizes the "Sectionalized-type construction" of the dam, but there is also a strong emotional component to the experience; awe of the human effort that built it, and recognition of man's smallness and vulnerability as it towers above the ship.

With a candour that would have been unthinkable in Soviet times, my guidebook added, "The absence of a drainage system in the foundation should be considered an unfortunate design decision: only a grout curtain was provided for reducing seepage under the dam."[5]

Visiting Zaporozhia and the Island of Khortytsia

Shortly afterwards, the ship docked at the city of Zaporizhia (which means "behind the cataracts"), and I was met on the dock by Stanislav, a local historian who works as a guide at the Cossack Museum on Khortytsia Island. He sported a Cossack moustache and a forelock, called "oseledets" in Ukraine.

Driving through the nondescript industrial city that was famous for the production of the Zaporizhitsa motorcar — a sort of Soviet

Beetle and the cheapest car they produced — I was reminded of a Ukrainian friend whose boyfriend owned one of the vehicles.

"My mother was insistent I should marry him on account of his politeness," she recounted to me. "He always opened the car door for me. What my mother didn't realise was that the workmanship was so poor; he was the only one who could do it! In all other things, he was a real rascal."

Between the fifteenth and seventeenth centuries, three big players came to dominate the political and cultural scene and to fight over their borderlands near to the Dnipro valley, which they referred to by the name "Ukraine." The Polish-Lithuanian Commonwealth adopted Catholicism, and their southern territories, which now form part of Ukraine, were exposed to the humanist influences of the Renaissance, such as secular literature and the arts, and later to the Reformation. In the south, the Tatars of Crimea, vassals of Ottoman Turkey who were mostly descendents of the Mongol armies emerged as a powerful enemy. In the northeast an alliance of Moscow princes consolidated control and slowly removed the yoke imposed by the Mongols.

It was in the borderlands, at the confluence of these three great powers, that the Cossacks (from the Turkic word Kazak meaning "free man") emerged as the only people able to colonize the open, fertile plains. And in the 1550s, Prince Dmytro Vyshnevetsky founded a Cossack fortress called Zaporizhska Sich on Khortytsia Island.

Today, Khortytsia is within sight of the mighty Dnipro Hydroelectric Dam, and the narrow, twelve kilometre long island has the full status of a national cultural and historical site.

Slavery: "Harvesting the Steppe"

On the way to the Cossack Museum on Khortytsia Island, I asked Stanislav why the Cossacks alone were able to colonise these lands.

"Slavery," he replied without hesitation.

Perhaps he had misunderstood my question.

"After Africa, the second greatest source of slaves was from the lands that now constitute Ukraine," he continued. "Some scholars estimate that more than three million people, predominantly Ukrainians, but also Russians, Belarusians, and Poles, were enslaved during the time of the Crimean Khanate which was between about 1450 and 1783. The majority were exported via Kefe, the modern day town of Feodosiya, in a process that the Tartars called, 'harvesting the steppe.'"

His reply surprised me. "Because of this threat the Poles and Moscali were prevented from extending their influence southwards towards the Islamic lands, and from extending their agriculture into warmer climes. They deployed tens of thousands of soldiers and fortified their towns and cities to resist the annual raids, but the slave tax revenues collected at Kefe show that about twenty thousand captives made it to market each year, though thousands more would have died brutally during the journey."

"And the Cossacks avoided capture?" I queried.

"Sometimes they were threatened directly, but at other times they supported the Tartar expeditions and received payments for the transit of slaves through the areas they controlled. The trade ceased when the Crimea was finally annexed by Russia in 1783."

Our conversation reminded me of some earlier research I had done. A Lithuanian tradesman, observing the business in the early seventeenth century, wrote:

> When the slaves are led out for sale they walk to the marketplace in single file, like storks on the wing, in whole dozens, chained together by the neck, and are there sold by auction. The auctioneer shouts loudly that they are 'the newest arrivals, simple, and not cunning, lately captured from the people of the kingdom of Poland, and not from Muscovy; for the Muscovite race, being crafty and deceitful, does not bring a good price. Sometimes beautiful and perfect maidens of our nation bring their weight in gold.[6]

One such maiden who attracted the eye of the Ottoman Emperor Suleyman the Magnificent was a Ukrainian girl called Roksolana, who was also known as "The Laughing One." She was captured just south of Lviv in what was then the Kingdom of Poland. Her red hair, green eyes, and incessant laughter soon won her the heart of the great ruler, and when she converted to Islam in 1530, they were married and had three sons and a daughter. It was the first time in history a Sultan had married a slave. Roksolana used her advantages to educate herself, and she became a shrewd politician who accompanied the Sultan on his tours and managed affairs when he was not there.

In what was perhaps her greatest intrigue, she convinced the Sultan that Mustafa, his son by another wife and heir to the empire, was plotting against him. The Sultan had his son strangled with silk, and when the Sultan died, one of Roksolana's sons, Sellim II, became the leader of the Ottoman Empire.

Cossack Horsemanship

As we approached the museum on foot, I could recognize a chancellery, a smithy, a tavern, and an open-air horse theatre. Stanislav wore the traditional dress of the Cossacks — an intricately embroidered white shirt and baggy loose-fitting trousers tied at the waist by a long, wide belt called a *kuntush*, which protected his torso and, centuries ago, would also have indicated his rank.

We took seats overlooking the horse arena where Cossacks were practicing their acrobatics, and Stanislav explained why the Cossacks are such a strong symbol of Ukrainian identity.

"The Cossacks tried to establish a way of life that was distinct from the great powers of their day. They held prominence for more than four centuries, and, being descended from the indigenous people and those who passed through the steppe, they symbolize the multiethnic mix of modern Ukraine. They were free-spirited, self-reliant, and not prone to domination. They weren't displaced people forced to live on the steppe, like some suggest, but they choose to live here because of its beauty and abundance. Nowadays people relate to their values of freedom, equality, and fraternity."

Fifty metres ahead of us, the Cossack horses trotted slowly into the ring, their calm progress barely hiding the high mettle of their alert eyes, stretched ears, and tensed muscles. The Cossack riders started to rehearse a series of moves not unlike those of a break-dancer one might see on Kyiv's main streets, falling to the ground, springing up, spinning on their back and shoulder blades. But whereas a break-dancer has the pavement as a platform, the Cossacks have wild animals beneath them.

"The horses need to be as well trained as their riders," Stanislav explained. "The rider must develop complete trust with his horse and great patience is needed. Special saddles with handholds and hidden straps are used to communicate with the horse."

His gold earring glinted. I had read that a Cossack wore an earring in his left ear if he was the last child in his family.

"The horses probably have blood lines as diverse as the Ukrainians," he speculated, "containing the blood of Magai, Karabakh, Turkmen, and Persian-Arabian horses."

The first move was called "the whirl," which is similar to "the windmill" move of the break-dancer. The forward-facing rider jumps off the galloping horse, then springs from the earth to land backwards on the horse before spinning on his shoulder blades on the saddle in a whirling motion. It clearly requires tremendous strength, agility, and balance.

Deception and concealment from the enemy is a part of the Cossacks military strategy, and in a move called "wings," the rider hangs horizontally behind one side of the horse so that it looks to be riderless.

The most dramatic move involved the rider putting both legs on one side of the horse, and then falling backward over the other side, causing me to take a sharp intake of breath. With his arms flailing just above the ground, and one leg waving limply in the air, the manoeuvre feigns the death of the rider, so that the horse can approach the enemy position.

The Cossacks at Sea

As we talked, I realised that it is a myth that the Cossacks fought mostly on horseback or, indeed, that they fought only on the land — a myth perpetuated, perhaps, by Pushkin's remark about Cossacks being "always on horseback, always ready to fight, always on the alert."

"At the peak the Cossacks probably had a fleet of three hundred 'Chaikas.' Enough to be an important force in the Black Sea," Stanislav reflected.

The Chaika (meaning "Seagull") was built from wood and reed, and would last only a few seasons. Each boat varied in size, from fifteen to twenty-five metres long, weighed a maximum of forty tons, and was equipped with eight to twenty pairs of paddles. A cloth spar sail on a folding mast provided additional propulsion, and the boat could achieve seventy kilometres in a good day. The larger boats would carry small canon that had been looted from other ships, but otherwise they would use pistols, side-arms, and bows.

The Chaika exhibited good seaworthiness, could navigate shallow rivers and be rowed onto a beach, which made it ideal for raids. The low-lying posture of the boat coupled with its high manoeuvrability allowed the Cossacks to make numerous daring attacks on the Tartars and the Turks, and to record many successes. Though they could never be an equal match with the Turkish fleet in direct confrontation at sea, the element of surprise and the boat's mobility enabled them to attack the outskirts of Constantinople in 1615.

According to naval tradition, a country can claim to have had a navy from the date of its first naval victory; otherwise the date of its establishment is the date the fleet is inaugurated. In 1992, President Leonid Kravchuk hastily produced a decree to establish a Ukrainian navy, but he ignored, or was ignorant of, a Cossack victory in 1492. As a result, Ukraine has one of the youngest navies in Europe, rather than one of the oldest!

Cossack Hetmen

As we strolled around the replica fort, Stanislav told me about the most important Cossack leaders and their influence on Ukraine's history. "The main hero, and for many 'The Father of The Nation,' was Bogdan Khmelnytsky, who became Hetman (Leader) of the Zaporozhian Cossacks. It is this figure who sits astride a horse in front of the Saint Sophia Cathedral in Kyiv, and his face graces five hryvnia banknotes.

"In 1648, Khmelnytsky, who is sometimes compared with Oliver Cromwell, launched an uprising involving the peasants and his Tatar allies that redrew the map of Eastern Europe. The Polish army was crushed, and an autonomous Cossack state was established."

Stanislav's remarks reminded me of something I had read about Khmelnytsky's victory over Poland being aided by hundreds, if not thousands, of agents working under cover. They masqueraded as beggars, pilgrims, and monks, and were trained to recall well rehearsed stories, if captured, in order to deceive their adversaries. As such, Khmelnytsky must have been one of the earliest proponents of psychological warfare. The establishment of the Cossack state allowed Khmelnytsky to develop his own administrative structure and a foreign policy, and the Cossacks took on the role of Ukraine's political class. Within a few years, however, he was betrayed by the Tartars, and war resumed, forcing him to seek an anti-Polish alliance first with the Ottoman Empire, and finally with Moscow. This was the fork in the road.

Stanislav now provided additional information on this subject. "Khmelnytsky negotiated the Pereiaslav Treaty, and in 1654 the Cossacks were put under the protection of the Tsar. Historians, politicians, and ordinary folk discuss to this day whether or not this was a terrible betrayal of the hard fought freedoms of the Cossacks or a necessary expediency."

As we approached the wooden museum building, he continued his narrative. "The treaty had been negotiated on the basis that the Tsar would respect Cossack self-rule. But within a few years the Tsar signed a separate treaty — the Andrusovsky Treaty — with Poland, and this declared that right-bank Ukraine was part of Poland, while left-bank Ukraine had been 'reunited' with mother Russia. This division still influences the balance of political power in Ukraine today."

I knew that the Tsar's action corresponded with the view that only Russia was the true political heir of Kyivan Rus. Later both Russian Imperial historians and Soviet historians adopted the view that Khmelnytsky was a Russian national hero for bringing Ukraine into the union of all three Russias: Great Russia, Little Russia, and White Russia. Khmelnytsky had shown that an independent state was possible and then lost it. Apart from a few months in 1919, amidst the chaos of war and revolution when Ukraine briefly achieved independence, it would be three hundred and thirty-seven years before Ukraine could claim to be an independent state.

Despite the various peace treaties over the remaining forty years of the seventeenth century (a period known as the "Ruin"), all the powerful neighbours of Ukraine used the steppe as a battlefield. In 1709, it was left to Hetman Ivan Mazepa to make the last (and unsuccessful) attempt to break away from Russia.

The inside of the museum was adorned with thousands of Cossack artefacts. A minibus had arrived with a group of tourists and they were now taking their seats for a presentation of dancing. On weekends they have hundreds of visitors from the cruise boats, but mostly they are Ukrainians. As we took our seats as far from the noise of the music and dancers as possible, I asked Stanislav if an educated statesman such as the Tsar had not outwitted Khmelnytsky in negotiating the terms of the Pereiaslav Treaty. He plucked at his drooping Cossack moustache.

"Firstly, let me say that the negotiations were made through interpreters since the Cossacks did not speak Russian. So, perhaps yes, that was one source of confusion. But it is another myth to believe that the Cossacks were peasants. The foot soldiers were, of course, but the Cossack elite were mostly from noble families and one of the most prominent examples was Pilip Orlik."

In 1710, Pilip Orlik wrote *Pacts and Constitution of Laws of Troops of Zaporozhje*. It is believed to be the first constitution ever written — preceding both the French and the American constitutions by about seventy years — and it contained two revolutionary and fundamental ideas: election of all government officials, and the abolition of serfdom. Such ideas were an anathema to Poland and Russian, which operated hereditary systems, and they rejected the Cossack's renewed demand to establish a Ukrainian state.

Orlik was a close friend of Hetman Ivan Mazepa, one of the richest men in Europe and owner of twenty thousand estates. Mazepa was a faithful ally of Tsar Peter I for more than twenty years, but in 1707 he turned against the Tsar after he refused to send soldiers to protect Ukraine from the invading armies of Charles XII of Sweden. Mazepa believed that the Tsar was obligated to do so by the Pereiaslav Treaty, and as retribution Mazepa sided with the Swedish monarch. Tsar Peter I was now forced to challenge the attackers, and when Charles' army was defeated at the Battle of Poltava, both Orlik and Mazepa were forced to flee to Turkey.

When Ukraine gained independence in 1991, Mazepa became a national hero because he was the first post-Pereiaslav Treaty Hetman to try to break away from the orbit of Russia. In the ever-shifting interpretation of Ukrainian history, Mazepa is regarded by many as a hero for trying to gain independence but failing, whereas Khmelnytsky, who achieved independence but then lost it, is regarded as a traitor.

Music, Dancing, and Painting

The bandura musicians and dancers took their places on the stage and gave us a show that must have been similar to that experienced by Mazepa.

The bandura is a folk instrument unique to Ukraine, similar in appearance to a large mandolin, and in timbre to a harpsichord. From the fifteenth to the nineteenth centuries it was played by Kobzars (wandering minstrels) and Cossacks who sang psalms, chants, and epic songs called "Dumy," which recalled their adventures with the Tartars, Poles, and Moscalis.

Practitioners of the bandura argue that it has evolved perfectly suited to expressing the character of Ukrainian songs, and musicologists argue that there are a number of characteristic Ukrainian melodic phrases that had an impact on European classical music, and which appear in the works of famous composers. Tchaikovsky, Beethoven, and Litzt, for example, wrote music about the Cossacks, perhaps influenced by their servants' folk songs or, in some cases, friendships with Ukrainian Hetmen.

Cossack dancing is exuberant, characterised by running, leaping, and the difficult movement called the "prysiadka," where the dancer assumes a squatting position with his knees turned out, back erect, and hands placed on his hips. It reflects the spirit of the fearless soldier and expert horseman, and Cossack dances show more than a hint of classical Russian ballet choreography, serving as a reminder that it was these folk dances that appeared before ballet.

"It is said that the dances increase in speed as one travels southward to the warmer climate of the Black Sea," Stanislav remarked as the powerful and colourful performance got underway with an arrangement of typical Ukrainian steps in which a boy offers a gift to his girl, and she accepts it.

In addition to dancing, the Cossack life also comes across very strongly in Ukrainian literature and painting. There were very few occasions when Joseph Stalin commented directly about art or a specific artist, but such an occasion was the Moscow Art Exhibition of 1928. In a show of modesty, he walked from the Kremlin and queued alongside the ten thousand or so visitors for the opening ceremony. He declared to friends that the exhibition was "generally good," and that his favourite painting was the large canvas called *Zaporozhian Cossacks of Ukraine Writing a Letter in Reply to the Sultan of Turkey* by Illya Repin, Ukraine's greatest painter. Later, when Repin fled the Soviet regime for self-imposed exile in Finland, Stalin showered him with gifts and tried to lure him back, but Repin never succumbed.

The picture that moved Stalin took thirteen years to complete and shows a group of Cossacks being cheered on by others who are composing a rude letter in reply to Sultan Mohammed IV's demand that they submit to his rule. Repin painted figures of different nationalities with different costumes, postures, and expressions, and the composition radiates a sense of irreverent camaraderie.

As the Cossack dancers brought the concert to a close by performing the high-kicking Ukrainian national dance called "The Hopak," I was reminded of Repin's painting of the same name. It is a joyous and exuberant canvas that exhibits the vitality of the dance.

"Ukraine in his paintings is all beauty, joy, happiness, a grand and even reckless struggle against powerful enemies. Russia is wallowing in ugliness and cruelty," judged one observer when comparing Repin's canvases painted in Russia with those he painted in Ukraine, and about Ukraine.[7]

For contemporary Ukrainians, particularly those from central and western regions where Cossack values are held more firmly, this is a sharp observation that encapsulates concisely the spirit of Ukraine.

STEAMY BUSINESS

JUST TO HOLD *DAS KAPITAL*, written by Karl Marx and published in 1867, and to flick through its densely-packed pages, you know it will be a long and tedious read. I confess to never having read the book: it demands more from me than I'm willing to give and yet I recognise that its influence should not be understated.

Marx saw capitalism as the exploitation of the working class by the employing class to create profit. He conjectured that profit would decline over time, crises were inevitable, and capitalism would become unstable and collapse. For him, and those who followed his ideas, capitalism was an evolutionary phase on the path to something better.

Economists and Business Cycles

Ukrainian-born Mikhaylo Tugan-Baranovsky (1865–1919) was bold enough to put forward a different view. He produced the first coherent "Economic Theory of a Business Cycle" by arguing that business cycles are driven by investment; over investment will lead to recessions, and under investment leads to a pick up in the issue of credit followed by economic activity. Contrary to Marx, he argued for a wave-like pattern of business activity in which equilibrium was the norm and crisis was a deviation from it, albeit recurring and periodical. If given the proper inputs, he reasoned, the cycle could be held in a particular phase.

Tugan-Baranovsky's work became familiar to the Austrian economist Joseph Schumpeter who was teaching in the town of

Czernowitz, in what is now western Ukraine, and in 1911 Schumpeter wrote the *Theory of Economic Development*. He argued that entrepreneurs provide the fuel for spurts of economic growth through technical and financial innovations and, in turn, these sustain profits. He was also the first to label the four phases of a business cycle as boom, recession, depression, and recovery.

Schumpeter was a colourful personality who immodestly confessed to three wishes in life: to be the greatest lover in Vienna, the best horseman in Europe, and the greatest economist in the world. History barely records his success in the first two endeavours, but in the third he was supreme. When *Forbes* magazine compared Schumpeter with the British economist, John Maynard Keynes — both had been born 100 years earlier and just a few months apart — Schumpeter overshadowed his rival. [1]

In 1924, the Russian economist Nikolai Kondratiev, one of Tugan-Baranovsky's students, published his theory that Western capitalist economies have long-term (fifty to sixty year) cycles of boom followed by depression. He also argued, in contradiction to Stalin's views, that there was a place for small capitalist enterprises to operate within the Soviet system. Stalin was displeased. Kondratiev was imprisoned for eight years, and on his release in 1938 he was retried, sentenced to a further ten years' imprisonment, and presumably on a whim was executed by firing squad on the day the verdict was issued. "Kondratiev Cycles" are nowadays recognised as a means to describe the movements of many variables such as oil prices, interest rates, and stock markets.

So it was that in a small part of Eastern Europe a group of economists defined the theories of entrepreneurship and business cycles that much of the world would follow for the rest of the century. Ironically, Ukraine was prevented from experiencing a free market cycle for most of the twentieth century.

On a cold February evening I meet a friend on Maidan Nezalezhnosti (Independence Square) in the centre of Kyiv. Andrei is a successful businessman and a student of the prestigious Lviv Institute of Management, the first school of its kind to open in

Ukraine. He promised to be my guide through the unsanitary world of Ukrainian business and the sanitary world of banya. Dirtied by the former, I would be cleansed by the latter.

The banya, a steam bath of 40–50° Celsius and a relative humidity of approximately 90 percent, harkens back to an age when bathing was an irregular affair. It continues to be popular with the generation of Soviets who lived in communal apartments without baths or showers and, though no longer a hygienic necessity, it remains a source of relaxation, rejuvenation, and communion. In the same way that the kitchen or the crèche is female turf, the banya is predominantly a male domain.

Catherine II banned mixed bathing in 1743. Public baths such as the Central Public Bath, our destination and Kyiv's last remaining public banya, are open to men and women on alternative days. According to some, all key business decisions are made in the banya, and when Viktor Yushchenko became president he kicked-off his corruption clean-up campaign with an informal ban on visiting the banya by government officials.

To the uninitiated the banya can be quite daunting. Just entering the massive, impersonal, and windowless building and breathing the warm humid air of the changing room, which is reminiscent of a holiday camp toilet, is unnerving. Nor had I been reassured by the entry for "Banya" in the *Great Soviet Encyclopedia*[2], which refers to bath houses as disinfectant stations and auspiciously informs the reader that such establishments will usually issue clean underwear to customers.

Like a boy attending his first day at school, I committed to follow Andrei through whatever Bacchanalian ritual might exist beyond the shower room door. Carrying a zinc bucket, a birch brush called a "venik," and a felt hat, I followed him into the steam room wrapped in a dishcloth-sized towel.

We sat on a bench in the sanctuary of the banya. Within minutes tiny beads of perspiration formed on Andrei's shaven head. He frowned and the beads coalesced. Moments later he wiped his brow.

From Sugar to Stock Exchanges

By the seventeenth century Western Europe had a well developed system of commerce and manufacturing and the arts were flourishing. But in the Russian Empire it was a different story: commerce was underdeveloped, manufacturing was confined to small workshops, and literature, painting, and music were centred on the church. Peter the Great sought to modernize but it was not until the emancipation of the serfs in 1861 that factories resembling those of their rivals in the West were built, particularly for sugar and grain processing.

Some of the richest Kyivan families made their fortunes in the sugar business and either lived in Kyiv (the Tereshchenkos, Brodksys, Zaytsevs, Galperins, Khanenkos), or had their offices located there (the Bobrinskys, Branitskys, Yaroshinskys). Jews, in particular, played prominent roles and the philanthropy of the sugar families enabled dozens of buildings to be built including schools, hospitals, churches, banks, and stock exchanges.

The legacy is very apparent today as you walk through the city centre. The Kyiv State Bank at Institutskaya 9, for example, built in the style of the northern Italian Renaissance, is one of the most beautiful buildings in Kyiv. The first stock exchange was established in Odesa in 1796, followed a few years later by exchanges in Kyiv, Kharkiv, Kremenchuk, and Berdychiv. (By comparison, the regional exchanges in Manchester and Liverpool in England were established only in the 1830s.) Surprisingly the Ukrainian exchanges remained open until 1930, long after the Bolsheviks came to power.

How Central Planning Came About

"How do you feel?" asked Andrei.

He lifted my arms to see if they were sweaty and let them slap down against my torso, much like a Babushka (or old lady) at a market might do when inspecting a plucked chicken.

"It's time to head to the cold pool," he said, leading me to the shower room for an ablution. "It will give you a floating, buoyant feeling." By then my breathing had already become a conscious rather than an unconscious effort.

"How did business cope during those tumultuous first two decades of the twentieth century?" I enquired as we relaxed. I noticed then that many of the baby blue tiles of the shower area were missing, exposing the mouldy signature of tile cement.

"The Bolsheviks didn't invent state ownership, or central control," Andrei said, "and nor were they the first to appoint managers who lacked basic skills to manage businesses and who made irrational decisions. These had also been characteristics of the Tsarist officials."

But as he explained, there were profound changes. A large proportion of the business class had emigrated or had died fighting in World War I, and a disruptive Civil War had followed. So, the starting point for building the economy was not a good one.

For the first few years to 1920, the Soviets bought out the former capitalists but encouraged them to continue managing their enterprises under the direction of workers councils. In this way all enterprises comprising ten or more people were "nationalized," and the basis for the Central Planning System — the behemoth of the Soviet economy through to the 1980s — was established.

By 1921, industrial production in Ukraine was just ten percent of pre-World War levels. With wholesale nationalization clearly failing, Vladimir Lenin ordered an about-turn called "The New Economic Policy," and the government began denationalizing small industries. Within a few years the number of small businesses grew to over one hundred thousand, and before the end of the decade Ukraine's gross domestic product would attain pre-World War I levels.

A dilemma the Soviets faced was graphically referred to by Lenin as "the scissors;" industrial prices were increasing along the rising open top blade whilst those of food were dropping along the bottom blade. With nothing affordable to buy, the farmers were not taking their agricultural produce to the cities and the manufacturers were selling very little. After Lenin's death, Joseph Stalin sought to close the scissors by selling manufactured goods at below cost price by increasing food prices, and also by bringing private enterprise back under state planning.

Overnight, company balance sheets became an incidental art form and this unsustainable balancing act was to be a bulwark of Soviet policy for the next sixty years.

Andrei and I returned to the steam room and I noticed that the banya was heated by a huge gas-fired furnace that occupied an entire wall and was accessed by a small metal door a few metres from where we sat. The high-heat and method of producing steam in this sort of banya is said to vaporize the water to smaller particles and to produce a more pervasive heat than can be achieved with saunas. The seating consisted of a series of wooden terraced benches in the shape of a small amphitheatre. The higher one went, the hotter it got, and a small increase in altitude could mean a big difference in temperature.

In the higher elevations I spied many men large and small, hirsute, and corporally-bald. One man lay prostrate; another was beating his companion with a brush of birch. Reciprocity appeared to be very much a part of the communal bathhouse spirit, with the old educating the young and the middle-aged shepherding the elderly through the experience. As we took our seats on the second row I noticed a lucky man who was being beaten by two friends.

Communist Millionaires

Everyone knows that in the Soviet Union private enterprise was illegal until Perestroika, and yet through other sources I had been told that Ukraine had already several hundred millionaires (measured in US dollars) by the time the system collapsed.

"How could a businessman become a millionaire and lead that sort of lifestyle in the Soviet Union?" I asked Andrei, who smiled at my naivety.

"The rich couldn't spend the money beyond owning their own apartment, rather than living communally, eating and dressing well and taking holidays in Crimea. Perhaps they would buy additional apartments using the names of relatives, but they avoided things that attracted too much attention. This was especially true of those in business in the 1950s and 1960s. But by the 1980s their children were becoming less concerned about concealing their wealth and this was a driving force behind Perestroika."

I recalled that with hindsight it was now clear that Perestroika fed two contradictory demands that were its downfall. Civil society had hoped that it would bring greater democracy, whereas the rich thought it would legalize their privilege and enable them to live openly. The tension created by the open display of wealth quickly led to a rise in criminal violence and gangs that nowadays so epitomizes the post-Soviet republics.

Andrei continued, saying, "Most of those who became businessmen after World War II had been marginalised by the Communist Party. Perhaps they were Jews who were prevented from taking responsible positions in Government or others that didn't have professional or academic standing. As the Soviet archives continue to be opened, legal cases are now coming to light of businessmen who amassed millions and were arrested, tried, and in some cases executed. In a society where everything was regulated, knowing that you had achieved something provided a tremendous inner freedom and defined who you were."

"But how did they become rich?" I wondered.

At that moment one of the older men opened a hatch and threw water into the opening. The roar of steam being created temporarily drowned our voices and moments later a wall of heat hit my body, searing my skin. Surely this was how the universe had originally come into being, I thought.

"How did they do it?" Andrei repeated my question as my heart felt like it was trying to explode through my rib cage. I was convinced I was going to have a heart attack.

"They manufactured consumer items, known by everyone as 'left-hand goods.' Not cars or refrigerators since these would have attracted attention, but clothes, shoes, and small manufactured goods for use in the home. You see, private suppliers could produce fashionable items very quickly whereas state factories took years to change what they produced. The main centres in Ukraine were Kyiv, Odesa, and Dnipropetrovsk, but it was widespread."

Over the next few minutes, Andrei explained how the deceit worked. A few families managed dozens of illegal businesses with a turnover of millions of roubles. The manager of a legitimate factory, say a factory making clothes, would set up a parallel workshop under the same roof. Such an enterprise would bribe dozens of people outside the factory, but most importantly a senior party official in the regional or national administration who would act as their "Godfather."

The manager would bribe the central planners who were setting the official production quota to give him more machines than he needed to fulfil the quota. The planners would also overestimate the time it took to make a garment in his factory, so creating time in which to make illegal goods. They would overestimate the materials needed to produce each garment — cloth, buttons, zips and so on — so that there was surplus available for "left-hand goods."

The factory would also play a role. Workers were paid extra by the manager to label a garment as large size even though it was a small size. This would save material and the factory would be paid the amount for a large garment. If the manager needed to raise money from the central budget, he would perhaps falsify the work done to maintain the factory. So for example, he might claim that the machines were overhauled or the factory had been painted. Of course, the work never happened.

More creatively, if the planner wanted to increase production he would be given permission to take on extra workers. He would receive money to pay these workers, but in reality they did not exist or they never turned up for work. The existing workers would simply produce more, forfeiting quality if necessary.

Some time later I would meet a woman who received a pension for a job she never had. In fact, she never once turned up for work. The factory manager kept the salary and, on the basis of her fictitious employment, he claimed one lunch each day, safety work clothes, medical expenses, and an annual holiday to a sanatorium in Crimea. "The spin-offs were almost endless!" She laughed at the reminiscence.

And whilst visiting the city of Lviv, a man confided that in the 1970s his brother bought a small illegal engineering business in the city. For all practical purposes the business didn't exist. It had no premises or assets, accounts, confirmation of turnover, or register of the creditors and debtors. Yet it lived under the umbrella of a state business. His brother paid some of the money immediately and the remainder was held back for a year just in case the seller had lied about something. "We thought we could always go to his house and break his legs," the man had said with a smile, making light of a serious matter.

Such a transaction, based on unwritten rules, was not dissimilar to the Law Merchant that operated in Europe in the early Middle Age. Yet, here it was, operating throughout the second half of the twentieth century.

The shadow-manufacturing system Andrei described is not unlike a story told by Odesa-born lawyer Konstantin Simis in *The Corrupt Society*.[3] Simis recounts the story of two Jewish brothers who operated an illegal network of companies, protected by a high official, in the 1960s. One day a journalist working for the newspaper *Izvestiya* was tipped off about their business and their subterfuge began to unravel. The brother's "Godfather" was offered a bribe of half a million roubles to save the businesses but they realised that one of the brothers (as it turned out the younger, crippled one) would have to be sacrificed if the business was to remain intact. The journalist's story whipped up such intrigue and hatred in the hearts of ordinary Soviets that when the swindler was prosecuted the court was packed. Reportedly, the Jewish millionaire owned two dozen suits and over one hundred imported ties.

The younger brother was tried along with twenty-eight accomplices and he was sentenced to fifteen years in a labour camp. He died seven years later and the illegal business continued in operation.

After Andrei and I had navigated our way around the flagellating couples to one of the higher benches (and to higher temperatures), I was instructed to lie down. The pressure on my eardrums jumped.

"I'll show you how the brush is used," Andrei said innocently. The birch brush or "venik" had been soaking in the bucket and was soft. He began to methodically slap my skin explaining that it improves blood circulation and intensifies capillary activity. The most surprising effect was not the sting of the impact, as I had expected, but the wave of convective heat associated with the swinging motion.

Painful as this was, Apostle Andrew who visited Kyiv and the banks of the Dnipro witnessed altogether more terrifying spectacles. As he wrote in the twelfth century in the *Primary Chronicle*:

> Wondrous to relate, I saw the land of the Slavs, and while I was among them, I noticed their wooden bath-houses. They warm themselves to extreme heat, then undress, and after anointing themselves with tallow, take young reeds and lash their bodies. They actually lash themselves so violently that they barely escape alive. They then drench themselves with cold water, and thus are revived. They think nothing of doing this every day and actually inflict such voluntary torture upon themselves. They make of the act not a mere washing but a veritable torment.

As I lay on the bench gradually succumbing to the rhythmic lashing, I found it difficult to comprehend the extent of the network of falsification and deception in business dealings. Though it required the complicity of millions of people, a precondition for its survival was total corruption in the ruling class.

The Soviet *Dictionary of Foreign Words*, published at about the same time, defined corruption as "Venality and misappropriation of funds by public figures, politicians and civil servants in the capitalist world."[4]

This was a travesty, and an absurd attempt to suggest that socialists are incorruptible. And just when the dictionary sought to obscure the reality, the true extent of the rot within the Soviet system was becoming apparent to more and more people.

Transition to a Market Economy

"Following the death of Stalin in 1953, the collective leadership experienced a sense of panic, and there was no longer a helmsman," Andrei said as he continued his story.

"Recognising that they could no longer control the masses through repression and terror, they conceded that they should do more to produce consumer goods. Though the centrally planned economy was able to achieve limited goals well, particularly in heavy industry and munitions, it did not adapt well to more complex goals that required shorter design lead times and a flexible approach to sourcing materials.

"Under Brezhnev the official economy could no longer function without the parallel 'left-hand goods' economy which was increasingly controlled by gangs. There was nothing the authorities could do short of turning upside down the system which, of course, happened in 1991.

"There was a brief window of opportunity in which to control the mafias who were gaining power in Ukraine's cities. Yuri Andropov, the longest serving KGB chairman (1967-1982) who went on to briefly lead the Soviet Union, attempted to do so but when the trail of bribery led right back to the heart of the Kremlin, Leonid Brezhnev stopped his work and the mafia began to grow unchecked."

"Turn over," Andrei ordered.

Somehow, being naked in front of another man is less strange when he's beating you with a brush and constantly checking your breathing. More akin to being at the doctor's, where nakedness becomes perfunctory. In fact, as Andrei explained, going to the bathhouse is commonly regarded as the "people's first doctor," vodka being the second, and raw garlic the third.

The sound of evaporating water roared through the banya once again and a fresh wave of heat enveloped us. "Sit up slowly. Time for you to beat me," Andrei said.

Aficionados had their own pattern of rinsing, steaming, and dunking and they employed a variety of beating styles. I decided to use the motion I would use to swat a mosquito, a sort of flick of the wrist. But beating proved to be much harder than being beaten. Not just physically, but also mentally as I fought the competing emotions of wanting to do a good job on my first attempt and wanting to inflict pain on the man who had brought me to such a near-death experience. As I thrashed away, I was thinking about other things Andrei and I had discussed earlier.

Observers of business life since the 1980s generally agree that the most pernicious element of the Ukrainian landscape has been the rise of the business-political nexus — the alliance of the former Communist Party elite, members of the law enforcement agencies, security apparatuses, and gangs of organized criminals. They are commonly referred to as Ukraine's mafia.

In the early 1990s they infiltrated the privatization process that was the method used to transfer state-owned businesses into private ownership and which had the potential to make ordinary Ukrainians richer. Andrei was one of those who had embraced the dramatic changes, though with difficulty. The vast majority of people, however, simply watched and waited. They tried to continue their lives as before, turning up for work but not being paid, and holding on to what little they had. Seventy years of conditioning had left them wondering if the processes unwinding socialism might be reversed, particularly by the intervention of the security forces. But the mafias had no such concerns and they were very busy.

Andrei had explained how the process had echoes of the New Economic Policy of the 1920s when the government thought it could control the process from the centre and have an orderly transfer of businesses from state ownership into private hands. Both times they were wrong. "Try to imagine what would happen if your government announced that it was going to reallocate ownership of every business, property, apartment, and house," he said.

He tried to get up to make a gesture but I beat him back down and, more calmly, he continued our bath-house discussion. His large, almost hairless body was a lesson in history with its several incision scars, tattoos on his forearms, and a red birthmark the size of a hand on his lower back.

"The government gave every Ukrainian adult privatization certificates which gave them the right to a share of the business or factory they worked in," he said. "These certificates were a great hope of ordinary people but their value never exceeded ten dollars and was soon two dollars. The people entrusted with the process of managing the share issue massively violated their obligations. They never issued the certificates to the right people, they stole them, they forged them, they told people they were worthless, and bought them for a pittance."

I was already aware that companies were sold in exchange for privatization certificates or at auction but that these processes were deeply flawed. We know now that the auctioneers were bribed, the time of auctions was changed at the last minute, bidders were prevented from entering the auction house, and people were disqualified from bidding for spurious reasons. Often the process was accompanied by violence and contract killing.

Though the number of contract killings in Ukraine is unknown, a figure of five thousand is sometimes quoted. Whatever the loss, Ukrainian friends confirm the dismal fact that the going rate to hire a hit man was as low as five hundred dollars.

Andrei turned over and winced with pain. Perhaps it was a physical pain or the result of recalling memories. "In more complex scams," he continued, "the managers of a business would make it appear worthless perhaps by cancelling contracts with customers, removing machinery, or piling debt onto the business. They would then buy it very cheaply and a short while later it would be running successfully. Often the families of businessmen would be threatened if they didn't give up control to the mafias. Many were scared into just walking away. What we can say that is positive," he said, finding a silver lining, "is that by the late 1990s privatization achieved the goal of establishing a private sector but at the cost of disillusioning ordinary people."

Not surprisingly public support for fast-track privatizations and market reforms diminished substantially. Ukraine had been viewed as the most promising of all the former Soviet Union countries for the development of a stock market, and, with a five million dollar loan from France, a stock exchange was established in 1991. But it didn't live up to early expectations and for a while there were only two stocks traded and the exchange operated for less than one hour per week. By day the prestigious building was an under-used trading floor and at night it was hired out for parties and art shows.

"There were several problems," explained Andrei. "Firstly those companies who wanted to trade on the exchange were probably successful because they defied layers of rules and regulations. But listing meant that they had to open their books to scrutiny."

He looked askance to ensure I had understood his code words for, "they avoided paying their taxes and fulfilling other obligations."

"Secondly, there was no one to buy shares. Ordinary Ukrainian people had and still have no idea how to make money from money."

During Soviet times the only option to "grow money" was a deposit account at the Soviet State Savings Bank. Such an account offered three percent annual interest, and the rate never changed over several decades. Those that did trust their money to banks lost almost everything in the 1990s through the combination of inflation and the theft of bank assets. Only now people are learning how to make money from property, and share ownership is still a pipedream.

Today the PTFS stock exchange trades over three hundred stocks. In 2007, the index growth of 135 percent was the world's second highest, and in 2008, as credit problems surfaced and recession began to bite, it was one of the world's worst performing markets. On reflection it is probably good that less than one person in a hundred owns shares in Ukraine.

Oligarchs

"Let's go cool down," said Andrei, perhaps cognizant that my swatting action was becoming increasingly absentminded and inaccurate. I emerged from the shower for the last time, scrubbed, polished, purged, relaxed, and heady. Opening a small bottle of vodka that he had taken from his bag, Andrei poured a couple of shot glasses, handed one to me, and we toasted our womenfolk. "It's time to visit the second doctor," he said, referring to the comment he had made earlier about the banya, vodka and garlic. "Understanding the future of the Ukrainian oligarchies is the key to understanding the future trends of the Ukrainian economy.

When the dust settled on the privatization process it was clear that a handful of businessmen had consolidated power. In 2003 eighteen of Ukraine's strategic businesses were sold and fourteen of them were acquired by the country's three largest financial industrial groups headed by Viktor Pinchuk, Rinat Akhmetov, and Ihor Kolomojsky.

At 42, Tartar Rinat Akhmetov is Ukraine's richest man. His father was a coal miner so he grew up in poverty. Just how he acquired his early wealth is not clear, as is the case with all the richest men in Ukraine. But in the mid-nineties he established a successful bank and took over the presidency of the Shakhtar football club in Donetsk following the murder of its criminal boss owner. Later he established his business empire, System Capital Management Corporation (SCM), which rapidly became a very aggressive player in acquiring hundreds of companies involved in iron ore, coal, steel, energy generation, insurance and banking, and leisure businesses.

Victor Pinchuk is Ukraine's second richest man. He was born in a Jewish family which moved to the industrial town of Dnipropetrovsk after he was denied the right to study in Kyiv. Pinchuk also happens to be son-in-law of Leonid Kuchma, who was president from 1994 to 2005. After independence, Pinchuk created Interpipe, an industrial and media conglomerate centred in Kyiv.

The reclusive Ihor Kolomojsky, who comes in at number three on the rich list, heads the Privat Group which includes PrivatBank and significant interests in the metallurgical and mining industry. They are headquartered in Dnipropetrovsk.

As Andrei explained, the most vulnerable is probably Pinchuk now that Kuchma is gone and because of the Krivorozhstal scandal.

In 2004, the steel company Krivorozhstal was sold to a consortium of Interpipe and SCM for just eight hundred million dollars. Mittal Steel, one of the world's largest steel makers, had offered one and a half billion dollars but Ukraine's State Property Fund, which oversaw the process, rejected the offer on a technicality. The clear implication was that the Fund had been bought off by the consortium. Following the defeat of President Kuchma by Victor Yushchenko, the privatization was annulled in early 2005 and the steel company was re-auctioned. This time, Mittal won with an offer of over three billion dollars, still regarded by some analysts as a bargain.

Though the sale provided much needed cash for the state budget and was popular with the public, the uncertainty caused by the unravelling of the process was unnerving for business. The government appeared bereft of a consistent strategy for business. Would Yushchenko rescind earlier privatizations, perhaps hundreds of them, because they were unfair? That would lead to legal challenges with the oligarchs and could deter foreign investment. Or would past misdemeanours be overlooked if the oligarchs agreed to work towards building a nation? After months of wrangling, the parties settled — with varying degrees of commitment — on the latter option. Theft was legalized in order to preserve some bigger interest.

As Andrei refilled our glasses, I reeled off a list of the other top Ukrainian names on the rich list and asked him for his comments. "Russia's economy may be ten times bigger than Ukraine's but Ukraine has a higher percentage of billionaires," I said.

He pondered my comments. "Well, you're making a common mistake. You've excluded those men who were born in Ukraine but live in Russia and are counted in Russia's total. If they're included I suspect Ukraine has more billionaires per head than all but the USA."

Mikhail Fridman, for example, grew up in a Jewish household in Lviv but it seems he has never regarded himself as Ukrainian. His earliest entrepreneurial exploits included window washing and running a discotheque. Viktor Vekselberg, also from near Lviv, recycled copper from cables used in the oil industry. He received wide media attention when he bought the Forbes family's Fabergé collection for an estimated one hundred million dollars in 2004.

I was reminded of a joke popular some years earlier. When a rich businessman was asked whether the dodgy privatizations that had made him rich had been fair, he replied indignantly, "Of course not. Several other oligarchs took control of bigger oil companies than mine."

We laughed and marvelled at the unfairness and mind-blowing arbitrariness of it all. (Laughing is a common Ukrainian reaction when others might think a more appropriate response would be to cry.)

"We're back where we were more than one hundred years ago," Andrei observed wryly. "This kind of robbery is what the sugar barons did."

"You know," I said as we polished off the last of the vodka, "French novelist Honore de Balzac said something that is relevant to Ukraine, today."

It comes as a surprise to most people to learn that Balzac conducted a fifteen year romance, mostly through correspondence, with Ewelina Hanska who lived in Ukraine. Despite rapidly deteriorating health he came to marry her in the city of Berdychiv in 1850. But their union was brief and he died five months later. In his novel *Le Père Goriot* — which in contrast to *Das Capital* I have read with pleasure — he rages against Parisian society which he considers is in love with money only, and he concludes, "Behind every great fortune lies a forgotten crime."

A MEDAL AT ANY COST

YOU KNOW THE KHARKIV-MOSCOW TRAIN is about to depart from platform six when you hear the playing of the march *Slavic Woman's Farewell*, composed in 1912 by the Russian Vasily Agapkin. On this particular November evening the temperature was close to -20° Celsius and only a few people lingered on the platform to say their farewells.

An old man shuffled along selling snacks, each shoe wrapped in an old rag tied on top in a large bow to provide traction on the slippery platform. A woollen hood cloaked his head. At this temperature, breath condenses quickly and any exposed facial hair — beard, moustache or eyebrows — is soon encrusted in fine ice. He appeared to shiver as another gust of wind swept along the platform, blowing loose snowflakes into tight whorls.

The strident march echoed eerily as the tinny sound was played through speakers located along the platform. After boarding, the carriage doors were slammed shut, each sounding like a military salute, and the train glided almost silently away from the station platform.

Why the music was playing at all, no one could really tell me. Perhaps it was that Kharkivians still consider themselves to be part of Russia, I suggested to my fellow passengers. After all, no anthem is played for trains departing to, or from Kyiv, and in the 1990s Boris Yeltsin had been petitioned strongly, though unsuccessfully, to adopt *Slavic Woman's Farewell* as the national anthem for the new Russia.

"It's something to do with the Great War," offered one passenger, who recited words from one of numerous versions of the song: *The moment of departing is here. You look into my eyes with alarm. I sense your beloved breath. Far away the storm is already gathering.* The compartment was bustling with activity. I had booked a second-class ticket because thirty US dollars for a journey equivalent in length to the "Caledonian Sleeper" (London to Glasgow) seemed a bargain to me. It soon became clear I was in the company of sports people, and most of the nine 4-berth compartments were occupied by gymnasts, their coaches, and family members.

Ukraine Won the Olympic Games

For many decades, Soviet sport and, in particular, the Soviet Union's performance at the Olympics, was admired and envied by the West and especially by Americans. After all, it was the only arena, apart from the conquest of space, in which the USSR has been able to demonstrate superiority over its great rival, the USA. At European or World Cup football, the Soviets have never achieved the winning consistency that they achieved at the Olympics.

Sport became an ideological battleground and Soviet Olympic success seemingly verified the superiority of the communist system. But behind the label "Soviet" lies the truth that, of the more than one thousand medals the Soviets won in the summer Olympics, one in three was won by a Ukrainian. Moreover, Ukrainians comprised at least one-quarter (and sometimes more than a third) of the Soviet athletes at each Games, even though Ukraine had only one-seventh of the population of the Soviet Union. The fact of the matter is that, without Ukraine, the Soviet Union would not have won a single Olympic Games. Perhaps in recognition of this, at five of the nine summer Games they attended, the team flag bearer was a Ukrainian.

Within the confined space of the compartment, I struggled to unroll the mattress and to make my shoulder-high bunk bed. After watching with amusement, one of my fellow travellers, a sports coach called Maxim, stepped forward.

"It's quite easy, look," he said, throwing the sheet and then the blanket with the flourish of a magician and tucking them under the mattress. "It's one of the most useful things I learned as a Pioneer," he added proudly, referring to the organization for children operated by the Communist Party.

"And the least useful?" I asked half jokingly.

"Oh, that would be dismantling and rebuilding a Kalashnikov rifle in total darkness."

The provodnitsa, a rake-thin woman in her forties, came to collect the tickets and to take our orders for tea and coffee. Her working life comprises living in a small compartment at one end of the carriage, checking tickets, tending the samovar, and generally keeping passengers in order. Cynics would say that her only function is to lock the toilet door whenever you need it most.

Each carriage has a toilet at each end, and the advantage, for those who chose to travel first class, is that there are only two bunks in each compartment, so eighteen people share the facilities. In third class — which I've never experienced — all the internal walls have been removed making space for fifty-four wooden bunks. String vests, chubby grandmothers, noisy children, and unpleasant odours are an inescapable part of the third class experience.

When travelling by train, none of my fellow passengers were able to explain satisfactorily why in the classless society of the Soviet Union there are so many classes of compartment. This group was no different and, after the introductions and small talk, the conversation soon turned to sport and, in particular, the Ukrainian Olympic stars.

Great Olympic Moments

"Bubka and Latynina are the two I remember most," said the coach with enthusiasm. "We were spellbound." I knew he was referring to pole-vaulter Serhiy Bubka, who set thirty-five world records and was repeatedly voted the world's best athlete; and gymnast Larisa Latynina, who won more medals than anyone else.

"I'll never forget the 1988 Olympic Games held in Seoul," he continued. "It was a balmy September evening, the balcony doors were open, and we were crowded around my parents' colour TV." (At the time it would have cost the equivalent of three months salary.)

"A Ukrainian had already won the gold medal for the high jump when Bubka entered the Jamsil Stadium in front of a crowd of one hundred thousand people. The atmosphere was electric," continued the coach.

"Bubka always chose a heavier and stiffer pole than his competitors, and his success lay in his unusually strong arms, fantastic acceleration over twenty-two strides, and technique for planting the pole. In a straight race he could run the hundred metres in 10.45 seconds; he was a natural athlete."

He paused, recounting his feelings from twenty years earlier. "The wining jump was over in a few seconds. I held my breath as Bubka planted the pole beneath the bar, forcing it to bend. Pole and vaulter momentarily stopped before the pole whip-lashed him skyward and he twisted over the bar, set at 5.90 metres. He had won the gold medal and the stadium and households throughout the Soviet Union erupted! Soon afterwards he became the first man to clear six metres — for decades considered impossible — and is the only man to vault 6.14 outdoors." He breathed deeply, contentedly, as if it were his own achievement.

Pole vault, with its practical origin as a means of crossing rivers, was the sort of sport the authorities wanted people to appreciate. It required speed, strength, precision, and intellect. In contrast to the javelin, discus, hammer, shot put, and so on, which are highly regulated, the pole can be of any length or material of the athlete's choosing. The limits are set by what one can lift and its flexibility and strength. If it snaps (the athlete's nightmare), there's a good chance he'll end up looking like a piece of shashlik on a skewer.

I learned later that Bubka was the first generation of Soviet sportspeople to take advantage of sponsorship, and each one of those fourteen centimetres above six metres earned him an estimated US$40,000 US from Nike.[1]

It was sport that provided the first big popular cultural breakthrough following the establishment of an independent Ukraine;

winning the Eurovision song contest was the second breakthrough. Every year of this decade, a Ukrainian has set some sort of world record, though 2004 is probably the most memorable year. Yana Klochkova, four-time Olympic champion, was named the world's best swimmer; Vitali Klitschko won the most prestigious World Boxing Council super heavyweight title; Andriy Shevchenko was honoured with Europe's most prestigious Golden Ball soccer award, and Vasyl Virastuyk was named the planet's strongest man.

In the Atlanta, Sydney, and Athens Olympics, Ukraine won sixty-nine medals, and in Athens in 2004, Ukraine was placed twelfth out of just over two hundred countries. Their Olympic success has been creditable when you consider that they are grossly under-funded, a fact which came to prominence during the 2004 Olympics. Prime Minister Viktor Yanukovych promised to pay each gold medal winner US$100,000, but he and nearly two hundred officials who attended the games partied hard, causing the State Committee for Sport to become bankrupt. Incidentally, the offer was a far better deal than was on offer in neighbouring Belarus, where gold medal winners received a lifetime supply of sausages. Two years later, Ukraine was still only able to allocate less than four dollars per person for the provision of all sports facilities in Ukraine.[2]

The Provodnitsa

The provodnitsa returned with lemon tea, and we paid her for the beverages and for the bedding (which is usually charged separately from the ticket).

The role of the provodnitsa has been immortalised in Ukraine and Russia by Verka Serduchka in the TV programme, *Sleeping Car.* The part of Verka is played by the Ukrainian male actor Andrei Danilko, and the TV show takes place in the studio-based mock-up of a sleeping compartment. There, in a carnival-like atmosphere, the provodnitsa interviews famous guests referred to as "passengers." Verka talks in Surzhyk, a cross between Ukrainian and Russian, and the word literally means a low grade mixture of wheat and rye flour.

Part of this program's appeal is that the viewer is never sure where the train is headed or how the show will end.

Danilko achieved wider recognition — notoriety even — for being voted second in the 2007 Eurovision Song Contest, dressed in drag and singing a song with ambiguous lyrics. To add to the controversy, the official video of the song contains lots of pornography.

Ukraine is split over the characters played by Danilko; some members of Ukraine's Parliament have denounced him, whilst others praise him. Those looking for deeper meaning in the character of Verka insist that he gets to the heart of what it means to live in Ukraine today. According to this view, his use of Surzhyk shows that Ukraine is as much Russian as it is Ukrainian, and the train's lack of direction mimics the country's search for a destination. To top it off, his acerbic, frenetic, and comic approach to the show is said to reflect Ukrainians bittersweet attitude to its newfound identity.

The faint yellow glow of streetlights became less frequent as we left behind the suburbs of Kharkiv. The view was replaced by the silhouette of bare trees, many adorned with large spheres of mistletoe.

Olympic Games History

Though Russia was among the founding members of the modern Olympic Committee in 1898, and they won their first medals at the Games in London in 1917, the Soviets withdrew on the basis that it was a bourgeois sports organization. It was only thirty-five years later that they decided to take part in the 1952 Helsinki Games. Given that the Soviet Union chose to isolate itself from the Western democracies in almost every aspect of life, it was a remarkable about-turn that they chose sport as the arena in which to exhibit the superiority of their ideology. After all, the spontaneity and the outcome of sport is a difficult thing for the state to control.

Just how the Soviet Union reached this momentous decision, and what followed, is as much about the evolution of sport in Ukraine as it is about the Olympics. In the nineteenth century, sport in the Russian

Empire was confined to the military and landed gentry who engaged in the pursuits of hunting, fishing, and shooting. For peasants, there was little time or opportunity for such pleasures, and though frowned upon by the authorities, the most common sporting pastime was wrestling, which was well established in cities and rural areas and was particularly associated with the travelling circus.

Two of the most famous wrestlers of the time were the Ukrainians, Ivan Poddubny and his wife, Masha Poddubnaya. He was a six-time world wrestling champion, and some say he was unbeaten for twenty-five years. Not to be outdone, his wife was women's world champion six times and her trademark, according to circus posters of the time, was to take on any other woman.

With the development of stronger commercial links with Western Europe by the turn of the twentieth century, foreign sports such as football, tennis, skating, fencing, rowing, and gymnastics began to take root, particularly in the trading cities of St. Petersburg and Odesa. British sailors visiting Odesa are generally given credit for introducing football as early as the 1860s, and the first newspaper account of a football game appears in the Lviv Gazette in July 1894.

Just prior to World War I, football leagues had been established in Odesa, Kyiv, Kharkiv, and the Donbas, but the organisation and facilities were primitive. When Kyiv played St. Petersburg in 1911, the Kyivans met the opposition team (who had paid for their own tickets) at Kyiv railway station and provided them with dinner, bed, and breakfast. The next day some three-thousand people — the largest crowd in the home team's history — stood on the chalk touch line of an improvised football pitch and watched the home team win 3-0. It was a foretaste of Kyiv's importance as a football city.

Russia's early experience at the Olympics was mixed. Only six athletes had attended the 1908 games and the Tsar had had to sponsor the team for the 1912 Games. The following year, he decided to hold the 1st All-Russian Olympics in celebration of three hundred years of Romanoff rule, and a five-thousand-seat stadium was built in Kyiv to host the track and field and cycling events. As part of the event, a five hundred kilometre motorcycle race was run from Kyiv to Chernivtsi, and it was probably the first point-to-point timed motorcycle race in the world.

With the October Revolution came change. Though both socialism and sport were products of industrialisation and urbanisation, they were rarely associated together in the early years of the Soviet Union. We know Lenin had a positive view of sport, but since few of the Soviet Union's first leaders played sport of any sort, short of agreeing that "capitalist sports" were to be avoided, there was no clear policy.

Ukrainian-born Anatoly Lunacharsky, who held the post of the Soviet People's Commissar of Enlightenment and was responsible for culture and education, was one of the few who displayed any interest. In 1922, he invited the mother of modern dance, Isadora Duncan, to the Soviet Union to build a new approach to dance and gymnastics. But she was soon dismayed by the authorities' lack of commitment and, having stayed just long enough to get married to the poet Sergei Yesenin, a man 17 years her junior, she departed within two years.

Some Communist extremists advocated the dismantling of all stadiums and promoted the invention of new games devoid of competition, based on pageants, mass rallies, and excursions, whilst for those trying to establish the Pioneers and the Young Communist League (the Komsomol) sport was to be an ideological foundation stone. But these utopian approaches only survived until the 1930s when the foundations for the next six decades of Soviet sport were established.

"Passports ready!" the provodnitsa shouted as she knocked on each compartment door and headed off to lock the toilet door.

The train slowed to a crawl as we arrived at the last station on the Ukrainian side of the border with Russia, and the Customs Officials who were gathered there in small groups stubbed out their cigarettes and got ready to board. The compartment door slid open, and a burst of cold air preceded a lady with orange bouffant hair. A few minutes later, after checking our passports and baggage, she left.

"Did you know she's wearing a wig?" asked the young athlete Vasili on the upper bunk opposite. I shook my head in surprise and he explained that many women who work in cold temperatures wear a wig for warmth. "It's a practical solution to an annual problem," he said.

Fifteen minutes later we rolled forward a few kilometres to the border city of Belgorod for a customs check on the Russian side of the border. This time it was a disagreeable, bald Customs Official who was clearly shaken by the laughter that followed his entrance.

Sometime in the early 1930s, Stalin and his colleagues realised that the Soviet Union needed to change its attitude to sport. Out went isolation and non-competitiveness, and in came all manner of competitive sports, the official encouragement of leagues and trophies, and participation in specially selected international sport organisations. By the middle of the decade the demand for world records became a constant theme.

In Ukraine the effect of these actions was obvious to everyone. Twenty-thousand-seat stadiums were built in Kyiv, Kharkiv, and Odesa and these became the homes of club teams. Leagues were introduced in basketball, wrestling, shooting, ice hockey, boxing, and football — the so-called "major sports" — but other sports also benefited. In 1937, Ukraine hosted the world's longest cycle race, the 14,317 kilometre run from Odesa to Vladivostok.

As far as we know, Joseph Stalin was not a fan of sport, though he did often watch the annual parade on Red Square on Physical Culture Day. This was an orchestrated piece of political theatre that masqueraded as a sporting pageant and involved thousands of athletes. For weeks before the 1937 parade, for example, members of the Spartak Society sewed a huge green carpet (136 x 64 metres) for use as a football pitch, and stored it in the GUM department store opposite the Kremlin. On the day, seven goals were prearranged for the thirty-minute match so Stalin would not become bored whilst watching from on top of Lenin's mausoleum.[3] Perhaps it was here that he saw the enormous potential of sport to create propaganda value.

For the next decade he openly denounced the Olympics as a "bourgeois club," and refused to join the movement. He recognised that his teams needed international competition in order to establish their ability, but he was concerned about the effect losing would have on the West's perception of communism. In his memoirs, Minister of Culture and Sport Nickolai Romanov recalls, "In order to gain permission to go to international competitions I had to send a special note to Stalin guaranteeing victory."[4]

Romanov must have been only too aware of the price of failure since Stalin's purges had already claimed the lives of five Ministers of Sport and countless officials and players.

The Soviet Union declined to attend the London Olympics in 1948, but their observers deduced that they would have been second to the USA had they taken part. Stalin was encouraged by the news and agreed to join the Olympic movement so that they could participate in the next Olympic, at Helsinki, but only on the condition that his officials promised him victory.

Memories of Olympic Games

After clearing customs at Belgorod and travelling for awhile, it became late and my companions and I were ready to turn in for the night. Impervious to the cold, Vasili stripped off his shirt and stretched, his muscles bulging and coiling like snakes. As I lay on my top bunk I was reminded of my first rail journey in the Soviet Union in 1981.

It was on the Trans-Siberian Railway, a journey of almost mythical proportions in which I clickity-clacked my way around almost a third of the globe. Depending on where one lived in the Soviet Union, most citizens had a rail journey of 12 to 148 hours in order to get to Moscow, and railways have always been connected with the national interests. If the Tsars had managed to connect the Crimea by rail to the Empire's heartlands, for example, the Russo-Turkish war would have had a different end, and a more reliable rail system would also have had a profound impact on World War I and the Civil War that followed.

Once the early risers start to go to the wash room and compartment doors are slammed, sleep becomes impossible for just about everyone. A cold, restless night interrupted by occasional stops and the incoherent blaring of tannoys (the platform public-address system) meant I was not in the best of moods. Our provodnitsa brought tea and we shared our prepacked breakfasts. I joined the communal affair with as much enthusiasm as I could muster.

"What did you think about the Soviet performance in the Olympics?" asked Vasili as he chewed on a meat pie.

"I know the world was astounded by your performance at the games in Helsinki," I replied.

Initially the Soviets had claimed overall victory but later conceded to the USA by a whisker. It was a remarkable debut, but the promise of victory to Stalin had not been kept so he disbanded the disgraced football team which had lost to Yugoslavia. Tito's Yugoslavia had just broken from the Soviet Union and Stalin was angered by both the political and sporting defeat.

Continuing, I added, "Four years later you won both the summer and winter Olympics, which demonstrated your superiority over the Americans." They considered my response and their faces beamed with delight.

"When I was a teenager, I knew that the Soviet Union was one of the greatest sporting nations and that you were consistently good at all the Olympic sports. I assumed that just about everyone played sport."

Vasili nodded.

I must have been just one of millions of people who held this view and the implied message that communism was a success and that it bred determined, healthy, and patriotic people. This, of course, was exactly the view that the Kremlin wanted to everyone to hold. For the most part, Soviet athletes upheld this wholesome view of Soviet sport, and those transgressions that did get reported in the West appear, with hindsight, as an amusing commentary on the attitudes of the athletes.

Watch Your Hats, Girls!

In 1952, the first Soviet gold medal was won by a burly schoolteacher from Kyiv, Nina Ponomareva, who threw her discus 168 feet and 8½ inches. She was in the spotlight again in 1956 when the Soviet team withdrew from the White City Games in London after she was accused of stealing five hats from the C&A store on Oxford Street, which were described as "One red woollen hat and four feathered half-hats of varying colours."[5]

On arriving in London the athletes were given a spending allowance by their Soviet managers. Intent on purchasing items rarely available back home, Nina and her girlfriends went shopping for lipstick, earrings, and fancy hats. The C&A store guards, of whom Nina was completely unaware, arrested her after seeing her secrete the hats in two bags and, not knowing who she was, they charged her with shoplifting. The Soviet officials in London insisted that no one should be sent to court unless their guilt had already been proved and they were further outraged when the British officials refused to intervene in the judicial process.

"Having considered all the evidence," said Magistrate Clyde Wilson, 'I must find the case proved ... I realize the fallibility of human nature. The hats displayed constitute a considerable temptation to women. I think the interests of justice will be served if I discharge the prisoner absolutely on payment of three guineas costs."[6]

It was about US$9.

The following month she walked onto the field at the Melbourne Olympics to friendly shouts of "Watch your hats, girls, here comes Nina!"

Cheating: a Medal at Any Cost

Behind the Iron Curtain, more serious transgressions of the Olympic spirit were now being planned. Perhaps only a few people were involved during the 1950s and 1960s, but within a few decades most of the athletes — and many close observers — knew that hypocrisy, corruption, and cheating permeated the Soviet system.

Mindful of my limited knowledge about the Olympics; I decided to qualify my teenage view. "Now I'm not so sure about the Soviet victories," I reflected as we tidied up the breakfast table.

"What do you mean?" Vasili countered.

"Well, the philosophy of, 'a medal at any cost,' meant that the Soviet Union used professionals when the rules required everyone to be amateur, and there's also the issue of drug use."

After an uneasy pause it was the coach who answered.

"Our sportsmen were registered as workers at factories and institutes, but everyone knows that they never worked there. But isn't that the same as an American sportsman going to study at a college that has elite sporting facilities? He gets a degree not because he's good at philosophy but because of his sporting success.

"Anyway, in the 1970s the 'amateur' requirement was dropped and we still carried on winning. As for drug taking, there were cases but I don't think it was widespread, and all countries did it."

Sport played anywhere is about identity. But in the Soviet Union sport was something that Soviet citizens chose to do or watch, rather than being told to do by the authorities. As such, it was an especially personal and satisfying experience in which the process of choosing ones own heroes was beyond the reach of the authorities. Despite the authorities' insistence that individual results were a product of the Soviet system, ordinary people still idolized Olympic sports people.

I neither knew the facts well enough, nor was prepared to challenge their strongly held beliefs. But having researched the subject, there appears to be overwhelming evidence that Soviet sport was managed in order to achieve a policy of "a medal at any cost." In particular, three Ukrainian sportsmen, presumably tired of having to compromise their integrity, were among the first to speak out against the hypocrisy and mendacity of the bureaucratic Soviet sports machine.

Yuri Vlasov is a five-time Olympic gold medal winner who held thirty-four world records and became the first man to clean and jerk 200 kilograms. Participating in the Super Heavyweight weightlifting class, and wearing his characteristic rim spectacles, this enormous bear of a man is widely regarded as one of the weightlifting greats. (His father, the Soviet Consul General in Shanghai, was executed by the Chinese as a spy.) As Chairman of the Weightlifting Federation,

Vlasov openly expressed concern about the use of drugs and the damaging role that some coaches played in Soviet sport. He named the members of the Soviet Sports Committee who first introduced anabolic steroids in 1968, and he also claimed that as early as 1959 he had overheard a cycling coach telling the Minister of Sport that without amphetamines they could expect no medals. Shortly afterwards amphetamines were made available.[7][8]

For his candour, Vlasov was ostracized. Though it was the period of Perestroika, references to his Olympic successes were erased, and the TV film of him carrying the Soviet banner at the Rome Olympic was edited to exclude him.

Another prominent Ukrainian sportsman to openly criticise the Soviet Union's use of growth stimulants, growth retardants, and anabolic steroids was Igor Ter-Ovanesyan. Born in Kyiv of Armenian ancestry (*Ter* means terror in Armenian), he participated in five Olympic Games and was the only Soviet to ever hold the world long-jump record.

In the wake of the Ben Johnson drug scandal, Ter-Ovanesyan launched a campaign against drug taking. In particular, he drew attention to scandal of giving child athletes drugs, and advised, "Society needs proper legislation to combat this evil, seriously punishing athletes and doctors, coaches, and drug suppliers."[9]

A few years later the Americans admitted that the CIA had recruited US sprinter David Sime to persuade jazz-loving Ter-Ovanesyan to defect. During a dinner the two sportsmen were tentatively discussing the defection when, according to an agreed plan with Sime, a CIA agent, referred to as Mr. Wolf, joined the pair of them. But it turned out to be a miscalculation. When Mr. Wolf started to talk in an Armenian dialect, Ter-Ovanesyan, thinking he had been set up by a double agent, stood up abruptly and left the restaurant. The deal was off![10]

The third sportsman to speak out — but this time about the restrictions placed on freedom of speech — was Vladimir Maslachenko, one of the Soviet Union's most famous footballers. Born near Dnipropetrovsk, Maslachenko had tried his hand at football, volleyball, basketball, athletics, and ping-pong before settling for football goalkeeper. Noted for his courageous and acrobatic style, he played eight times for the Soviet national team and participated in two World Cups.

In an article in Moscow's *Sobesednik* magazine, he recalled that sportsmen and journalists were invited to a meeting with the Minister of Sport just before the World Cup in Spain. The Minister explained that they were forbidden from discussing that Soviet sportsmen were paid professionals who were rewarded with cash payments for exemplary performance; that the Olympic Committee was run by government officials who knew about and sanctioned drug use by the athletes; that the security forces were the real sponsors of Dynamo sports club, and that they shadowed all athletes whenever they travelled abroad.[11]

A number of other people interested in Soviet sport have also written on the subject, in particular James Rhiordan. He explains that the policy of "a medal at any cost" required the Soviets to be good at all sports, and this meant that funding was given to a select group of people at the top of those sports. Scarce foreign exchange was spent to ensure that medals could be won in fencing, canoeing, diving, sailing, and equestrian events — sports that Soviet citizens never showed an interest in doing, let alone watching. (Beyond football, basketball, and ice hockey, other sports had a smaller fan base than in the West.) This use of resources meant that local sports facilities were either poor or nonexistent and directly contradicted the Soviet's avowed aim of "sport for all."[12]

Facilities for players and spectators did improve gradually. Kyiv constructed the hundred-thousand-seat Republic Stadium in the 1960s, for example, but they remained poor compared with other countries. By the collapse of the Soviet Union, there were still only eight stadiums in the entire USSR with capacities above fifty thousand, compared to nine in the State of California alone, and only two thousand swimming pools compared with the million plus in the USA, and just one hundred indoor skating rinks compared with ten thousand in Canada.[13]

European Cup 2012

The provodnitsa walked past the compartment shouting, "We arrive in 15 minutes."

Outside, densely-packed grey buildings and factories seemed intent on spilling onto the railway line. Occasionally, I noticed multicoloured rugs and carpets hanging from apartment balconies; people insist that the sub-zero temperatures and a dusting of snow draws out the dirt.

"You're all excited to be hosting the European Cup in 2012?" I said as the train slowed to a crawl. My question was greeted with laughter.

"Most of the oligarchs own football teams," responded the coach, "and so building the four stadiums should be achievable, but funding the road and rail infrastructure, hotels, and things like security and policing may be more problematic."

We talked then about the building of the infrastructure, which will require significant funding, dedication, and team work and, therefore, it is no surprise that there is apprehension about a repetition of Eurovision 2005 in Kyiv. On that occasion, visiting guests had to live in tarpaulin tents because of the lack of hotel rooms.

Indeed, there are few reasons to be optimistic. The people who run Ukraine today also run Ukrainian sport and, as in the old days, sport is as politicised as ever. Shaktar Donetsk, the football team aligned to President Leonid Kuchma and Viktor Yanukovych, faced a quandary when Viktor Yushchenko's Orange Revolution was born. Temporarily, Shaktar Donetsk changed their orange strip for a white one. Sportsmen have also taken political sides, either willingly or unwillingly. The Klichko brothers boxing duo bravely took the side of the underdog Yushchenko in 2004, whilst the footballer Andriy Shevchenko appeared on TV looking as uncomfortable as a hostage as he read a script in support of Yanukovych.

As the train suddenly juddered to a halt within sight of the platform, the coach laughed and said, "You know, the state of sport in Ukraine reminds me of an old joke. Stalin, Khrushchev, and Brezhnev are riding in a train which stalls, and they turn to Stalin for guidance. He commands immediately, 'Shoot the engineers, exile the crew, and get someone new.' The train leaps forward, but soon afterwards, it stalls again and Khrushchev takes control. He pardons the exiled crew and returns them to their jobs. The train lurches forward but inevitably stalls once more. Brezhnev ponders for a moment and orders, 'Everyone, pull down the blinds and we'll pretend we're moving.'"

FEAST OR FAMINE

IN RECENT YEARS Kyiv has developed a labyrinth of subterranean shopping malls. Rather than build upwards, architects and builders have burrowed into the rich black soil. On a cold winter day, when outside temperatures are -20° Celsius and half a metres of snow lies on the ground, it can be quite comforting to descend into this brightly lit world of designer goods and cafes.

"Good morning!" I shouted to Yuri as I approached the baker and his daughter, Polina, in the subterranean shopping mall. I had agreed to meet them outside the premises where they were establishing a high-class, artisanal Ukrainian bakery. It was located in the recently built Metrograd shopping mall, a leviathan construction built by Indians to cater to the boom in consumer spending in the post-Soviet economy. The enormous site is located in central Kyiv between Metro Teatralno and Metro Palats Sportu, and it is one of thirty malls to have been built recently. Despite this surge in development (only slowing with the onset of the global recession), the city is still regarded as a potential retail developer's heaven because Kyiv has only 50 percent the retail space per person of Moscow, and only 20 percent that of Prague.

Yuri's thick glasses were perched on the end of his beaky nose. "Come this way," he said. "The designers are here."

He steered me through a narrow wood panel door that hid the refurbishment from the shoppers. "Are the contracts signed?" I enquired.

"No, we still need to finalise arrangements with the Fire Service."

This sounded ominous. I'd first met Polina and her father some six months earlier. She managed a bakery located on the ground floor of the apartment building where I was staying. The move to Metrograd was to be a big step, especially in view of high rents compared to other sites in Kyiv. Metrograd was going to cost more than one hundred dollars per square metre per month, and that would mean selling an awful lot of premium-priced bread.

At first, I didn't understand the economics, so Yuri explained to me the hidden costs of doing business in Ukraine. The final straw that persuaded him to move from his old site was a suggestion (read *demand*) from the fire service that he should make a contribution to the Firemen's Retirement Fund if he wanted his licence renewed. Similar requests had already come from the local building administrators, the police service, and various local gangs offering to "help him" stay in business.

No, he assured me, shopping malls are expensive but most of their tenants are foreign companies and the hidden costs are already taken care of. The sweet smell of warm bread wafting up the staircase of the old apartment block would be missed.

Three designers were busy measuring the area and discussing the location of the serving counter. A wood-burning stove would be installed, if the Fire Service allowed it, but most of the bread would be baked off site. Yuri explained that the proposed design maximised the retail space but gave the customer an engaging retail experience. The concept was meant to be "sticky." Not with warm, egg-wash buns, but in terms of retaining customers by encouraging them to visit time and time again. Only ten years earlier such jargon would have meant nothing — after all we're talking about a bread shop and what could be more Soviet than that, right? — but this is the new Ukraine. And these are the new consumers.

He guided me through the building debris, chatting as we walked. "There are French bakeries in every city in Ukraine and, of course, the standard Bread Factory No.1 and Bread Factory No. 2 etc., but we believe our shop is the first Ukrainian up-market bakery focusing exclusively on traditional breads. You can buy Ukrainian bread in every corner shop, but you'll only find basic black and white breads, perhaps five varieties, whereas we'll have forty."

The words tumbled out excitedly from beneath Yuri's croissant-shaped moustache. "I've heard it said that the Danish people have many different words for snow. Well, in Ukraine we have dozens of words for the types of loaves that we produce. And, of course we have so many proverbs." He paused to reel off a few: "Bread is the head of everything; borrowed bread lies heavy on the stomach; don't say you're full if you haven't touched the bread; it's better to live in troubles and need than to eat soldiers' bread."

The Breadbasket of Europe

Ukraine is famous as the breadbasket of Europe, and historically bread and wheat products are very important to their cuisine. Ukraine provided a quarter of all grain produced in the Soviet Union and half of the grain that was exported each year. The country also influenced others: a descendent of Ukrainian wheat, called "Red Fife," is the genetic parent of virtually all wheat grown on the Canadian prairies.

Bread's significance is ingrained in the culture, and no important event can take place without it, whether it's a major festival, a birth, christening, marriage, or death. Wheat has been grown in the rich deep black soils of Ukraine for more than three thousand years, and rye, which is used in making the famous black bread, was introduced soon after. Two and a half thousand years ago when Ukraine was known as "Scythia," Greek cities such as Chersonese (near Sevastopol) were established on the Black Sea coast for grain export, and it is likely that Socrates and Plato ate bread made from Ukrainian wheat. Greek imagery is still strong today in Ukrainian design motifs.

To put that into some historical perspective, the potato only reached Ukraine three hundred years ago, followed by corn, tomatoes, pumpkins, beans, cayenne peppers, cocoa, and other plants.

"Tell me, do you really think you can pay the rent selling bread?" I expected a robust response from Yuri and his answer hinted that there was more to the venture than simply money.

"I tell you, we are losing our food history and culture. The idea that a common and relatively cheap item, such as bread, should be revered sounds quaint in this age of global trade and brands, but this is how to understand a Ukrainian. Put him in New York and he will crave Ukrainian bread no matter what his wealth. It is still the key to our hearts."

He pondered for a moment, then added, "People buy foreign breads firstly to experience them, and secondly to make a statement about their wealth. But many comment about their fluffy nature, their lack of capacity to sustain the body, and a lack of taste."

Local interest in bread is certainly high. Ukraine is one of only two countries in the world to have a national bread museum, the other being in Portugal. The Kyiv-based museum, which has had more than two million visitors, contains hundreds of examples of regional breads. Naturally, a yeasty smell pervades the museum, but one of the most memorable breads I saw had no smell whatsoever. It was baked more than ten years ago in Zhitomyr from an original World War II recipe, and it is called "Leningrad Blockade Bread." The ingredients are low quality flour, malt, bran, and paper. Ukrainian bread was also taken into space by Soviet cosmonauts: each "loaf" weighed 4.5 grams and they were eaten in pill form to help maintain energy levels.

Polina entered the small space clutching a couple of bags of loaves. Her narrow face was accentuated by her large and sombre eyes that were seemingly without pupils.

"Here we go, let's taste!" she said. Each day she was buying bread from nearby competitors for her father to try. He tore open one of the white loaves and buried his nose in its doughy cleavage.

"Additives!" He exclaimed. "Bread is more important than wine, and it appeals to the senses in the same way. Our wheat produces a hay yellow crumb, and is long in the mouth and rich. It has an intense scent of herbs and a slight acidity. Often the nose has notes of fennel and other herbs. You know, it's particularly well suited to sourdough baking methods, where small differences in the wheat do not affect the end result, but this has been doctored, probably to increase shelf life."

He frowned and broke off some crumbs, and examined them like a jeweller might inspect diamonds.

Bread for all Occasions

Evidence that Ukrainian bread has long held a place of reverence in society is reflected in the name for wheat grain, which means "all of divinity" in Ukrainian. Flour was originally ground manually between two rounded grindstones known as *querns*. But in the thirteenth century the manual process was gradually replaced, at least on the commercial scale, by water-driven and wind-driven mills. When the wheat is ground a single time, the flour retains all its constituents and it is used to bake whole-wheat products. Repeated grinding and sifting produces finer flour that can be used in baking white bread. White bread is common in the southern and south eastern regions, whereas a darker sour rye bread is more common elsewhere. Rye bread is based on a sourdough starter rather than yeast, and it imparts a mild, vinegar flavour. It is the perfect accompaniment to such Ukrainian favourites as borscht, homemade sausages, and salo — pig fat that is commonly doused in salt and eaten cold, raw, smoked, fried, or boiled.

In some communities, bread continues to be offered as a sign of hospitality at various social functions. Commonly, a circular bread and salt are placed on an embroidered cloth called a *rushnyk* (as shown on the book cover). Each guest is invited to break a piece of bread from the loaf, and to dip it into the salt whilst bowing slightly to the host. The bread represents a warm welcome whilst the salt symbolises friendship that will never sour or be corrupted by time.

Yuri was deep in discussion with the designers when I asked his daughter, "Have you completed the design for the wall panels?" A month previously we'd met at the library where she'd been researching images of bread in paintings, from which to make a wall panel for the shop.

"Not yet, but we think we'll use 'Soviet Loaves.'" I nodded in agreement. Ilya Mashkov's imposing 1936 oil painting titled *Soviet Loaves* (145cm x 175cm) is one of the best depictions captured in paint, and it shows perhaps forty different types of bread. Mashkov built up to this doughy tour de force by prototyping his subject in numerous smaller bread paintings, such as *Still Life with Loaves of Bread* and *Moscow Food*. These esoteric paintings seem to confirm that, deep in the soul, it is bread that defines our sense of well being.

Polina flicked through the folder of design plans, and stopped on the page showing the image. "Yes, it's the perfect image for our bakery; it captures the history and variety of our bread."

Yuri chirped in, seemingly conducting two conversations simultaneously. "Look, there's the Paska, the Kolach, the Korovai, the Babka, the Dyven, the Lezhen ... ." I followed his finger as he pointed to the various types.

Paska is a rich disk-shaped bread decorated with crosses, rose twists, and pinecone shapes that is prepared at Easter. Traditionally, it is carried to church in an Easter basket to be blessed by the priest and then eaten at home. Babka is also an Easter bread, but it is softer and lighter than Paska, and contains dried fruit and fruit zest. It is baked in a tall cylindrical pan and sometimes glazed with icing. Some historians believe that the name derives from the word "Babushka," and its diminutive "Baba" meaning grandmother, and that it originated at the time when women priests were authority figures in the early church.

Kolach is round-shaped bread usually eaten at Christmas or at funerals. The dough is braided with three strands representing the Holy Trinity, and then formed into a circle, a symbol that indicates eternity. At Christmas a candle is lit in the centre of the Kolach, and left to burn all night. At funerals a Kolach, as large as a metre in diameter, is the centrepiece of the dinner table. Guests are given their own smaller Kolach, and it is traditional to place a loaf over the heart of the dead person to provide sustenance in the afterlife.

Many of the breads are elaborately decorated, and in rural areas this became an art form practised by Ukrainian women. It is best seen in wedding breads, of which the Korovai is the most common. Like the Kolach it is round, and like the Babka it has rich ingredients. But it is intricately decorated with symbols that reflect beliefs and rituals. Cone shapes represent fertility, doves represent love, thorns represent the problems of marriage, a turtle warns a wife not to become lazy, and a hedgehog reminds a husband to be gentle with his wife.

The preparation of the Korovai is also steeped in tradition. Ideally, it is to be made by seven young women selected from seven happily married couples. They should take water from seven different wells and use flour from seven different fields, eggs from seven different birds, and so on for each ingredient. Dough sculptures and structures are put on the bread and the culinary extravaganza is decorated with periwinkle and glazed, or even shellacked, in order to preserve it. The whole process is a family and community effort — albeit without the help of men — and it is a symbol that everyone accepts the married couple. Alcohol and traditional songs lubricate the elaborate baking process, as shown in this verse:

> Herbs in the garden,
> Seeds behind the shed;
> And at the bride's home,
> Two are about to be wed.
> We have flowers for the bouquet,
> And all the older cooks we need,
> But who will bake the korovai?
> And who will drink the mead?
> The young women will work the dough and knead;
> The old women, they will drink the mead.

The Holodomor

After a few moments' thought, I aired my reservation about the image Polina was considering for the wall panels. Yuri was nearby, listening.

"I think it's a wonderful picture to use," I offered in support. "It expresses the notion of the abundance, wealth and beauty of bread.

My only hesitation is that Mashkov painted it just shortly after the Holodomor."

The term Holodomor is used exclusively to apply to the 1932-33 famine that occurred in Ukraine. The word comes from the Ukrainian words "holod" meaning "hunger," and "mor" meaning "plague," and is commonly described as "murder by hunger."

"That was typical of the Soviet system," Yuri replied solemnly. "It was always necessary to show abundance when there was scarcity, show unity when there was disarray, to show colour when there was darkness, and to show that it was strong when in reality it was weak. The painter, no doubt, painted such a composition to save his own life."

He paused, then added, "That just adds to its poignancy as part of our culture."

I asked Polina for her view of the Holodomor. "I don't know what to think," she replied. "We don't talk about it in our family and I wasn't told about it at school. It's just our history and we can't change it."

She sighed, flicked her hand through her short blonde hair cut back in a wave — the latest style in Kyiv — and looked towards her father. For once he was silent.

Most observers agree that the famine was caused artificially by Stalin's policies. Historians estimate the number of Ukrainian deaths to have been between five and ten million people, which puts it on a par with the Holocaust. As an example of man's inhumanity to his fellow man, the Holodomor is one of the most shocking examples.

The first Soviet Ukrainian official to admit the existence of the genocide was Volodymyr Shcherbytsky, the Head of the Communist Party of Ukraine. On December 25, 1987 he confirmed that there had been "famine in some localities of Ukraine."

It took more than seventy years for the Ukrainian political leadership to have the courage to recognise the famine, and many in the Russian leadership still dispute the causes. Ukrainian schools are still uncertain about how to teach it.

Though the subject is complex and emotive, it's worth spending time to understand the Holodomor. From the mid 1920s the Soviet Union had ambitious industrialisation plans, and agricultural reform was seen both as a necessity to feed the workers of the industrial centres and to earn export cash from selling wheat overseas. Stalin encouraged a policy of "collectivisation" to consolidate individual land and labour into collective farms, but whilst the policy was voluntary, progress remained slow. By 1929, less than six percent of Ukrainian peasant households and arable land were collectivised, and so Stalin imposed the policy.

Stalin believed that if the peasants were left alone they would never produce the surpluses that were required for export and be able to fund the massive industrialisation plans, nor would they be willing to sell their produce at low prices. What was needed, he reasoned, was a class struggle in which the richer peasants, or "Kulaks" (who he believed were hoarding grain and organising resistance), were eliminated as a class. With the Kulaks removed, the poor peasants would see themselves as equal partners and would work towards achieving the wheat production targets. But the reasoning was flawed. The great majority (95 percent) of peasants were very poor, and few willingly gave up their land and livestock for what was on offer.

A decree in January 1930 established the target date for collectivisation as spring 1932, but just two months later Stalin claimed his officials in the countryside were already "dizzy with success," and that nearly half of peasant farms had been collectivised.

The twenty-five thousand officials were mainly made up of "socially conscious" party supporters who came to be known as the "twenty-five thousanders." They visited each village and tried to encourage groups of ten or twenty households to give up their land and livestock and to form a collective. In return, the collective was allowed a small garden on which to grow their own produce, and they could keep any grain that was above the annual quota.

It was not an attractive proposition, reminding many of serfdom under the Tsars. Most peasants killed their livestock and resisted the change, or agreed to join a collective whilst the officials were in their region only to revert to their old ways when the officials left.

As a result of this direct resistance, many peasants were murdered and more than three-hundred thousand Ukrainians were exiled to beyond the Urals and to Central Asia, with thousands dying during the gruelling journey.

The wheat crop was good in 1931 and expectations for the crop the following year were also high. But when it became clear that the crop would not meet the plan, the remaining kulaks were blamed and swift retribution was imposed. A resolution was passed in November that urged the Soviet security forces to increase their effectiveness. Two of Stalin's closest supporters, Vyacheslav Molotov and Lazar Kaganovich, visited Ukraine many times to ensure the quotas were being met, and they ordered the seizure of all food from every house, even if there was no grain to be collected.

The following year, the government passed a law concerning public property rights which was commonly called "Law of the Wheat Ears." It imposed a minimum prison sentence of ten years for any theft of public property, including the theft of a single ear of wheat. Within five months more than fifty thousand people had been sentenced, of which more than two thousand were executed.

In January 1933, Stalin and Molotov signed Decree Number 3861 that obliged the security forces to set up barricades at Ukraine's national borders, and in large cities such as Kharkiv, to prevent people crossing the borders. It also prevented any external communication of the famine, and prohibited foreign journalists from entering the country. A month earlier the government had introduced new identity papers and registration requirements. Tickets to travel by rail, for example, could only be purchased if approved by the authorities.

Actions such as these support the critics' view that far from trying to alleviate the famine conditions, Stalin was purposefully pursuing a policy of subjugation of Ukrainians. His supporters point to his apparent acts of compassion, such as an emergency distribution of grain in one district, or grain handouts to foreign workers helping in the construction of major Soviet engineering projects. But such acts were small in number, narrow in scope, and limited in effect.

Grain exports dropped from nearly five million tons in 1931–32 to less than two million tons in 1933-34. But it is harrowing that there were grain exports at all, given the appalling conditions being endured by the peasants: Ukrainians were dying at the rate of twenty-five thousand per day, one thousand per hour, or seventeen every minute. For comparison, six thousand people per day were killed during World War II.

In recent years a small number of books have been published containing interviews with survivors, and they make distressing reading. Here is an extract from a BBC New Kyiv report which gives a flavour for the material covered by the researchers:

Seventy-five years ago, Ekaterina saw seven members of her family and almost all of her neighbours starve to death.

"Don't go near the priest's house either — because the neighbours there have killed and eaten their children." Ekaterina Marchenko recalls a warning from her mother.

"Of our neighbours I remember all the Solveiki family died, all of the Kapshuks, all the Rahachenkos too — and the Yeremo family — three of them, still alive, were thrown into the mass grave."

Ekaterina, her mother and brother, survived by eating tree bark, roots and whatever they could find — but she says starvation drove others to terrible deeds.

"One day mother said to us, 'children, you can't take your usual shortcut through the village anymore because the grandpa in the house nearby killed his grandson and ate him — and now he's been killed by his son ... .'"[1]

A few years after the Holodomor, a census was conducted of the USSR. Ukraine's population figure should have shown an absolute decline as a result of the millions who died, and it should have shown a relative decline, against the other republics, because of the lower birth rate during the famine years. The figures were never published, however, because Stalin suppressed them and ordered many of the census officials to be shot. Two years later, in 1939, a "corrected" census was issued which, many believe, was doctored. It showed that the Ukrainian population fell by only three million whereas the Russian population increased by sixteen million between 1926 and 1939.

Collaboration for Silence

Another troubling aspect of the Holodomor is the number of bystanders who did nothing. European governments and the United States government received numerous contemporary reports about the unfolding tragedy, but choose not to say anything in public.

But a few brave and honest souls did talk about it openly. The English journalist Malcolm Muggeridge was the Moscow reporter for the *Manchester Guardian*. Defying the travel ban and going to Ukraine in 1933 to see for himself, he reported, "They [soldiers] had gone over the country like a swarm of locusts and taken away everything edible; they had shot and exiled thousands of peasants, sometimes whole villages; they had reduced some of the most fertile land in the world to a melancholy desert."[2]

Muggeridge was a great friend of George Orwell, the author of *Animal Farm,* and if you've read the book you've also read about the Holodomor, perhaps without realising it. But it was Gareth Jones, a Welsh journalist, who is credited with first publishing the news. Ukraine's Ambassador to Great Britain referred to him recently as "Ukraine's unrecognised hero." Jones was inspired to go to Ukraine because of a family connection via his mother. She had been the tutor of some of the grandchildren of steel industrialist John Hughes. In March 1933, shortly after a visit to Germany to meet Adolf Hitler, Jones visited Ukraine and filed a report that appeared in several papers, including the *Manchester Guardian* and the *New York Evening Post.*

His report opened with the sentences, "I walked along through villages and twelve collective farms. Everywhere was the cry, 'There is no bread. We are dying.'"[3]

Jones was banned from visiting the Soviet Union and died, in mysterious circumstances, two years later after being kidnapped and shot whilst reporting from Mongolia. There were suspicions that Stalin's secret police organization was responsible.

Walter Duranty, a Liverpool-born reporter for the *New York Times* in Moscow, challenged Jones' article in a published reply under the heading, "Russians hungry, but not starving," and quoted a Kremlin source as saying, "Russian and foreign observers in country could see no grounds for predications of disaster."[4]

The previous year, Duranty had won the acclaimed *Pulitzer Prize* for his reporting of Stalin's industrialisation programme. Subsequently, Duranty revealed that he did know the full extent of the famine and many believe that he lied in order to maintain his coveted access to Kremlin insiders. According to US journalist Eugene Lions, the Soviets were able to elicit tacit collaborations from the American press because of an upcoming show trial of British engineers employed by the Vickers Electrical Company. Lions put it quite bluntly: "Throwing down Jones was as unpleasant a chore as fell to any of us in years of juggling the facts to please dictatorial regimes — but throw him down we did."[5]

In 2003, the Parliament of Ukraine passed a resolution declaring the famine of 1932–1933 an act of genocide, and a Joint Declaration at the United Nations has recognised the Holodomor as a great tragedy. The Russian Federation, however, officially denies that the Holodomor was an ethnic genocide and considers that Ukraine is trying to politicise the event.

For Ukraine's President Yushchenko, this is precisely the point; politics drove the genocide, and the political aim was to exterminate Ukrainian people.

Some six hundred people died in Yushchenko's home village including his grandfather. But when asked if an apology would be forthcoming, Victor Chernomyrdin, Russia's Ambassador to Ukraine replied, "We're not going to apologise ... there is nobody to apologise to."[6]

Kazimir Malevich and Suprematism

Whilst doing research at the library for paintings of bread, Polina had come across a reference to a Ukrainian painter named Kazimir Malevich. Though many outside Ukraine regard him as one of the most influential figures in twentieth-century art, she confided to me that she had never heard of him. The education system had no curriculum that included abstract art, suprematism, futurism, and so on. The only art-ism taught was Socialist realism. Malevich's place in this story is relevant because he painted what art experts consider to be the only painting to portray the Holodomor that has survived.

Kazimir Malevich was born near Kyiv in 1878. As one of six children, he spent his early years living in the villages of Ukraine, close to sugar beet plantations where his father worked. During this time, the young Kazimir developed an interest in peasant ornamental art and, in particular, the peasant art of decorated walls and stoves, and embroidery.

After studying at the Kyiv School of Art he moved in 1903 to the Moscow Institute of Painting, Sculpture and Architecture. There he worked with various modernist styles, such as those of the impressionists, fauvists, and cubists, before arriving at a style of geometric abstraction which he called Suprematism. Within five years he had his first exhibition and he exhibited with Vasily Kandinsky and with fellow Ukrainian Mikhail Larionov. Larionov was joint founder of two important and radical artistic groups, which he imaginatively called *Jack of Diamonds* and *Donkey's Tail*. He was the founder of the movement of Rayonism, which was an important step in the development of Soviet abstract art.

Malevich is credited with having painted the first geometric, totally non-representational picture, *Black Square* (1915). Suprematism asserts that the effect of colour creates a sensation that is the starting point behind all art. So, in *Black Square* the contrast between the colour black on the white background stimulates the brain and produces the emotion that is the basis of art.

How Malevich arrived at this style is not documented, but there are similarities between Ukrainian folk art and Suprematism. Both are concerned with geometrical composition, primal colours, and cosmic symbols. Conjure up an image, for example, of the Ukrainian peasant dress of red shapes embroidered on a white cotton background, and you may see a connection.

Following the Revolution, Malevich and his colleagues were in demand by a regime that was open to new ideas, and he was given the creatively titled position of Director of the Division of Visual Arts of the Russian Commissariat of Enlightenment. But the period of enlightenment was not to last. Storm clouds were gathering, and it would not have gone unnoticed to Malevich how his exhibitions of abstract work contrasted with those showing more convention works. Stalin, in particular, was growing dissatisfied with art that he could not comprehend, and he saw such paintings as an ineffectual tool for propaganda. So when Malevich travelled to Germany in 1927 to take part in one-man exhibitions where he met many of his contemporaries, including Jean Arp, Kurt Schwitters, Le Corbusier, and Walter Gropius, he had the foresight to leave many of his paintings with his friend, Hugo Haring. These later found their way to the Stedelijk Museum in Amsterdam.

Back home there would soon be no audience for *Black Square*. Malevich's Moscow exhibition was criticised, and when it moved to Kyiv Art Gallery in 1929, the Director was arrested and imprisoned. Malevich began to backdate his paintings so that he could not be accused of continuing a style that was disapproved of. But he was arrested for three months in 1930, and much of his work in Russia was destroyed then or confiscated. When he was released he continued to paint, but in a "safer" representation style.

His haunting painting, *Running Man* — or as it is also known, *Peasant Between a Cross and a Sword* — was completed in 1932 and is regarded as depicting the horror of the famine that struck Ukraine. This small painting, which hangs in the Musee National d'Art Moderne in Paris, shows a puppet-like peasant dressed in green and white running through an empty land, his hands and feet the colour of black earth. On the horizon is a cross, and behind him hangs a sword covered with blood, suspended between two peasant houses. The sword points to a single sack of grain. The land on which he runs is coloured red. There is no sun; the only yellow colour is along the bottom of the picture, buried beneath the earth.

Malevich died a penniless artist, and he was buried in a coffin that he had already painted with supremacist motifs. His work was also figuratively buried with him and only re emerged with Glasnost.

The Record Obliterated

If "Running Man" is the only surviving depiction of the Ukrainian famine, the question must be, *why?*

Throughout history there have been artists who have been willing to create images out of horror, or those that fly in the face of official policy, so it beggars belief that all Soviet artists working in the 1930s would toe the party line or flinch in the face of horror. Artists recorded just about every significant event in the twentieth century.

In fact, there are numerous surviving examples of art depicting a less severe famine in Ukraine in the 1920s, including a set of postage stamps issued by the State showing the horror as a means of raising famine relief. So the subject matter itself was not taboo.

A more likely explanation for the absence of artworks is that the artists were terrorised by the regime and when artworks had been created they were either destroyed by the artist, his family, or friends, or were destroyed by the Soviet state. Such was the power of the terror that reigned in Ukraine in the 1930s.

Yuri and Polina spent the rest of the afternoon discussing the plans with the designers, and we all met again a few months later at the "Day of Bread and Harvest" on Sofia Square. The bakers of Kyiv baked the world's biggest round loaf, and together with a few thousand attendees, we each ate a small slice of Ukraine's history.

Yuri gazed at me over half-frame glasses perched delicately on his beak-like nose. "Don't tell me," I forewarned, as the words formed on his lips, "the quality of bread is the quality of our life!"

POLITICIANS AND PARTISANS

MANY OF THE IMPORTANT leading political figures of Ukraine in the twentieth century were Tsarists or Communists, but among them were also Democrats, Republicans, Revolutionaries, Anarchists, Partisans, and Conservatives. They included the Jew, Leon Trotsky, who whimsically assumed the surname of his jailer; Lazar "Iron Man" Kaganovich, perhaps the most ruthless executioner of Stalin's policy who admired the literary works of a Ukrainian nationalist; The "Butcher of Ukraine" Nikita Khrushchev, who often visited Taras Shevchenko's grave and praised the great poet; and Leonid Brezhnev, who used tax receipts from the sale of vodka to fund his invasion of Afghanistan and inadvertently created a condition between socialism and communism called alcoholism.

Without doubt, it was the post-World War II leadership who defined the complex course of history leading to the independence of Ukraine in 1991. But let's start the story in the early years of the century.

Nowadays few people recall that it was the peasantry who swung the balance of power away from the Tsar towards the revolutionary camp, and that the vanguard of the Russian Empire's peasantry came from Ukraine. Uprisings by Ukrainian peasants began in the west of the country as early as 1903, and it was the Volhynian Regiment of Grenadiers whose rebellion in early 1917 unseated the Romanoff dynasty and led to the abdication of Tsar Nicholas II.

At the same time that my weary grandfather was returning from the Western trenches of World War I to rebuild his life in England, a civil war engulfed Ukraine that would turn the country into a raging inferno for the next four years. At least six armies engaged in a bloody version of musical chairs on Ukrainian lands, with Kyiv changing hands more than a dozen times before the Bolsheviks took the seat of power.

Despite the bloodshed and the transitory nature of the political administrations, the period has huge significance for Ukrainians. It was a time during which they declared independence and during which eastern and western Ukraine united, a time when Ukraine was recognised by foreign powers and a time when heroes were wrought.

Foremost among them was historian Mykhailo Hrushevsky, and though his political career is controversial, as a historian and statesmen he is one of Ukraine's most important figures. It is his avuncular bearded face that today adorns the 50-hryvnia note. Shortly after the February revolution in 1917, (when the Provisional Government, led by Prince Georgy Lvov, and the Congress of Soviets, led by the Bolshevik Vladimir Lenin, were vying for power in Petrograd), the Central Council in Kyiv elected Hrushevsky as the President of the Central Council, and Ukraine declared autonomy from Russia.

By October, the Provisional Government had been overthrown and the Russian Empire ceased to exist. It was, perhaps, the most consequential event of the twentieth century, referred to by Mikhail Bulgakov as "the great and terrible year." Considerably agitated by Kyiv's errant behaviour, Lenin declared a Soviet Ukrainian Republic with the city of Kharkiv as the capital, and asserted that Russia would not be great without Ukraine and that he would teach Ukrainians a good lesson.

Ukrainian Independence

Hrushevsky declared a fully sovereign Ukrainian state in January 1918. His political colours were those of a democratic idealist, and he spent most of his time establishing a national academy of sciences, two universities, and a state library — laudable institutions which continue to function today — but he left Kyiv undefended against Leon

Trotsky's advancing Red Army. With the attackers on the doorstep, the Kyivans hastily put together a unit of five hundred students to stop their advance. But it was an unrealistic objective that resulted in a shameful massacre at the Battle of Kruty, and the story was kept a secret by the Soviet authorities for many decades.

Most of the prominent government figures, including Hrushevsky, fled the city, but it didn't deter the rapacious Red Army from taking brutal reprisals on the civilian population. The Ukrainians first real stab at ruling themselves was proving challenging, and realising his inability to retake Kyiv without support, Hrushevsky approved the signing of the Brest-Litovsk Treaty with the Central Powers (Germany, Austria-Hungary, the Ottoman Empire and Bulgaria) whereby they offered military protection in return for Ukraine providing food aid.

Four hundred and fifty thousand soldiers from the Central Powers made short work of retaking Ukraine. But it soon became evident that the Ukrainians could not deliver their side of the bargain, and Hrushevsky's Central Council was overthrown in a coup that brought ex-Tsarist General Pavlo Skoropadsky to power, supported by the conservative German administration. Skoropadsky, a man of Cossack descendency who gave himself the title of "Hetman," proved to be a competent administrator. Ironically, given his pro-Empire credentials, he was the only leader during the Civil War who proved capable of fomenting any stability in Ukraine.

Bigger picture events, however, dominated his brief tenure. By late 1918 the Central Powers had lost World War I and the Germans were forced to withdraw from Ukraine, leaving the door open to a group of Ukrainian nationalists referred to as the Directorate, led initially by Volodymyr Vynnychenko, and later by enigmatic Semen Petylura. Supported by thousands of battle-hardened rebel veterans and Ukrainian forces, such as the Sich riflemen and the Zaporozhians Corp, the Directorate built on the peasants' disgust at the Hetman's attempt to reintroduce landlords and used it as a platform to re-establish the Ukrainian National Republic.

Anarchists and Anarchy

The situation throughout Ukraine was dire. Ukraine was officially at war with the Bolsheviks (the "Reds") to the northeast, and the confederation of counter-revolutionary forces (the "Whites") to the southeast, which was being led by generals Denikin, Wrangel, and Kornilov. They were fighting to establish a non-Bolshevik democratically elected Russian government. In the southwest, Romanian forces laid claim to territory, as did the Poles to the northwest, and throughout the country local agitators were leading marauding bands whose allegiance changed on whim. One such agitator was Nestor Makhno, who became one of the twentieth century's leading anarchists.

In 1989, the influential weekly, *Literary Gazette¹* magazine, with a circulation of several million copies being published under the watchful eye of The Writers' Union of the USSR, published an astonishing mea culpa about the life of Makhno — hitherto described as an outright enemy of the people and presented in Soviet films as a half-comic, half-tragic bandit. This was just the sort of revelation that created such chaos for The Central Examination Board for History and disrupted the school exams mentioned earlier.

Makhno's philosophy was the non-recognition of authority, and during the Civil War he saw the opportunity to create a free Ukraine starting in his home district of Gulyai Pole, a remote area just north of the Sea of Azov.

Anyone in any doubt as to the inhumanity of civil war should to read Dietrich Neufeld's first-hand account of the atrocities committed by Makhno's men on a community of Mennonite farmers.² As the frontline of fighting flowed more than a dozen times across their villages like a tide of evil, the farmers were forever accused of colluding with the "enemy," and were raped, brutalized, and murdered by men intent on debauchery for its own sake.

The issue that the Soviets had hidden for decades was that Makhno never hesitated to come to the aid of the Bolsheviks when they needed help. In 1919, Makhno's army practically saved Moscow from being taken by the Whites — thereby saving Communism — and the following year Trotsky's Red Army defeated the Whites only with Makhno's assistance. Then, with his enemies defeated, Trotsky's reward to Makhno was to put a price on his head and he was forced to flee.

Several years later Makhno surfaced in Paris, working at menial jobs in theatres or at the Renault Car factory. Having led Europe's largest anarchic community in the early twentieth century, he would live his remaining years in near poverty, supported by the Spanish anarchists who embraced him as a hero, but consumed with the bitterness of defeat.

The Union of West and East Ukraine

Compared with the chaos reigning in the territories of the former Russian Empire, towards the west things were more orderly. In the dying days of the Austro-Hungarian Empire, one of the Central Powers that had been defeated in World War I, the nationalist liberation movement in Galicia established the Western Ukrainian People's Republic. Based broadly on Austrian laws and the pre-existing administrative structure, the Republic moved swiftly to open missions throughout Europe and in those countries where Ukrainian emigrants lived, in particular, Canada, the USA, and Brazil.

Fleetingly in January 1919, the Western Ukrainian People's Republic joined forces with the Ukrainian National Republic, creating for the first time the political union of an independent Ukraine. But it was to be both symbolic and short-lived. Though Ukraine sent representatives to the Paris Peace Conference in July — whose remit was to define the new world order — the conference outcomes ignored the existence of the newly independent Ukraine whilst supporting the birth of Poland, Lithuania, Latvia, and Estonia.

Lacking recognition by the European powers, and weakened by fighting on so many fronts, the Ukrainian National Republic, led by Symon Petliura, gradually lost ground to the stronger Bolsheviks. Before being forced to flee Ukraine, Petliura's government relocated to three other cities, each further westward. In 1920 Russia signed the Riga Treaty with Poland, whereby Russia recognised Poland's claim to Galicia in return for recognition that the rest of Ukraine would be taken by the Russians.

Ukraine had rendered a great service to Europe, but the Europeans either didn't recognise it or ignored it. While the Ukrainian steppes smouldered with rebellion, Ukraine could not be used as a safe starting point for the communist invasion of Europe, and red Russia and red Hungary, led by the Bolshevik leader Bela Kun, were unable to unite. Had they done so, the history of Western Europe would undoubtedly have been different.

Symon Petliura fled to Paris where he continued to lead the Ukrainian National Republic in exile. He was assassinated by a young Jewish Ukrainian, and the trial at the Court of Assizes in 1926 — one of the few in France to be composed of a popular jury — gripped all Europe. The killer's demeanour was described wonderfully by *TIME* magazine:

> Short, ugly, he yet commanded the attention of the whole court, for he told his story, not as do many prisoners, shamefaced and haltingly, forced to reveal their crimes and motives by harassing lawyers — no, watchmaker Schwartzbard openly confessed with gleaming eyes and hysterical mien, his body trembling with passion, how he slew Symon Petliura to avenge the deaths of thousands of Jews slain in pogroms, which he charged Petliura instigated.[3]

Miraculously, given Schwartzbard's admission of guilt, he was found innocent. It was a verdict that made Jews rejoice and shocked many who believed that the only explanation was that the Soviets had manipulated the French judicial system.

Joining the Soviet Union

Many Bolsheviks believed that they "solved" the question of a Ukrainian state in 1921 when they established the Ukrainian Soviet

Socialist Republic, and in the following year joined it with the other Bolshevik-controlled states of Belarus and Transcaucasia (Azerbaijan, Georgia, and Armenia) to form the Soviet Union.

The Civil War had forged a new Ukrainian consciousness in the peasantry and city dwellers that had previously been germane only to the intellectuals. This time they had fought not for Tsar or Bolshevik, but for their homeland. The promise that the association of Soviet Republics would be based on "voluntary centralism" (that is, they could opt out later) suggested it was an idea worth going along with. But whilst Ukraine had the features of a sovereign state (including territory, a constitution, a language, administrative units, a flag and a national anthem), its freedom was soon curtailed and it became wholly beholden to Moscow.

"You could be forgiven for thinking that the early Soviet leaders would look favourably on Ukraine since three of the six leaders of the revolution were born here," a retired professor in Kyiv told me, referring to Leon Trotsky, Grigory Zinoviev, and Anatoly Lunacharsky.

"But foremost they saw themselves as Communists and revolutionaries, and somewhere behind they considered themselves as Russians or Russian Jews. Being born in Ukraine was as incidental as being born on a Tuesday."

Trotsky, a Jew born with the surname Bronstein, and who whimsically assumed the surname of his prison jailer when he was incarcerated as a youth, viewed himself as an internationalist. As he wrote in his autobiography, "In my mental equipment, nationality never occupied an independent place, as it was felt but little in everyday life. It never played a leading part — not even a recognized one — in my list of grievances."[4]

With the death of Lenin in 1924, Trotsky found himself on a different side of the ideological fence from Joseph Stalin. Whilst Trotsky remained wedded to the notion that world revolution was a prerequisite for a true socialist society, Stalin was progressively moving towards his big idea of building "Socialism in One Country." He could do without those who still carried old ideological baggage, and Trotsky was exiled.

In exile, Trotsky was passed around like a hot potato, first to Turkey, and then to France and Norway before being invited to Mexico by President Cardenas, who sent his luxurious railcar, "The Nobleman," to transport Trotsky from the coast to Mexico City. But the distance from Moscow failed to quell Trotsky's revolutionary spirit and Stalin realised the error of allowing his most indefatigable critic to go free.

Despite having a guard of six men, Trotsky knew he lived on borrowed time remarking often to his wife, "We have been spared another day." They both took comfort in the fact that you can kill a man, but not his ideas.

As it happened, the fateful year was 1940. On August 20, Ramon Mercador (also known as Monard), drove the pick of an ice axe into Trotsky's head. Mercador spent the next twenty years in the comfort of a Mexican jail cell, fully carpeted with TV, good food, and creature comforts such as a weekly private visit of his common-in-law wife. If there were doubts about the identity of his paymasters, they were dispelled on Mercador's release when he was flown to Cuba in the company of two diplomats from Czechoslovakia.

The importance of Jews like Trotsky to the establishment of the Soviet Union is well recorded. In 1918, for example, Robert Wilton, a correspondent of *The London Times* in Russia, reported that, of the 384 Commissars, more than 300 were Jews and only 13 were Russians.[5] Their participation was so clear that Winston Churchill described Communism as a "Sinister confederacy of international Jews who have gripped the Russian people by the hair of their heads and have become practically the undisputed masters of that enormous empire."[6]

Today, Ukraine has the fifth-largest Jewish community in the world, and the Ukrainian contribution to Israeli politics is unsurpassed. Three of the first four prime ministers of Israel were born in Ukraine, including "Iron Lady" Golda Meir, the world's first female Prime Minister to hold office without any prior family connection.

Kaganovich and Khrushchev

Of the original founders of the Soviet Union, only Stalin now remained alive. He would go on to lead the Soviet Union until 1953. Of the men who survived in his shadow, Lazar Kaganovich and Nikita Khrushchev both held the post of First Secretary of the Ukrainian Soviet Socialist Republic and would make the challenge for ultimate power following Stalin's death. Though both were ethnic Russians, Kaganovich was born in Ukraine, and Khrushchev was born within a stone's throw of the Ukrainian border.

Kaganovich, who earned the nickname "Iron Lazar" for his personal loyalty to Stalin, died at the age of ninety-six years, and he was one of the few people present at both the creation and the fall of the Soviet Union.

His survival is remarkable given that, by 1953, he had become Deputy Premier (and the last remaining Jew in the hierarchy), and had executed Stalin's wishes unreservedly, including orchestrating the artificial famine in the 1930s. Despite his lack of a formal education — he worked at a shoe factory in his youth — at the age of just thirty-two years he was leader of the Ukrainian Republic and rigorously implemented a strict policy of Russification (though he spoke fluent Ukrainian) and purged many officials as "Ukrainian Nationalists."

It was Kaganovich who was responsible for employing jug-eared Nikita Khrushchev. Like his mentor, Khrushchev had very little formal education, but his loquaciousness, bluntness, and folksy humour endeared him to Kaganovich and others, including Stalin. Khrushchev drank prodigious quantities of yorsh (a potent mixture of beer and vodka), and played the Ukrainian flute. Stalin would occasionally demean Khrushchev by ordering him to perform the hopak, the traditional solitary dance of the Ukrainian peasant.

During World War II, Khrushchev masterminded the political strategy in Ukraine and, within certain limits, he promoted national sentiment to win the war. Whether or not he was being hypocritical we do not know, but as this extract of a wartime speech shows, he was not averse to drawing images of Ukrainian heroes in order to galvanise the people of Kyiv:

> Comrades, workers, peasants, intelligentsia of the Great Ukrainian People.... . The cursed enemy has captured part of our native Ukraine by a perfidious attack. This cannot frighten our mighty militant people. The German dog-knights were slashed by the sword of the warriors of Danylo of Galicia, by sabres of Cossacks under Bohdan Khelnystkyi, and the Kaisers hoards were destroyed by the Ukrainian people under the leadership of Lenin and Stalin in 1918.[7]

Unlike faceless bureaucrats before him, Khrushchev didn't hide behind the Kremlin walls and could occasionally be encountered inspecting damage on Kyiv's main street, Khreshchatyk, wearing an indecently shabby raincoat. Through actions such as these, people, particularly those in eastern Ukraine, began to regard him as Ukrainian. Whereas independence was anathema, "statehood" was something that he was willing to propagate though not to the extent demanded by nationalists such as Stepan Bandera.

Bandera and the Nationalists

During a visit to Lviv, I came across the bronze statue of Bandera standing on a metre-high marble plinth surrounded by a dozen or so wreaths of bright plastic flowers. Only recently erected, the statue bears no epitaph, just a plaque that states his name. His clean-shaven appearance and attire of suit, tie, and long overcoat creates an impression that repudiates the view held by some Poles, Jews, and Russians that he was a bandit and mass murderer.

It is only when you espy the two policemen assigned to protecting the statue that you realise that Lviv City Council has made a bold statement, and that Bandera remains a source of considerable disunity. He is a political hero for some and a barbarous enemy for others.

"We were taught that he was a gangster," said my companion from Kharkiv on seeing the statue.

"Who's causing trouble?" I shouted to the policemen.

"The Polish," one replied, "mostly."

The Polish occupation of the western Ukrainian territories in 1919 was as brutal as the Soviet occupation of the East. By June 1919, more than one-quarter of a million people — more than six percent of the Ukrainians in Galicia — were in Polish internment camps with property either sequestered or destroyed, and Ukrainian cultural achievements were annihilated. Bandera, a 10-year-old boy, learned early of the savagery of the Polish "Borderlands Policy" which included the ruthless purge of the education system of anything Ukrainian.

Within fifteen years, at a time when the Polish Interior Minister was continuing to apply "pacification measures," Bandera was appointed the head of the Organisation of Ukrainian Nationalists (OUN) in Ukraine, which was led by Colonel Yevhen Konovalets who was living in exile in Vienna. About the measures, the *Manchester Guardian* reported, "There can be no doubt whatever that these were the most drastic measures of oppression ever heard of in the history of the civilised world."*8*

Bandera responded with force, by ordering the assassination of the Polish Interior Minister and attacking the Soviet Consulate in Lviv. But in the reprisals that followed, his headquarters was discovered and he was sentenced to death, but later commuted to life imprisonment in Warsaw. Not long after, Konovalets, OUN's leader-in-exile, was assassinated when he accepted a booby-trapped box of chocolates from Pavel Sudaplatov.

Sudaplatov, who was born in eastern Ukraine, was the man in charge of the assassination of Trotsky, and he was also head of a special laboratory whose role was to examine the action of poisons on humans.

After having spent three years in solitary confinement, Bandera was released by the German soldiers who captured Warsaw. His association and cooperation with the Germans was one that would earmark the nationalists for severe reprisals by the Soviets when they incorporated Galicia into the Ukrainian Soviet Socialist Republic. But at the time it was an opportunity.

Galicia was freed from Polish occupation and the OUN was able to advance into Soviet Ukraine. Marching eastwards, just days ahead of the main body of the German army, some twenty thousand OUN soldiers marched to the Don River and Crimea, occasionally being captured by advancing Gestapo forces and often being killed by the retreating Soviets before finally being overtaken by the German advance.

With Lviv free from Polish control, the OUN established a provisional government in June 1941 and, at a ceremony blessed by the city's highest dignitaries, declared the restoration of the Independent Ukrainian State, which was headed by Jaroslaw Stetsko.

Despite significant loss of life, the OUN plan of aligning itself with the Germans had worked, but they had made one serious misjudgement: establishing a Ukrainian state was not on Hitler's agenda. The unrepentant Bandera was interned shortly afterwards in the concentration camp for political prisoners in Sachsenhausen.

Roman Shukhevych, a leading member of the OUN, who is perhaps more famous under his General Taras Chuprynka pseudonym, took control and became commander of the Ukrainian Insurgent Army (UPA). Its forces numbered more than two hundred thousand men at its peak.

There is significant controversy about what happened in the following two years. It is clear that the UPA colluded with the German army against the Bolsheviks; the Germans both trained and armed the Ukrainian insurgents. But there is controversy about who murdered four thousand Jews in pogroms in Lviv and one hundred thousand Poles in Volynia.

Successive and exhaustive investigations have failed to show any direct involvement of the UPA in these acts[9] and, controversially, President Viktor Yushchenko awarded Shukevych Ukraine's highest title of "Hero of Ukraine." In response to criticism, particularly from Israel, he responded:

No archive can today attest to any punitive action in which the fighters of the UPA and other similar organizations participated. I understand how stereotypical the strength of Soviet-like propaganda is, however we have the right to state, that there is another truth.[10]

As for Bandera, he was released by the Gestapo at the end of 1944, and he lived in Munich under the name of Popel. One day fifteen years later, he was about to drive from his apartment, accompanied by his security personnel, when he realised he had forgotten something. Without his guards, he returned to the stairwell of the apartment block and was killed by a man who fired a cyanide pellet into his face. It was revealed later that the assassin was a KGB Agent and fellow Lvivian named Bohdan Stashynsky, who was working on instructions from Nikita Khruschev. Stashynsky was a career assassin, and was last known to be living under a new identity in South Africa.

Khrushchev Emerges Triumphant

On the day Stalin died, the women cried incessantly and people gathered in the streets, lost for words.

"Our guiding light in the Great Patriotic War was no more," lamented one old lady. "We went to the railway station to buy tickets to Moscow, but we were prohibited from travelling."

When I told her that more than a hundred people had died in the crush to see his body, she bemoaned that she felt more ashamed for not trying harder to go.

The official line of the ruling Politburo was that the leadership were adopting a more collective approach in the post-Stalin period. But behind the scenes each was working to his own agenda. After an abortive coup attempt, the power base of Kaganovich fell apart. But Khrushchev, initially an outsider in the stakes for power, worked tirelessly to promote to positions of influence Ukrainians loyal to him.

When I lived in Moscow, a nephew of Khrushchev occupied an apartment below mine. He recalled to me one day (whilst his dog urinated on a tree that his uncle had reportedly planted) how Khrushchev had sprung one of the twentieth century's greatest surprises: his denunciation of Stalin in the "Report on the Personality Cult and its Consequences," the so-called "secret speech" made to the 20th Party Congress in February 1956. For nearly four hours, several thousand attendees listened in deathly silence to the anxious voice of Khrushchev.

"It was audacious because he didn't call Stalin's actions misjudgements, but crimes," his nephew told me. "It changed the course of history because it later emboldened Gorbachev, and other 'children of the twentieth congress' to push ahead with reforms two decades later. They learnt an axiomatic truth of Russian history that liberalisation from above will be thwarted by lesser party functionaries unless the leader builds a pact with the people. A truth, incidentally, learned by Viktor Yushchenko during the Orange Revolution."

Though Khrushchev's hands were as bloodied as Stalin's, his speech avoided his own formidable culpability and sealed his control of the Soviet Union, which lasted until a coup in 1964 by neo-Stalinists who viewed the speech as the cardinal sin.

During that decade of power, Khruschev took the people on a reckless, vodka-primed roller coaster ride of success and failure. His massive construction project to build the ubiquitous five-story apartment blocks that dominate city skylines (known as "Khrushchevkas"), and his allowing peasant farmers to keep home-grown produce were universally popular moves. His promise of a consumer heaven and the luxury of "almost three pairs of shoes per year" by 1965 aroused a sense of optimism about the future. And within one year of his introduction of a law allowing the workers to change their jobs, half the entire workforce had done so. Releasing prisoners from the gulags, and allowing the publication of Solzhenitsyn's, *One Day in the Life of Ivan Denisovich* had narrower appeal, but were seen as positive. There was also much to dislike about Khrushchev's era of "the thaw."

"How could Khrushchev claim that he loved the Ukrainian people, and they loved him," asked one pensioner in Kyiv, "when he deported a quarter of a million Ukrainians, and transferred half of our tractors to Siberia for an abortive experiment to grow corn? He wasn't called the 'Butcher of Ukraine' for nothing."

To this litany, the international observer might add that Khrushchev also brutally crushed the Hungarian Revolution in 1956, built the Berlin Wall, and put nuclear missiles in Cuba.

Brezhnev and the Workers' Paradise

Just about every history book describes "the Brezhnev years" as a period of stagnation; a time when ordinary Soviet citizens realised they were falling behind the Western capitalists, and when the authorities understood that they were incapable of changing the centralised, heavy industry-based economy to one that produced more and better quality consumer goods.

Ironically, however, it was also the period looked upon with greatest nostalgia by ordinary working class Ukrainians because they (temporarily) attained a lifestyle that some called a workers' paradise.

Brezhnev, an ethnic Russian born near Dnipropetrovsk, owed his advancement to Khruschev who recognised his ability after he was appointed to manage Ukraine's third largest city and its major industrial region at the age of just thirty-three. Both men were given to fits of anger, but Brezhnev's tantrums were often accompanied by tears, and he was a strenuous greeter, pulling his audience towards his medal encrusted chest in a bear hug and planting kisses on their cheeks. His sartorial elegance — beautifully tailored single-breasted suits and flat-top Homburg — contrasted markedly, however, with Khruschev's slovenly appearance. Brezhnev appeared so rarely without his medals that when it happened the workers often jested, "He's left them on his pyjamas!"

Inwardly, however, they were quite different, and Brezhnev believed ardently that his mentor had moved too far, too quickly from Lenin's ideals. In 1964, he was a member of the triumvirate of conspirators, including Premier Alexei Kosygin and fellow Ukrainian Nikolai Podgorny, which forced Khrushchev into retirement. Initially the triumvirate shared power, but Brezhnev, who was viewed by some as an insignificant figure, gradually elbowed out his rivals without resorting to the bloodletting of the Stalin era.

The policies, unrealistic experiments, and promises of Khrushchev were reversed. Policies reminiscent of the Stalin years were reintroduced, and Stalin rejoined the list of acceptable leaders; a man who had done many good things during difficult times. Referring to Brezhnev's bushy eyebrows, workers quipped that he had outdone Stalin by cultivating two moustaches but, more seriously, they knew he had freed them from terror or unemployment.

"He increased wages every year," one metalworker informed me during a visit to Donetsk.

"Every New Year shop prices were reduced," recalled one middle aged woman shop assistant, "and we bought our first television and refrigerator."

And a former machinist in Kharkiv extolled, "We were strong internationally."

Party membership in Ukraine swelled to two-and-a-half million workers and more than 65 percent were ethnic Ukrainians. Among party bosses, nine out of ten members of the Communist Party of Ukraine Politburo were ethnic Ukrainians. It was the "meat in the sandwich," the scientists, intellectuals, and dissidents (all three groups of which were overly represented in Ukraine compared to others in the Republics) whose living standards and freedoms were squeezed. Official anti-Semitism was also commonplace.

Of course, the rigidity of the system and the lack of innovation — assisted by a level of alcohol consumption that was six times higher than in the 1920s — condemned Brezhnev's workers' paradise to extinction. But until 1982, the Ukrainian worker could sit in his newly built "Khrushchevka" with vodka shot glass in hand and watch TV images of Brezhnev offering "détente" whilst flexing his nuclear muscles, crushing the Poles and Czechs, and invading Afghanistan.

Ethnic Ukrainians Rule Ukraine

Part of this feeling of "good times" and "elevated self-esteem" can be attributed to the two ethnic Ukrainian men who ruled the Republic during this period: Petro Shelest, a colourful party boss (1963–1972), who defended the Republic's economic interests and culture, and then the more hard line, pro-Kremlin successor, Volodymyr Shcherbytsky (1972–1989). Both were proud that Ukrainian statehood had been achieved and they fought vigorously with Moscow in particular (as long as it did not upset all-Union matters) about investment and the workers' well-being.

Shelest is regarded as the more liberal of the two but, nevertheless, he had a divided personality. Oddly, he spoke Ukrainian in public and Russian at home. He wrote warmly about Ukraine's Cossack origins, and thereby highlighted a separate origin from the Russian people (much to the ire of some of Moscow leadership), yet he abhorred nationalism and supported the pro-Stalinist faction's overthrow of Khrushchev. His cognitive dissonance is most clear in a comment he made on August 24, 1991, the day Ukraine gained independence: "I don't know. Should I be please that my country has become independent, or should I be distressed that my other country which I have served all my life has perished."[11]

When Brezhnev died in 1982 — then the most powerful man on earth — Kremlin-watchers could neither agree on his wife's first name nor how many children they had, let alone understand how the politburo worked and who his successor would be.

Shcherbytsky adopted a more cautious approach to the leadership of Ukraine than Shelest, cracking down on dissidents but continuing to promote selective aspects of Ukrainian culture. This proved to be a sound strategy for his seventeen-year survival, and he continued to hold the position under the next three Soviet leaders: ex-KGB head, Andropov; septuagenarian Chernenko; and reformer Mikhail Gorbachev.

Shcherbytsky's downfall was what caused, in part, the downfall of the Soviet Union — Chornobyl. Like others, for several years he had been complaining to Moscow, which managed nuclear energy issues, about the inadequacy of the facilities and the people. In the days immediately following the accident on April 26, 1986, it is unclear exactly what role Shcherbytsky played, but it is clear that the administrative machine greatly underestimated the severity of the event and was slow to respond. He would later argue that Moscow prevaricated whilst radiation levels were rapidly rising. When he told Gorbachev that he intended to cancel the Kyiv May Day celebrations, Gorbachev replied that he would be expelled from the party if he did. Out of a sense of loyalty to the Party, perhaps for fear of loosing his power, or perhaps to demonstrate that all was well, he brought his family to the celebration.

All Ukraine's pre-independence leaders shared a common trait; a sentiment divided between the interests of Ukraine and her people on the one hand, and those of the Soviet Union (read *Russia*) on the other. Until independence, loyalty to the big brother had always prevailed.

IN SHEVCHENKO LAND

"HE WAS ASSASSINATED whilst writing a book about trees?" I looked askance at Natasha, my fellow passenger. The old minibus's progress along the potholed lane was both noisy and slow.

"Pomology," she said definitively, "The science of fruit trees."

"And the author Lev Symyrenko was shot by a sniper on Christmas Eve?" I asked incredulously.

"Yes, she said with mild exasperation, "Lev Symyrenko owned the estate that had the largest collection of fruit trees in Europe, about nine thousand varieties. The Symyrenko Rennet has won blind tastings all over the world. Anyway, you should know this, since the British Embassy is located in the family home in Kyiv."

"Really?" I replied, now weary after a gruelling tour and Natasha's almost constant commentary. We were on the final day of a tour of "Shevchenko Land," the verdant and gently undulating land between the cities of Uman and Cherkasy on the right bank of the mighty Dnipro. It is the birthplace of Ukraine's national hero, Taras Shevchenko, an illustrious romantic bard, accomplished painter, and baritone.

Shevchenko rebelled openly against the bondage of the people in the same way that Abraham Lincoln and Beecher Stowe (author of *Uncle Tom's Cabin*) had come out against slavery. The big themes of his work — alienation and dependency — continue to define the modern Ukrainian character. These often show themselves as antagonism

against big oppressors (such as Poland and Russia) that is balanced
with expressions of resentment about their dependency on these
powerful neighbours.

The Librarian

I first encountered Natasha on the decrepit staircase outside my rented
Kyiv apartment. She lived opposite, with her daughter, and she
worked as a librarian at the Vernadsky National Library of Ukraine,
one of the ten largest national libraries in the world. A few stairwell
encounters later she invited me for dinner and, tired of a diet of
sandwiches and bottled Guinness, I accepted readily.

Prim, contemplative, tidy, and bespectacled she was not;
bookish she was. The whole apartment, save for a few pieces of
furniture, was populated with books. They packed bookcases,
strained furniture and window ledges, and were piled everywhere on
the floor. As far as I could tell, every waking moment she held a
book in one hand whilst waving the other as she espoused Ukrainian
culture.

When I asked her about her job, she told me how it had been
transformed following the independence of Ukraine. "Most people did
the same job as before; doctors saved lives, coalminers dug coal. But
my job changed. It had been to restrict readers to accessing books that
promoted Russian culture whilst ensuring that those promoting lesser
cultures such as Ukrainian culture were unreachable. "Can you
imagine," she continued passionately, "the library has over ten million
books, and more than 90 percent are not even written in our national
language. Ask an Iraqi how he would feel if the occupying American
forces replaced of all their books with American pulp."

She stopped momentarily to take a breath.

"And not a single one of our forty-five thousand Ukrainian
libraries has a copy of the *Encyclopaedia Britannica*. But I digress. My job
was transformed overnight into promoting free access to ideas.
Initially people were sceptical because we had been a key part of the
State's apparatus of control, but now that's changed."

Months later and now better acquainted, she asked me if I wanted to join the tour of "Shevchenko Land."

"Those who want to understand the poet should come to his homeland." she said, quoting Germany's great writer Goethe. I felt I couldn't refuse.

Taras Shevchenko

So it was that on a pleasant September day, I found myself in the company of nine pilgrims in search of the spirit of their prophet. Day one was exhausting, uplifting, and at times awkward for me. But Natasha loved it.

We commenced by visiting Shevchenko's birthplace in the village of Morintsi. In a small clearing strewn with autumn leaves and dotted with pretty yellow flowers, a stone and metal obelisk had been erected where he was born. An Ethnography Museum is housed in a 100-year-old cottage nearby, and in the nondescript village centre there is a Shevchenko Memorial Room and a bust of Shevchenko. The village was doing its best to be "the" Shevchenko place to visit; but as I was to discover, so were a dozen other places.

Shevchenko was orphaned at the age of twelve when his father, whom Shevchenko often assisted in carting salt cross the region, quickly followed his wife to the grave. In the village of Shevchenkove, his childhood home has been reconstructed complete with a pond as depicted in one of Shevchenko's drawings. It was here, beyond the village, that he spent his joyless childhood tending lambs and going in search of "the pillars that held up the sky." Nearby are the graves of his parents, the ubiquitous museum, bust, and an oak tree planted by his descendents in 1914.

The Shevchenko surname is common throughout the region, and the Glory Odelisk lists the names of fifteen Shevchenkos that died in World War II. We took afternoon tea with the great-great granddaughter of the bard's brother, an event which led to tears, hugging, and much singing. It was a communal attempt to reconnect with a glorious past that left me marginalized and mosquito bitten. I found distraction in the old tattered Soviet guide book I carried with me. It declared proudly:

> During the years of Soviet power modern cities and villages have grown on the site of former miserable and wretched villages, described by the poet with suffering and bitterness. In this blossoming land resounding with songs, the people are as happy as Shevchenko once dreamt they would be.[1]

On day 2 of the tour, the mood on the bus was subdued. Sitting in the seats we had occupied previously, we embarked at a pedestrian pace across a landscape dotted with derelict wooden windmills; scenes of serene, timeless beauty.

With neither parents nor money, Shevchenko at the age of fourteen became a houseboy of his owner, Pavel Engelhardt, and he relocated with him to St. Petersburg. There he was apprenticed to a painter for four years. Whilst sketching St. Peterburg's landmarks, he met the Ukrainian artist Ivan Soshenko and, via him, was introduced to a number of influential people who took a liking to this exuberant and talented acolyte. In 1838, after failing to gain Shevchenko's freedom from Engelhardt through civil means, Professor Karl Briullov donated a portrait he had painted to a lottery and used the proceeds to buy Shevchenko's freedom.

During the following nine years, Shevchenko studied at the Academy of Arts and produced his greatest artistic and literary works, including *Kobzar*, a collection of poetry that craves freedom and social justice and protests ardently against the oppression of Ukraine.

Our first stop was the cheerless and modest white painted house of Shevchenko's master, Englehardt, located at the end of a long avenue of sycamore in the village of Budishche. As is the practice in Ukraine, the bottom metre of each tree had been painted white. Nearby stands a truly huge oak (it took six of us to encircle the trunk with outstretched arms) where, according to legend, Shevchenko hid his drawings and poems.

Numerous busts and icons later, we stopped in the ancient picturesque settlement of Lisyanka, which stretches along the middle reaches of the meandering Hnily Tikich River. The Polish and Tsarists troops executed sixty peasants here and, as a symbol of deep grief, the local girls plait black ribbons into their braids. Memories are well preserved in these parts.

That evening we gathered in the museum in Uman for a lecture about Shevchenko. Today, Uman is a popular tourist destination blessed by shady green streets and parks, but it is especially famous for the Sofiyivski Park, a gem of landscape gardening built around 1800 by Polish magnate Stanislav Potocki for his Greek wife Sofia.

Our lecturer explained that during one of Shevchenko's visits to Kyiv from St. Petersburg, he befriended Romanticist writer Panteleimon Kulish and Mykola Kostomarov. Kulish was the first to translate the bible into modern Ukrainian, and Kostomarov established The Cyril and Methodicus Brotherhood, a secret society whose aim was to overthrow the existing social order. In 1847, the society was suppressed; Shevchenko was arrested and sentenced to exile as a private with the military in Orenburg, a city on the Ural River fifteen hundred kilometres east of Moscow.

"Tsar Nicholas I gave *explicit* instructions," said the lecturer, emphasizing the adjective and thus the cruelty to the Tsar, "that he should be kept under the strictest surveillance, without the right to write, or paint."

But for a man with Shevchenko's gifts — painting, singing, and story-telling — there was always a ready audience in the remote outpost, and he was not inhibited from writing. His main burdens were boredom and the oppressive climate, but he wrote some of his most famous lines including this extract from, *My Testament*:

> It does not touch me, not a whit
> If I live in Ukraine or not,
> If men recall me, or forget,
> Lost as I am, in foreign snow,
> Touches me not the slightest whit.
> Captive, to manhood I have grown
> In strangers' homes, and by my own

Unmourned, a weeping captive still, I'll die …
But it does touch me deep if knaves,
Evil rogues lull our Ukraine
Asleep, and only in the flames
Let her, all plundered, wake again …
That touches me with the deepest pain.

Tsar Nicholas I died in 1855 and Shevchenko was pardoned two years later. During the next five years he was allowed to visit Ukraine only once, and spent most of his time in St. Petersburg, surrounded by friends and admirers.

In 1860, he celebrated Christmas with his old friend Kostomarov, "boisterously and involving much alcohol," according to our lecturer. But he was in a poor state of health then, and by February he was having acute breathing difficulties. His friends arranged for well-known doctors to attend him, but the day after his forty-seventh birthday, while propped up in bed and surrounded by his unfinished work, he died of a pulmonary edema.

It was also fascinating to hear how the Soviets recreated "Shevchenko" as an atheist and independence fighter who had converted "to a communist universalism" as a result of being in St. Petersburg and in exile. According to the *Great Soviet Encyclopedia*,[2] the secular bible of doctrine, Shevchenko was a romantic-turned-realist who fought both Tsar and church and inspired socialist revolution. The Encyclopedia ascribes his use of Christian motives in his poems as a metaphor for more important revolutionary ideas, demonstrating how easily politics and ill intent can reinterpret history.

Though the Soviets banned many of his works, they raised his profile by naming thousands of parks and streets after him (including some places in Lviv, a city of which Shevchenko adamantly disapproved because he considered it Polish). For the peasants deprived of religion, Shevchenko rose as a spiritual father who kindled hope.

Day 3, the final leg of the tour, was a day of two halves; educational and then emotional. We visited the Symyrenko Memorial

Museum and the remains of the estate where poor Lev was assassinated, and I learnt more about the sugar content of fruit than I really need for a happy life.

But the real purpose of the visit was to learn about his grandfather, Platon, one of Ukraine's first industrialists who is credited with building the first mechanized sugar refinery in the Russian Empire. It was Platon who gave Shevchenko, with whom he shared a Cossack ancestry, 1,100 roubles to publish *Kobzar*. Without this philanthropy, the book may never have been published because soon afterwards Russia banned the use of the Ukrainian language.

On such a sunny day with the bus windows lowered and the smell of freshly harvested fields in our nostrils, it was difficult to imagine that this region had been the site of a battle in 1944, referred to as the second Stalingrad. Some sixty-thousand German soldiers (though numbers vary widely, especially on the upside) were encircled in an area called the Korsun Pocket by the 1st and 2nd Ukrainian Fronts. The only means of escape was through a narrow corridor now referred to as "Hell's Gate" and, needless to say, tens of thousands were killed.

Following his death, Shevchenko was buried in St. Petersburg, but a few months later, fulfilling the wish he expressed in his poem, *Testament*, his friends transported his body in a metal coffin to Monks Hill (later renamed Taras Hill) overlooking the languid blue water of the Dnipro:

> When I am dead, then bury me
> In my beloved Ukraine,
> My tomb upon a grave mound high
> Amid the spreading plain,
> So that the fields, the boundless steppes,
> The Dniper's plunging shore
> My eyes could see, my ears could hear
> The mighty river roar.[2]

The police had searched the coffin for sabres and rifles but the real weapons Shevchenko left behind — his words — were unconquerable and mighty. During his lifetime his work was reviewed in the Russian, French, Spanish, and Italian press, and he was mentioned for the first time in the English-speaking world in a magazine edited by Charles Dickens. By the end of the twentieth century, his work had been translated into more than one hundred languages.

By mid-afternoon we arrived in Kaniv and there was a mood of anticipation in the bus. We climbed the hill, a gentle stroll of an hour or so. Until 1918 a simple Celtic cross had stood on his tomb, but in 1939 — with the Soviet re-branding of Shevchenko complete — the famous sculptor Matvei Manizer designed a series of granite steps leading to a seven-metre pedestal on which stands a figure of Shevchenko bowing his recalcitrant head in thought.

On top of the hill the mood was one of unbridled joy. Small groups of pilgrims dotted the site: some were singing gaily, others gathered around as someone recited verse, and others simply admired the breathtaking view of the river. A strong breeze was blowing. Shevchenko always had a deep concern for Ukraine's future, but he would have gladdened to learn that a hundred and thirty years after his death an even stronger breeze had blown away the shackles from his Cossack maiden.

Franko and Ukrainka

A number of Russian intellectuals recognized the talent of Shevchenko, but lamented that he had chosen to write his work in a peasant language. For them, Ukrainian was at best a dialect, and anything aspiring to a wide readership must inevitably be written in Russian. But, from 1860 onwards, there was a dramatic upsurge of work written in Ukrainian which fuelled the idea that Russia and Ukraine were fundamentally different. Whether we look at the growing interest in folklore, ethnography, secret societies, or the works of two great Ukrainian writers, Ivan Franko and Lesya Ukrainka, they all point to the slow but inexorable rise of a Ukrainian distinctiveness.

This was a paradigm shift for the Tsarist authorities, who viewed the growing sense of nationalism with concern. In 1863, the Interior Minister proclaimed melodramatically, "There never has been, is not, and never can be a separate Little Russian language."[3]

As often happens, however, prohibition increases the level of interest. The arrest and punishment of Ukrainian writers, coupled with the banning of books and public performances, broadcast their work more widely than they could have achieved alone. It also had the counter-intuitive result of bringing together people in Russian-controlled Ukraine and in Galicia (under Austro-Hungarian control). Ukrainian writers readily sought out Galician publishers and writers, particularly in Lviv, because they had relative free access to printing presses and to the literary community.

As the winter evenings grew longer, Natasha, her daughter Anya, and I spent more time together. After a day of research I would often knock on their door around 7 p.m. and, as is customary in Ukraine (no matter how frequently you meet), I would bear a small gift of food or drink, usually their favourite sweet red wine, called Kagor. In return I would receive a hearty meal and good company.

"Does it bother you that Ukrainian writers wrote in Russian and that some contemporary writers continue to do so?" I asked during a meal of meat dumplings.

"You need to be pragmatic," answered Natasha. "If it's the only way to get your message out — as it was for the Ukrainian dissidents in the late Soviet period — then clearly no. Some in the nineteenth century also saw it as expedient."

I injected a thought I had then. "I'm not sure who said, 'A language is a dialect with an army and navy,' but that obviously applied to Russian and not to Ukrainian writers."

"What helps make our three literary greats — Shevchenko, Ukrainka and Franko — so great is that they wrote almost exclusively in Ukrainian when such freedom of conscience inevitably meant persecution," Natasha continued. "Ivan Franko was Shevchenko's worthy successor, a brilliant talent who believed that whoever was willing to work should be given a chance to develop his potential. Do you know his poem, *The Eternal Revolutionist?*

Knowing my answer, she recited part of the poem:

Eternal revolutionist —
Soul that body spurs to action,
Progress, freedom, satisfaction,
He's alive, he's in our midst.

Eternal revolutionist —
Knowledge, freedom, thought and spirit
Will not let the darkness near it,
Won't be shackled by a mist.

Where in world is there such power
That could keep in its bower,
Could extinguish, could delay
This oncoming, dawning day.[4]

"Many believe that the civil war which burst open in Ukraine in 1917 grew out of the poetry of Shevchenko and Franko. Unfortunately, the Bolsheviks proved too powerful."

I knew Shevchenko's poetry called for his fellow countrymen to take up arms and to bring about civil war whilst Franko had simply stated that freedom was inevitable.

"Ukrainka must have been such a clever and precocious child," added Anya, referring to Ukraine's third literary giant. "Do you remember, Mama, how we used to recite her poem, *Hope*, when we were dispirited?"

No freedom have I, my good fortune has flown,
A lone hope is left, the one thing that I own,
The hope of returning once more to Ukraine,
To feast longing eyes on my homeland again,
To feast longing eyes on the Dnipro's rich blues,

And there live or perish, whatever ensues;
Feast my eyes on the steppe and the grave mounds I love,
Recall ardent thoughts and the dreams I once wove.
No freedom have I, my good fortune has flown,
A lone hope is left, the one thing that I own.[5]

Astonishingly, Ukrainka wrote *Hope* when she was just eight years old, having learned to read at age four. She was christened Larysa Kosach, and she and her mother invented her penname, literally meaning "a Ukrainian woman" to emphasis her roots at a time when the use of the language was banned. Her poetry was published in western Ukraine and smuggled into the Russian Empire and she became a leading figure in Ukraine's modernist movement.

Confusing Identities

"I was thinking more of Nikolai Gogol," I broke in, referring back to my question. He was born in Odesa and educated in Kyiv, and was fluent in Ukrainian, but wrote exclusively in Russian."

"The Father of Russian Realism," Anya sighed. "There isn't a single person in Moscow who doesn't believe that Gogol was Russian."

I could have added that the BBC and *New York Times* also often refer to him as "the Russian writer Gogol."

"Yes, it really matters," Natasha insisted. "If someone born in Wales and speaking welsh went to work in London for an English newspaper, you wouldn't insist that he was English, would you? Of, course not! And just because Gabriel Garcia Marquez writes in Spanish, it doesn't alter the fact that he's Colombian."

"But, mama," Anya said more calmly, "he was expedient and in the pay of the Imperial Court. The Soviets elevated him to the monolithic Russian writer and never gave him back, so to speak." Her ballet shoes, pink-footed tights and leotard were draped over a chair. The leotard filled out well in front, I thought.

"Anyuta, you know that's not true!" Her mother admonished her, calling her by a diminutive. "They had no one to give back — he never left! The French always referred to him as Ukrainian." She reached over and ruffled Anya's hair.

It was a topical discussion that mirrored televised debates that have started to emerge in Ukraine. In one discussion, a Russian spokesman said Ukrainians should stop trying to claim Gogol as a "trinket of national culture" (implying it is tiresome and petty), and the Ukrainians responded pointedly that the Russians should stop "stealing the family silver."

For his part, Gogol appeared well aware of the sensitivity of the issue when he wrote:

> I myself do not know whether my soul is Ukrainian or Russian. I know only that on no account would I give priority to the little Russians before the Russian, or to the Russian before the Little Russian. Both natures are too richly endowed by God, and, as if by design, each of them separately contains within itself what the other lacks — a sure sign they complement one another.[6]

Akhmatova: an Odd Bird

On another occasion Natasha and I went to a theatre on Franko Square to a poetry reading of the work of Anna Akhmatova. Theatre, which had a substantial following in Soviet times, remains a popular pastime because prices are generally still reasonable.

It is hard to imagine that this small square, located two minutes' walk from Khreshchatyk, Kyiv's main boulevard, was until 1900 a lake. The spring which fed the lake now feeds the cast-iron fountain in the centre of the square and, as a joke, the iron workers cast a grotesque portrait of the hated boss rather than a lion's head as decoration.

Akhmatova was born in Ukraine, educated in Kyiv, and relocated to St. Petersburg where she wrote in Russian. Her "Ukraineness" never seems to arise, and she is widely referred to as the "Queen of the Neva" and "Soul of the Silver Age," as the period came to be known in the history of Russian poetry.

"I didn't understand a word of that," I admitted to Natasha as we left the poetry reading.

"If you're trying to translate it into English to understand it, it's very difficult," she offered. "There's an economy of words, ingenious structures, and obscured allusions. She's an odd bird."

Indeed, but she had a remarkable life. She married a young poet in 1910 when she was twenty-one, but whilst on her honeymoon in Paris, she fell in love with Italian artist Amedeo Modigliani, for whom she posed nude. In 2007, as if to underscore her complete lack of a Ukrainian identity, a private company donated one those drawings to the Russian state as part of its Russian culture sponsorship. Her poem, *He Loved*, published as part of a collection of poetry, acknowledged her incompatibility with her husband:

> Three things enchanted him:
> White peacocks, evensong,
> And faded maps of America,
> He couldn't stand bawling brats,
> Or raspberry jam with his tea,
> Or womanish hysteria.
> … And he was tied to me.[7]

The collection was instantly popular because of the immediacy of the work and the intimate tone with which it described love and emotion. As Russia lurched from crisis to crisis (World War I, the October Revolution and Civil War, Stalin's Terror, and World War II), her poems changed radically, reflecting the trauma of the times. Yet the words were always simple and strong, jarring but undeniably poignant.

From "Russian" Avant-Garde to Socialist Realism

During the first two decades of the twentieth century under relatively benign conditions of the late Tsar period and the early Soviet period, literature and the arts flourished in Ukraine: Kazimir Malevich's Suprematism; Vladimir Tatlin's Constructivism; David Burliuk's Futurism; Alexander Archipenko's Cubist sculptures; Alexandra Exter's theatre art; and Mykhailo Boichuk's Monumentalism are some of the more prominent contributions by Ukrainians to the "Russian" avant-garde movement.

Many prominent institutions continue to classify these artists as Russian even when the artists promoted themselves as Ukrainian. For example, the exhibition catalogue accompanying the 2003 exhibition of Malevich's work at museums in New York, Houston and Berlin states, "Malevich is unquestionably the most celebrated Russian artist of his generation."[8]

In literature, numerous diverse movements also flourished, from the radical proletcult movement through futurism, and then to neoclassical. But the renaissance was temporary and was brutally squashed by the Stalinist terror. Mykola Khvylovy, the most prominent leader of the literary movement, committed suicide in 1933 in protest at the disappearance, imprisonment, or execution of his colleagues who were euphemistically described as having been "forced to leave the ranks." Writing in 1987, Nestor Luckyi states that the literary purges in Ukraine resulted in the death of two hundred and fifty-four writers and critics.[9]

The turning point in sentiment towards the literati came in 1932 when Politburo member, Andrei Zhdanov (a Ukrainian by birth), made a keynote speech authorising the dissolution of all literary organisations and the establishment of the Union of Writers, and in which he established socialist realism as the only acceptable aesthetic. Henceforth all art would be judged by its contribution to advancing communist ideals — it would need to edify as well as entertain — and the Union and its apparatus would control all publishing decisions including the allocation of paper to approved writers. In a move that provides rich opportunities for parody, one letter from the 33-letter Ukrainian alphabet was banned from 1933 until 1991.

As far as national libraries go, I doubt that The Vernadsky National Library of Ukraine is one of the most beautiful. Having opened its doors to readers in 1918, its current manifestation it is a twenty-seven-storey concrete tower which includes twenty-two specialised reading rooms. During a guided tour given to me by Natasha, I asked her to try to paint a verbal picture of what a library would have been like in the early Soviet period.

"Before the leading Bolsheviks became heads of state, they were journalists," she said, "and they knew the impact of propaganda. They knew how effectively it could be used against them if they gave this weapon to the public. Nadezhda Krupskaya, Lenin's wife, redefined the role of libraries as a crucial part of the ideological infrastructure of the Soviet Union, and she ordered the confiscation of all collections of over five hundred books on the pretence that they would be made available via libraries. In truth, many of the books were destroyed or consigned to storage."

"So what did most people read?" I asked.

"Well, families may have had a few books, but the Bolsheviks promoted short forms of propaganda such as newspapers, short stories, and posters through which they sent simple, consistent messages. And the radio also started to become accessible."

After World War II, the grey uniformity was slowly replaced by a more colourful literature. War time stereotypes and heroes became common subjects, as did the conquest of the arctic or the pioneers of the new Siberian cities. Boy-meets-girl stories were popular, but the twist was that they worked on a collective farm or in a factory.

"And what about the spread of factual information, like news?" I asked.

"Mass culture, including newspapers, did not faithfully report 'the truth' as you understand it, but rather a selection of items that demonstrated the ongoing success of the socialist program. Its role was to mould and inspire. The authorities were never ashamed of their monopoly of culture, and they even considered their policy progressive."

From Samizdat to Blogging

The death of Stalin in 1953 was accompanied by disquiet and a number of atypical books began to appear, such as *Thaw* by Ukrainian writer Ilya Ehrenburg[10] (from which came the term "Khrushchev's Thaw").

"And the 'swinging sixties' passed you by?" I asked as we as we approached the ticket catalogue of books. (Only books received after 1990 are catalogued electronically and simply locating a book about Ukraine can be very difficult because it might be catalogued under the key words of Russia, Kyivan Rus, Soviet, USSR, Little Russia, South Russia, Galicia, and so on.)

"We had pirate copies of the Beetles, Pink Floyd and others, and a movement called 'people of the sixties' flourished briefly with dissidents being prominent among its members. By the early 1970s, the Party Secretary of Ukraine was a hard-nosed man, and a period of suppression followed in which leading writers were shipped of to Siberia."

"Perhaps surprisingly," Natasha continued, "the collapse of the Union didn't lead to a revival of Ukrainian literature. The immense Kyiv publishing house which had published millions of books in over a hundred languages suddenly found itself without writers or readers. Many writers couldn't adapt to freedom because they were bereft of any original thoughts. The network of bookshops which had been exemplary in Soviet times disintegrated along with the book distribution system and so, nowadays, London has more bookshops than the whole of Ukraine."

Another key factor was the competition for customers' money from consumer goods or mass-media entertainments. The low arts such as romance novels, rock music, and blogs have done much better than prose or poetry. The blog has emerged as a sort of new Samizdat (the publishing system whereby forbidden literature was reproduced and circulated privately in the Soviet Union). Bloggers are the new dissidents!

We strolled through one of the reading rooms, now almost empty as we approached closing time. "Another surprising consequence of the break-up of the Soviet Union," Natasha added, "is that book writers have zero influence on public opinion but journalists can bring down a government. Under communism the opposite was true. There is no censorship of literature, but censorship of journalism is ubiquitous."

"So, what about the cutting edge of Ukrainian literature today?" I asked.

"Well, there are perhaps only a couple of dozen full-time novelists using the Ukrainian language. They are generally referred to as the '1984 Generation,' in a reference to George Orwell's novel, and they have a popular, dynamic style of sex, drugs, and rock and roll writing. The 'great' novel remains the Holy Grail for Ukrainian writers, but until we become surer of who we are as a nation and the values we share, my belief is that it will prove illusive."

TAKING THE MEDICINE

I THINK IT GOES WITHOUT SAYING that, for ordinary citizens, daily life in Ukraine is a challenge. One of the most worrisome events is the risk of falling ill and being transferred to a local hospital. The issue is not one of a lack of doctors or facilities. The Soviet system, whose legacy still prevails in today's unreformed health service, provides twice the number of doctors and beds per person compared with their Western European counterparts.

No, the key issue is medical competence and the *quality* of facilities. The last few decades have exterminated the professional dignity of the Soviet physician and nurse, and reduced their work to that of an underpaid worker with access to no (or at best, wretched) equipment. Partly as a consequence, many treatments have been (and continue to be) based on reasoning inferred from theory and physiologic principles rather than from clinical tests. Though in principle care is free, a city such as Kharkiv allocates just thirty dollars per person per year to its medical budget, less than one percent of that provided in most Western European countries. Nearly two decades after independence, Ukraine still lacks a national organization of physicians, and there are no trusted journals (such as *The Lancet* in England) that can serve as channels of education and communication.

For examples of the lack of professional competence, let's consider my own experience. When my wife needed an operation, I paid a hospital several thousand dollars in order to secure the best conditions and service. But just before the operation commenced, the nurse anaesthetist asked for more money in order to keep her in the operating room.

After falling and hurting my arm, I followed the common method of seeking a diagnosis from three different doctors before deciding whom I believed. One said it was broken and two said it wasn't.

The most vulnerable in society — older people and single mothers — fare even less well and are preyed upon by unscrupulous doctors. The most harrowing stories I hear (with disturbing frequency) concern doctors telling mothers that their child is in urgent need of medical treatment; otherwise the child will die. A mother, naturally distraught, and perhaps lacking both an education and a husband, does whatever she must to raise the money for the operation. The doctor then "operates" on the fictitious ailment and, by a miracle of modern science the child is cured. Even if the ruse is rumbled — and media stories show the occurrence of such traumas — there is almost no recourse since the Hippocratic Oath is unheard of in Ukraine. As President Victor Yushchenko once wryly remarked, one can contest the Ten Commandments in the Ukrainian courts of law and still win the case.

Healthier Times

But it was not always like this. Many people speak positively of the treatment they received under the Soviet system. Though the doctors were officious, they were regarded with great respect. They were also plentiful; at the peak the Soviet Union employed nine hundred thousand doctors, more than a quarter of the world's doctors. As a result the hospital was viewed as a caring establishment that gave people time and attention. Conditions that would require only outpatient treatment in the West, such as an X-rays, pneumonia, and even blood tests, would often require an official minimum stay.

Those requiring inpatient treatments would be admitted to the hospital assigned to their factory or district, and once admitted there was little motivation to discharge patients because the remuneration of hospitals and physicians was correlated with patient numbers. The patient also had little motivation to leave, because his salary continued to be paid in full, so long as the doctor said so. At the very least, this provided the patient a substantial convalescence and perhaps also a welcome change from the drudgery of working life at the local factory.

Even after discharge, the patient was often allocated to light work or offered rest in a sanatorium allocated to their factory or trade union. Most of the health resorts were located in Crimea partly because of the agreeable climate, but also because it is the location of most of the palaces and private mansions confiscated from the Tsarists, which proved ideal for conversion into rest homes.

Of course, all medical treatment was entirely free to the patient. To its credit, the Soviet Union took the socialisation of healthcare to a degree beyond any other developed country. Each institution or factory established a Social Insurance Bank, controlled by the workers, which collected funds from the employer. This money funded healthcare costs and, quite sensibly, doctors were kept away from any economic decisions. Progress was slower in the rural areas, but each village established a "Feldsher Station" that employed a midwife and a Feldsher (a sort of paramedic with two years' medical training). All told, this was an extra 2.7 million pairs of hands for the medical profession.

Wise Women

In the villages, the wise women, or *Babki* (also known as a Znakarki), vied with the Feldsher to provide treatment. These folklorists had an uneasy relationship with the Soviet medical system, but were never banished and still persist today. Several city-dwelling friends I consider to be highly educated have openly discussed visiting a Babki to cure a smoking addiction, insomnia, or to learn the sex of their unborn child. The Babki usually use blessed water or wax treatments to cure those ailments which respond poorly to conventional treatment, such as stuttering, irritability, bedwetting, chronic pain, and curses.

Amongst the former Soviet states, Ukraine has a particularly strong tradition of medical folklore. A louse eaten with bread is a remedy for hepatitis. The fresh air and outdoor life of the dacha are essential for health. Swaddling babies even on hot summer days is the norm. Drinking cold drinks is a sure way to get a sore throat. Applying onion juice in your nostrils cures the common cold — and as I have learned from personal experience — causes a burning sensation which should lead to it being classified by the United Nations as torture.

The upshot of all these facets of healthcare — the role of the family, the inference of the problem from theory rather than from tests, the absence of effective medicine, the importance of recuperative spa treatments, and the influence of folk medicine — means that the Ukrainian experience of healthcare is considerably different from that, say, of Western Europe.

But that is not to say it was without success. By the 1960s, Ukraine had eliminated epidemics, and the average life expectancy had risen from about thirty years just before the Revolution to an average of sixty-six years for men and seventy-four years for women, comparable with Western Europe. Sadly, things have gone backwards in the last four decades or so, and today Ukrainian life expectancy remains at the 1960 rates (having fallen in the 1990s) whilst the European Union figures have improved.[1]

I developed an interest in learning about the Ukrainian medical profession from a rather unexpected source. More than a year after commencing Russian language lessons with Mikhail, a sprightly 70-year-old doctor, he corrected my misunderstanding about his title. I had assumed, quite wrongly as it turned out, that he was a Doctor of Philology. Instead, he was a Medical Doctor who had specialised in tropical diseases. In the 1960s he had worked as a doctor in India in the footsteps of the Ukrainian physician Waldemar Haffkine.

Controlling Cholera

During the nineteenth century, five cholera pandemics ravaged much of Europe and Asia, and in the 1890s, the fifth pandemic was taking a heavy toll of lives, particularly in India. The bacterium that causes cholera had been isolated first by Italian anatomist Filippo Pacini some fifty years earlier, but no one had successfully used vaccines against the disease. Haffkine produced a culture of the bacterium, and in a calculated move (read *foolhardy*), he injected himself and confirmed the efficacy of the inoculation. He thus became the first person to develop and use vaccines against cholera and bubonic plague.

Haffkine moved to the Ganges-Brahmaputra Delta region of India and, by the turn of the century, more than four million people had been inoculated, leading to Haffkine being described by the great surgeon Lord Joseph Lister as "a saviour of humanity."

Some time later, Mikhail telephoned me to say he wouldn't be able to teach me for some weeks. When I pressed him for the reason, he revealed that he was lying in a hospital bed in Kharkiv with an undiagnosed illness of the stomach. I was worried; for his age he always appeared remarkably fit and alert. Knowing that his only son lived in a town some distance away, I realised he would need some support and so, largely on my insistence, we agreed that I would visit him whilst he was in hospital. For me, it was also a good opportunity to see inside the system.

The more I read and talked to people about the medical service in Ukraine, the more I came to understand that Ukraine had a glorious history of medical development, particularly between 1850 and 1940, but the contribution of Ukrainian physicians since then is largely unrecognised. We recognise the names of Frenchman Louis Pasteur and Englishman Joseph Lister, and we know they changed our lives. But perhaps we should also recognise the Ukrainian men who gave us the X-ray, the first epidemiology department, the word "antibiotic," the plaster cast, the first human kidney transplant, magnetic spin resonance, and skin transplants. And let's not forget the polyhedral chisel for skull trephination.

Medical discovery and innovation were stifled from the 1930s onwards largely because of one man: Joseph Stalin. This period saw Stalin's increasing persecution of the bourgeoisie and intellectuals, labels that attached easily to doctors because of their higher education and regular contacts with foreigners. His character was ruthless, adept, brutal, and cynical, and he was deeply mistrustful of everyone. Those doctors who were working to provide specific treatments — by definition, of benefit to a few rather than to all society — were particularly vulnerable. Community solutions gained favour, whilst treating a rare disease or developing an expensive treatment attracted criticism. So abortion, widespread inoculation, rest in a sanatoria, and tranquilising drugs became the prescribed solutions for the problems of birth control, public health diseases, recuperation, and psychiatric problems, respectively. One size had to fit all.

Persecuting Doctors

"Stop! Where are you going?"

I was leaving the foyer of the hospital on my way to Mikhail's ward. The officious voice of the babushka stopped me in my tracks and I was aware that I was suddenly the centre of attention.

"You must wear plastic overshoes," she barked on hearing my explanation.

She took my two-hryvnia note and thrust at me what looked like a pair of blue elasticised shower caps. Abstemious regulars were searching their bags and pockets for the pair they had bought on a previous visit. Like all arcane rules of the former Soviet system — such as not being allowed to wear an overcoat in a public building — the overshoe rule strikes me as being of dubious benefit. But I complied, nevertheless.

"So what's the diagnosis?" I asked Mikhail after having found the ward he shared with six others. I could see a drip feeding liquid into his right forearm, and a bucket lay next to his bed. I presumed he couldn't keep down his food.

"Oh, the doctor's still deliberating, but I have my own views."

I looked into his sunken eyes, no doubt the work of the triumvirate of tiredness, illness and old age. "Well," I said facetiously, "if you don't like the diagnosis, we can have the doctor shot."

Mikhail gave me a glance and winked. During one of my Russian lessons he had told me about how Stalin was complicit in the murder of many doctors during "show" trials. A trial of intellectuals and doctors in Kharkiv Opera Theatre, which only weeks before had been overwhelmed by the basso cantante voice of one of Ukraine's greatest singers, Boris Gmyrya, was a precursor to the more well known "Doctors' Plot" trial in Moscow in 1953. There, nine doctors, including six Jews, were accused of murdering Ukrainian-born Andrei Zhdanov, a close friend and probable successor of Stalin.

Reflexology and Conditioning

More pertinent to Mikhail as he waited the doctor's diagnosis, was Stalin's dismissal of his own personal physician, Dr. Vladimir Bekhterev, the inventor of the term, reflexology. According to rumours, Stalin was so incensed with the diagnosis that he had him murdered. Whatever transpired during their consultation, Bekhterev died the next day, no post mortem was conducted, and his name was deleted from textbooks and scientific literature.[2]

Bekhterev's greatest achievement, however, was in transferring Ivan Pavlov's work on the conditioning of dogs to humans. By doing so, he discredited the work of Sigmund Freud, which attributed normal behaviour to deeper sexual drives (and which was beyond the control of the state). According to some accounts, both of Freud's parents were born in eastern Galicia, now Ukraine.[3]

I glanced through the dirty windows of the second-floor ward in one of the various buildings that made up the hospital compound. A broken mosquito screen tempered the breeze that freshened up the otherwise dreary room. The hospital was laid out in the so-called "pavilion style," which consisted of many small blocks situated equidistant from each other so as to create the maximum isolation of the patients.

It had been years since the ward had received its last coat of olive green paint, and the previous weathered layers were in evidence around the wooden window frames. As is usual in former-Soviet public buildings, the bulky cast iron pipe work for heating — the diameter of a man's arm — snaked around the walls.

"If you can wait an hour of so you can accompany me to the X-ray room," Mikhail said. "It might be interesting and we can talk to some of the technicians."

"So you already have the blood tests?" I enquired, and he nodded. "Of course I'll join you."

The Secrets of Blood

It was during these visits that Mikhail revealed fascinating snippets of information about his earlier life as a doctor. Often he did not know the whole story himself. Either he'd forgotten, got the story mixed up, or only knew the official version. But on the subject of blood, he was well informed, and the information he provided fed my appetite for further research.

The name of the Ukrainian mostly closely associated with research into human blood is that of Kharkiv-born Ilya Mechnikov. Soviet historians had several reasons to cover up his name: he was from a bourgeois family, he had fled his homeland, he was active in the Jewish community, and he was an ardent supporter and colleague of Charles Darwin. But cover-up was difficult because he had been awarded the Nobel Prize in Biomedical Sciences in 1908 for his brilliant work, *Immunity under the Infectious Diseases*. Today his name is associated with universities, institutions, astronomical observatories, philately, distinguished prizes, street names, metro stations, and a mountain.

At just twenty-two years of age, he was appointed professor at the new University of Odesa. There he married his long-term girlfriend who suffered from tuberculosis and who had to be carried to church in a chair. By all accounts, it was rare to encounter such a gifted teacher, and he progressed rapidly up the educational hierarchy. But five years later his wife died. Driven to understand the immune system and burdened by unending research, he was already troubled by poor eyesight and heart troubles, and her death tipped him into attempting suicide by overdosing on opium. Such attempts would be a recurring feature of his troubled life.

Mechnikov was particularly interested in bacteria, the small one-celled creatures that are considerably smaller than red cells. In the 1860s, the French chemist, Louis Pasteur, had shown that bacteria could get into the body and multiply, causing many common diseases. The question on Mechnikov's mind was, "Why don't we all die of disease?"

During a pogrom of Jews in Odesa, following the assassination of Tsar Alexander II in 1881, he fled to Messina in Italy where he would make the discovery that would change his life. Whilst sitting on the beach to clear his mind, he idly poked small thorns into a starfish to observe its reaction. The next morning he observed that white cells had been carried by the blood in great numbers to the site of each cut. There was so much blood near to each cut that the pressure was causing them to appear red and inflamed. He conjectured that the white cells had destroyed the bacteria and prevented the infection from getting worse, and thus it was the white cells of the body that acted as the first line of defence against infection. This simple observation would have a profound influence on the direction of immunology and medical science.

Reinvigorated by his discovery, Mechnikov shook off his torpor and became the head the Scientific Research Laboratory for Louis Pasteur in Paris. There he proved his theory. Photographs taken at the turn of the century depict him as a sort of absentminded uncle figure; unkempt, heavily bearded, bespectacled but kind, smiling, and affable. Invariably his pockets were stuffed with papers and he wore a scruffy hat and galoshes even in good weather.

Though Mechnikov would not live to know it, he was the teacher of the man who became Hitler's doctor, Theodor Morell. Morell treated Hitler for nine years with some bizarre concoctions including bull's testicles, amphetamines, and material derived from animal intestines. He became a millionaire through the development of own-brand vitamin tablets, including a popular chocolate variety, and his best selling "Morell's Russian Lice Powder."

Discovering X-Rays

An hour or two later Mikhail and I made our way to the "Roentgen Kabinet" (X-ray room). As he sat in an invalid chair in the corridor waiting his turn, I could see just how frail he really was. His complexion was almost as white as snow.

He spoke to the technician and informed me that I could watch the process from the technician's cabinet. We were going to have a few interesting minutes. Though most of the world refers to X-rays as "Roentgen waves" after the name of the German physicist and Nobel Prize winner, X-rays were discovered seven years earlier than Roentgen's claim in 1887 by a Ukrainian named Ivan Pulyui.[4]

Pulyui's story is quite common for Ukraine. He was an outstanding scientist whose diverse achievements included the construction of Europe's first alternating current power plant and the translation of the Old Testament into Ukrainian. Yet the 1983 *Encyclopaedia of Ukraine*, compiled under the censorship of the Soviet Union, makes no reference to him.

"Why do you call this the Roentgen Kabinet?" I asked the technician after he had positioned Mikhail next to the vintage machine. Holding a lead curtain in front of his sex organ, Mikhail looked like a bandy-legged Daliesque bullfighter.

"Breath in, hold it," the technician barked as he peered out from above a green mask and pressed the button to emit the radiation.

"You don't know who invented the X-ray?" he said as he looked at me incredulously.

Though the three of us discussed the history of X-rays for the next ten minutes, the technician gave no ground. He was the expert, Mikhail was clearly suffering from the late stages of dementia, and I was a foreign novice. *Roentgen discovered X-rays.* Period.

Pulyui, the son of a minister, was born in 1845 at Hrymaliv in western Ukraine. Following his early education he made a two-month journey by foot to Vienna — railway construction would follow only a couple of decades later — where he studied theology for five years. It was during these years that he realised his passion lay in the study of science, and though his parents disowned him for rejecting his consecration to religion, he pursued his new vocation. For the next few years he studied philosophy, mathematics, physics, and astronomy, and then in 1873 he moved to the physics laboratory of the University of Strasbourg to study for his doctorate. Coincidently, Wilhelm Roentgen was an assistant in the laboratory and the two became acquainted and corresponded for a number of years.

In 1877, Pulyui constructed "Pulyui's Tube," a cathode ray tube, and two years later he created a vacuum tube. By passing electricity through the tube, he created cathode rays; and whilst performing experiments, he noted that photographic plates became black when exposed to these rays. Excitedly, he recorded a photographic plate of the radiation phenomenon. The description of the experiment and two exposed photographic plates, one of a guinea pig and another of a child's hand, were published in *The Herald* of Vienna Academy of Sciences in 1881. Eight years later the Physical Society of London published a translation of his monograph on cathode rays.

For the next few years, Pulyui became side-tracked on other projects, and it was during this time that Roentgen, to whom Pulyui had given examples of his cathode tubes, appropriated his invention. In October 1895, Roentgen announced the discovery of the radiation phenomena he called X-rays. Pulyui's wife, Catherine, later reported that her husband was in shock and kept repeating in confusion, "Oh, my lamps, my lamps."

Physicians in the United States were excited by Roentgen's paper, but when Frank Austin of Dartmouth College tested all the discharge tubes of both Palyui's and Roentgen's designs, he found that only the Pulyui tube produced X-rays. (This was a result of Pulyui's inclusion of a piece of mica to hold the samples of fluorescent material within the tube.) Palyui wrote to Roentgen asking him whether he had used his tubes. Roentgen replied more than a year later that he had not, but by this time the world's lexicon was already enriched by the term "X-ray" and Roentgen's name was on the Nobel Committee's short-list for a prize.

A New Word: "Antibiotic"

As if to confirm that the misallocation of credit is endemic in the sciences, the award of the 1952 Nobel Prize in the field of physiology and medicine to Selman Waksman shows the other side of the coin.

Waksman was born not far from Kyiv and, like Palyui, he is little known in his country of birth. Yet, he coined the term "antibiotic" and he is responsible for the discovery of streptomycin, which has proved to be an effective treatment of tuberculosis, a disease that over two centuries has killed more than one billion people — more than all the plagues, famines, and wars added together. (Today, ironically, tuberculosis is one of the main killers in Ukraine responsible for over 30 percent of prison deaths and 70 percent of HIV-related deaths.)

At the age of 22, Waksman left Ukraine for the USA, where he established himself as an eminent microbiologist. The purification of penicillin at Oxford University in 1937 added to his conviction that the soil would yield antibiotic-producing organisms, and he led a screening programme to identify them.

In 1943, Albert Schatz, an intense, skinny 23-year-old postgraduate student working for Waksman, isolated a new antibiotic. "I named it streptomycin," he told *The Guardian* newspaper in 2002. "I sealed the test tube by heating the open end and twisting the soft, hot glass. I felt elated, and very tired, but I had no idea whether the new antibiotic would be effective in treating people."

During the months that followed, tests showed outstanding results and Waksman, as Director of the screening programme, attracted growing media attention. It was convention that the credit for any success be given to the Director.

By the late 1940s, the royalties on the sale of Streptomycin probably exceeded US$700,000, and to his credit, Waksman gave most of the money to the Rutgers Research and Endowment Foundation. But Schatz, resentful that there was absolutely no recognition of his role, launched a publicly embarrassing lawsuit against his Director.

Though Waksman paid an out-of-court settlement, the scientific community closed ranks on Schatz and he was unable to find employment. Then, in 1952, Schatz suffered the final indignity when news came that Waksman would be awarded the Nobel Prize. Schatz lobbied against the award, but the "old guard" stood firm, expressing the view that Schatz had been privileged to work for the great man.[5]

Surgery

Mikhail was diagnosed as suffering from a duodenal ulcer, as he had expected. When I next saw him, his son had visited and had paid the doctor to do a good job and to provide the medical staff required for the operation. Beside the bed was a large bag containing all the material the doctor would need to perform the operation: drugs, syringes, swabs, and so on, which Mikhail's son had purchased from the dispensary located in the hospital entrance hall. He was now waiting his turn.

We talked about the routine operation and he was sanguine about the procedure. "I wish I could say it's the result of a lifetime of excess," he joked feebly. "But all will be well."

"Yes," I replied "Ukraine has a rich history of successful surgeons."

A few months later I was able to visit the Pirogov Museum in Vinnytsia, one of the centres of wealth during the Kyivan Rus period that was located in the Dnipro lowland on a promontory between two rivers. My Soviet guidebook gave equal space to Pirogov's museum and the Synthetic Fibres Plant built in 1959.

Nikolay Pirogov was Russian, having been born in Moscow in 1810, but apart from his first twenty or so years, he spent his remaining years abroad and mostly in Ukraine. In 1947, a museum was opened in his honour on his country estate, and in the same year Ukrainian film director Grigori Kozintsev produced a biographical film of his life with a score by child prodigy Dmitri Shostakovich.

Pirogov's claim to fame is that he is the founder of field surgery, having worked as an army surgeon in Crimea in 1854. He undertook forms of amputation that now bear his name, and he developed the concept of plaster casts and was the first to use anaesthesia in a field operation. Anaesthesia offered significant benefits over the more traditional method of sedating the patient by encouraging him to drink copious quantities of alcohol.

Pirogov attended four wars and, contrary to the view that triage was invented by the French during World War I, he used a five-category system of his own design throughout this time.

The museum, based around his country house and gardens, is an uneasy mixture. One moment you are seduced by the humanity of the man — a public servant who planted his own kitchen garden, devoted himself to treating those in need, and enjoyed leisure time around the piano with friends such as Pyotr Tchaikovsky. The next moment you are shocked by the sight of the gruesome tools of his trade and his graphically illustrated books such as *An Illustrated Topographic Anatomy of Sections, Performed in Three Directions through a Frozen Human Body.* On a page showing colourful cross sections of the body, the text said simply, "Not a single part of a human body has empty spaces in a normal state."

Today the 125-year-old mummy of Pirogov's body, quirkily described by the museum as "The oldest mummy in modern history," is kept in a special crypt beneath a belfry in the village centre.

Organ Transplants

The following day Mikhail informed me that he was scheduled for the operating theatre. The days without proper food were beginning to show in his energy level and attentiveness, but he wanted to tell me about the doctor he most admired, the transplant specialist Yuri Voronoy. It was a relative of Voronoy that had secured Mikhail's university entrance.) I guess it took his mind off the operation.

As we all know, transplantation has provided a rich and macabre theme for novelists and movie makers whose creations are often grotesque creatures that descend into madness, create havoc, or achieve immortality. An early example from Ukraine is Mikhail Bulgakov's 1925 novel, *Heart of a Dog.* (Bulgakov trained as a doctor before taking up a literary career.) The novel tells the story of a professor who implants the pituitary gland and testicles of a man into a dog, which becomes humanlike, secures a job in the Moscow administration, and turns the professor's house into a nightmare. The novel can be variously interpreted as, a warning against tampering with nature, a satire against Soviet attempts to create the "New Soviet Man," or a wry comment about the ability of a person with a dog's intelligence to achieve employment in the Soviet system. Whatever Bulgakov intended, his novel was banned and only published officially in the Soviet Union in 1987.

Pioneering medical work in transplantation in the early twentieth century probably provided the inspiration for Bulgakov's professor. In 1906, Mathieu Jaboulay transplanted pig kidneys into human patients. Three years later, Ernst Unger grafted a stillborn child's kidney to a baboon. But none of the operations were successful. More extravagantly, in the 1920s, Serge Voronoff, a Russian living in France, made his name and fortune by implanting thin slices of testicles from monkeys into the scrotum of thousands of men with the claimed benefits of improved longevity, sex-drive, memory, and eyesight.

But, out of sight from most of the medical world, it was Yuri Voronoy working in hospitals in Kharkiv and Kherson in 1933 who was the first to perform human-to-human kidney transplantation, and the first to use the kidney of a corpse for transplantation. Over the next few years he performed six similar operations, and though none achieved long-term success, his work was twenty years ahead of most others. It was only in 1954 that a successful transplant was made (between identical twins).

Voronoy's first donor was a 60-year-old man who had suffered traumatic brain injury and whose organ was taken six hours after his death. The patient was a 26-year-old woman whose kidneys had not worked for four days as a result of acute poisoning with mercury bichloride. The varied uses of this arcane chemical included photographic film processing, the treatment of syphilis, and use as a method of suicide.

The woman showed initial improvement following the operation, but she died two days later. This attempt, however, did convince

Voronoy that transplanted kidneys could function in a new body. His pioneering work would later be shown to have failed for two key reasons: firstly, the discovery that successful transplant requires that both the tissue type and blood type of the donor and the patient need to be broadly compatible; secondly, the discovery by Nobel Prize winner Sir Peter Medawar that patient survival is greatly enhanced if their immune system — which fights to reject the new organ — is suppressed by drugs. Nevertheless, Voronoy's pioneering work set the stage for the successful transplantation of an impressive menu of internal body parts, including the heart, kidneys, liver, lungs, pancreas, and intestine.

A few days later when Mikhail was recovering from the operation, I brought a bowl of water so he could have a hand and face wash and then tidied the sheets on his bed. Over the course of the week I'd been able to see firsthand how the ward operated. Compared to a western hospital, the most obvious difference is the lack of hierarchy. There is no matron or, for that matter, anyone else in charge, but there is a stratification of jobs. A domestic cleans the room and changes the linen each week. A general nurse ferries the patient around the hospital and brings the food (which is invariably the same for all patients irrespective of their illness). Specialist nurses give injections or set the intravenous drip. The night nurse takes the patient's temperature, and the doctor visits twice per day. If the patient is incapable, the patient's family needs to assist with washing, tidying the bed, and generally making the patient comfortable.

"How do you feel?" I asked Mikhail.

He had colour in his face now but his hair was ruffled, suggesting a restless sleep.

"I have a pain down my right side but otherwise everything seems okay."

"I guess it's because of old age," I offered absentmindedly.

"Is my right side older than my left one?" he quizzed. A glow rose up in his deeply wrinkled face, and when he embraced me for the first time, I knew everything was going to be all right.

RELIGIOUS WARS

"DO YOU BELIEVE IN RELIGION? You're an Old Believer, I bet."

"An Old Believer! Would an Old Believer have been drinking vodka with you?"

"True enough. But don't start fuddling my brains with your god talk. It makes me sick."

The young man spoke casually, in a rather flat voice.

"If I ever ran into that Christ of yours, I'd stick a knife in him right away."

"What for?"

"What for? Because he told all those fairy-tales, because he lied. No one's kind to others in this world. And your gentle Jesus taught people to be meek and mild. The bastard!"

The young man's voice was recovering its hard, aggressive note, but without the former elation.

- Extract from *I Want To Live* by Vasily Shushkin (1966).

Cult of Atheism

Although Albania was the only eastern bloc country to ban religion, the Bolsheviks made a serious attempt to eradicate it in Ukraine and the other Soviet republics. Believing Karl Marx's maxim that "religion is the opium of the people," they readily understood the ability of evangelicalism to galvanise people and religion's ability to forge bonds across international boundaries and political systems — forces which could derail their ambitions to build a socialist and atheist utopia. They believed that by tolerating the church but removing all financial support, it would wither away and be replaced by happiness in this life rather than the next.

In many ways they were simply replacing the structures. Lenin became the new God and his works the new bible, the Communist Party the new church, and the Politburo a new assembly of saints. Towards this end, successive decades from the 1920s onwards alternated between the discouragement of and the serious repression of religion.

The Soviet "cult of atheism" required that most religious buildings be destroyed, and a volunteer organisation called "The Society of the Godless" popularised scientific achievements as a counter to the myth of religion and desecrated buildings and sacred objects. It boasted several million members at its peak.

Foucault's Pendulum

After World War II, the Dominion Cathedral in Lviv — the most grandiose baroque building in the city — was chosen as the site for a Museum of Atheism and for Foucault's Pendulum; the only other such museum in the Soviet Union being St. Isaac's Cathedral in St. Petersburg.

The Dominican church was completed over the period 1747–1865 and the monastic order adopted the emblem of a dog lying on a book with a burning torch in its jaws, a sculptured version of which can be seen on the magnificent façade. Their purpose in building the church was to convey in stone the values which give life a purpose, including strength, beauty, and harmony. As you turn the corner into the small square housing the church, it does, indeed, take your breath away with its grandeur. The builders have managed to express something in stone that words can not convey.

"Foucault's Pendulum was suspended just there," said Viktor, a theologian from the Catholic University in Lviv, who was also my guide for the day, as he pointed to a spot in the cupola's heart, which was in dire need of restoration more than 40 metres above our heads.

Viktor had an eccentricity of appearance; black cassock, unruly hair, and a coloured backpack. He drew an imaginary wire towards the ground with a finger. Beneath the dome, eighteen restored statues of saints, made of linden wood and clad in gold, looked down upon us.

"A circular ridge of sand about three metres in diameter was placed on the floor, and the iron ball, larger than a football and with a nail protruding from the bottom, was drawn to one side and then released."

Today, the black and white tiled floor of the nave shows no remnants of this daily spectacle. "Because of the earth's rotation," Viktor explained, "the nail made a trace in the pile of sand and it took about thirty-five hours to complete one turn. The idea was that people would come to understand that there is a scientific explanation for everything and that this would stir doubts about God's existence."

A similar experiment conducted at the North Pole would complete the circle in approximately twenty-four hours; a sidereal day.

"How did people react?" I asked.

Viktor made a pained smile and folded his arms. "Well, I saw it many times in the presence of believers, and the laity was always enraptured by the movement and was deeply persuaded of the presence of a holy power."

Adjoining the church was the atheist museum that has now been converted into a museum of religion. Rather than encouraging no belief, Soviet atheism promoted a strong belief in the non-existence of God. The religious studies that were tolerated focused on the search for discrepancies in religious beliefs and objects, and it was these items that the Museum of Atheism had exhibited.

"One of my colleagues has done a study comparing the exhibits shown in the Museum of Atheism and the exhibits shown today in the Museum of Religion." Viktor looked up from the cobbled square outside the museum. "And you know what? The catalogues are almost identical. It demonstrates the universal truth that one man's proof is another man's disproof."

No where in the Soviet Union was it more difficult to win the war on religion than in Ukraine, which was referred to as the Soviet

Union's Bible-belt, and home to more religious establishments than Russia.

It is not possible to know exactly, but somewhere in the region of sixty thousand religious places of worship, including churches, mosques, synagogues, and monasteries were closed or destroyed between 1917 and 1989, and the majority of the clergy, perhaps significantly more than one hundred thousand, were killed or died in the gulags.

Ironically, the KGB, which perpetrated much of the destruction, and the Church establishment were the only substantial institutions to survive the collapse of Communism. More than one thousand years of Christianity in Ukraine could not be erased in a mere seventy years of Communism.

Adopting Christianity

Christianity was adopted by Kyivan Rus in 988 by Vladimir I of Kyiv because he thought that religion would be the best glue to unite the diverse and fractious tribes over which he ruled. He sent envoys to identify the best faith, and when they returned they recommended the faith of the Orthodoxy of the Greeks, reporting that when they attended the Divine Liturgy in the cathedral of Hagia Sophia in Constantinople, "We did not know if we were in heaven or on earth."

It was a choice that would indelibly mark Ukraine and Russia for all time.

As Vladimir's successors squabbled among themselves, the principalities to the north — especially Vladimir, Suzdal, and Moscow (in the land that would become Russia) — were growing stronger. In 1299, the Kyivan Metropolitan (the head of the ecclesiastical province and ranked next below the patriarch) broke canonical rules when he decided to relocate northwards to the city of Vladimir, and shortly afterwards to Moscow, without the prior permission of Constantinople. Over the next hundred years there was an exodus from Kyiv of scholars and church relics to Moscow. Breaking church rules again — and dubbed by some as the ecclesiastic crime of the millennium — Moscow announced that it would become independent of Constantinople and set up its own patriarchate, reputedly winning over the rebuked Constantinople patriarchate by bribing him with furs. This formally established the Orthodox Church in Moscow and, with their power on the rise, they made the Kyiv church a subordinate church in 1686.

In a twist of fate, the Kyivan founders of the Church in the eastern lands found themselves subservient to their errant children, a situation that would last for more than three hundred years. Perhaps understandably, therefore, some Ukrainian nationalists rebuke Russians for their short memories when they portray Russia as the mother of the Orthodox religion.

"If they look back a thousand years instead of a mere few hundred," rejoined Viktor, "they would see that Kyiv is the true mother."

Peter the Great brought the church under government control in 1721, and its moral authority declined for the next two centuries. For their part, the Ukrainian Cossacks repelled the encroachment of Roman Catholicism from the Polish in the north and also refused to accept the Muscovite Tsar-Pope. The idea of the subjugation of the church to the state was such an anathema to Ukrainians that the Metropolitan Peter Mohyla of Kyiv said he would rather die a martyr than join the Muscovite church.

As historian Alexandr Pypin noted:

> Moscow retreated more and more into her exclusive concept of the world, and at the same time fell into that religious and racial intolerance, which was destined to build a Chinese wall against foreigners and dissenters, engendered extreme racial arrogance, and eventually barred the road to enlightenment.[1]

In the lands that would become western Ukraine, religious evolution had been following a different model. Prince Vladimir's decision to adopt the Orthodox faith established an irrevocable schism with the Catholic Church, which predominated in the western lands and whose believers turned to Rome and the Pope for spiritual leadership. The fault line dividing the Roman Catholic west (characterised by papal infallibility, organisational unity, and respect for Roman law), and the Orthodox east (more closely associated with immutability of tradition, piety, and deep respect for spiritual principles), lay directly through Ukraine. For the next millennium it would meander east or west, but never by far, depending upon who controlled the land.

To add to the mix, in 1596, as part of the Union of Brest, many of the Orthodox bishops of the Polish-Lithuanian Commonwealth (including the territory of Galicia which today forms part of western Ukraine), decided to accept communion with Rome. The "Uniate" Church, as it became known, was a sort of hybrid; it formally recognised the Pope as the head of the church but maintained the traditional eastern rites.

When the Polish lands were partitioned by the Russian Empire and Austria in the late eighteenth century, those members of the Uniate Church who found themselves living in the Russian Empire were harassed because of their disloyalty. Kyiv fell under the control of the Russian empire and the leaders of the Uniate Church had to relocate hastily to the city of Lviv (then in Austria). Here, the administrators were much more supportive of the Uniates, and they encouraged the use of the Ukrainian language in church services and, in principle if not in practice, they placed the Uniate Church on an equal legal footing to the Roman Catholic Church.

The Uniate Church became the national church of Ukrainians in Galicia (and from now on I shall refer to them as the Ukrainian Greek Catholic Church), and many of their adherents were in the forefront of the Ukrainian national revival of the late eighteenth and early nineteenth centuries. Galicia remained an Austrian territory until the end of World War I when it was claimed by Poland, but in 1939, as Soviet troops forged westwards, it was annexed to the Soviet Union as part of the Ukrainian Soviet Socialist Republic.

Within the Soviet Union by the start of World War II, all the non-Orthodox denominations had been eradicated or were so repressed that they were operating illicitly and underground. The Russian Orthodox Church continued to operate with official sanction, but it also suffered heavy losses to the "cult of atheism." Across the fifteen Soviet Republics, probably only about five hundred parishes were open compared with an estimated fifty-four thousand before World War I, and a meagre four out of one hundred and fifty Bishops had survived.

World War II provided a small respite in the repression. Though Stalin had not changed his basic hostility to the Church, he realised quickly that in order to defend the motherland he needed to mobilise what remained of the Orthodox Church whose values still resonated with the peasantry. The Metropolitan in Moscow obliged by unambiguously calling on people to fight on the side of the (God-hating) Soviet regime, and by way of reward he was allowed to conduct Easter celebrations and other controls were relaxed temporarily. Behind closed doors the Church struck a deal with the devil; the opportunity to operate, albeit in a strictly controlled manner, in return for unswerving loyalty to the Communist Party.

Indeed, this Metropolitan rarely missed an opportunity to express his gratitude to Stalin, as is shown by a letter he wrote on the day after Stalin's death, in 1953:

> In my own name and in the name of the Russian Orthodox Church I express my deepest and sincerest condolences on the death of the unforgettable Joseph Vissarionovich Stalin, the great builder of the people's happiness... His death has been taken with deep grief by the whole of the Russian Orthodox Church, which will never forget his benevolent attitude towards the needs of the Church. His radiant memory will never be erased from our hearts. Our Church intones "eternal memory" to him with a special feeling of unceasing love.[2]

Such a shameful veneration was a betrayal of trust that many Ukrainians and Soviets would never forget.

City of the Lion

There is no better place to experience a microcosm of post-independence Ukrainian religious life than the city of Lviv, meaning "City of the Lion," located seventy-five kilometres from the European Union border. It is undoubtedly one of the most beautiful cities of Europe, and it owes its visual appearance more to Vienna, Budapest, and Prague than to Moscow or Kyiv. One hundred years ago, with the exception of Rome, it was the only city to have three Catholic archbishops in residence: a Roman-Catholic, an Armenian-Catholic, and a Greek-Catholic archbishop. The city also had Russian Orthodox and Protestant Churches and one of the largest Jewish communities in Eastern Europe. Today there is a bewildering choice of five cathedrals and more than fifty churches.

But you don't need to be religious to enjoy the city. As a close friend who lives in the city told me, "You don't come here to look around. You come here to be inspired."

The city's roots are very tangled. It was founded prior to 1250 as a fortress to defend trade routes by Prince Danylo Halytsky for his son, Lev (meaning "Lion"). Its favourable location between occident and orient and between Scandinavia and Byzantium meant that it rapidly assumed commercial importance. It was successively besieged or controlled by Lithuanians, Rumanians, Turks, Cossacks, Swedes, Poles, and Austrians and always had a cosmopolitan population.

The city's architectural styles reflect this diversity, with gothic, renaissance, baroque, classicism, Biedermeier, art-deco, and Soviet-style buildings jockeying to catch your attention. Voids between densely packed buildings, created by war and destruction, have been filled by constructions of a later style, and the whole assemblage of churches, mansions, and domestic dwellings of the old city has been granted UNESCO World Heritage status. It is truly an open-air museum.

In Lviv old traditions mix with the new. McDonald's is only a few doors down from a Viennese coffee house, and Skate-boarding youths from Ivan Franko University weave around Nuns wearing tunic and veil on their way to vespers. On the city outskirts, row upon row of poorly maintained Soviet apartment blocks, indistinguishable from Kyiv or Moscow, are being interrupted by the construction of new residencies.

St. George's Cathedral

Heading for Ruska Street, Viktor and I walked three hundred metres southwards from the Dominican church across the Market Square, which boasts nearly fifty baroque and rococo landmarks built between the sixteenth and the nineteenth centuries. This is one of the oldest and narrowest streets in the city, and the tram lines (a much later addition, of course) physically overlap each other so that two trams cannot pass each other at the narrowest point.

Viktor's cassock billowed theatrically as we disembarked from a tram near to St. George's Cathedral, which stood outside the medieval city on a high terrace. An Orthodox church was founded on the site in the fourteenth century, but following the Union of Brest — which was proclaimed on this site — the church transferred to the Ukrainian Greek Catholic Church. The new church, built between 1744 and 1774, is regarded by many Ukrainians as the citadel of the Christian spirit in Ukraine. With its ornate carvings, the architecture is a pearl of the late-baroque style in stone and brick.

"It was in this church," lamented Viktor, "that the Soviets convened a Council in 1946 to proclaim the annulment of the Union of Brest. There were no Catholic bishops present since they were all imprisoned, and it was a renegade Ukrainian Greek Catholic priest named Gabriel Kostelnik who officially offered to liquidate the Greek Catholic Church."

Gathering his thoughts, he continued. "It was a setup, of course, and soon afterwards, all the Church's property was confiscated and the clergy tortured. The Ukrainian Greek Catholic Church was forced underground for more than forty years after that."

Nearly three thousand parishes and more than four thousand churches were seized, and whilst some were used for Russian

Orthodox Church services or put to alternative uses, such as cinemas or storage, most were destroyed. As a result, more than four million Ukrainian Greek Catholics no longer had a working Church. Thousands of priests, monks, nuns, and seminarians were arrested and killed, fled the country, or were "converted" to Orthodoxy in order to avoid persecution.

"Is it not true that the Ukrainian Greek Catholics sided with the Germans during the war, and that this in some ways vindicated the Soviets actions?" I asked.

"Certainly the Russian Orthodox Church claims that the Catholics were under instruction from The Vatican to support the Germans. They also claim that Metropolitan Sheptytsky, whose body is buried in the crypt, had blessed the 14th SS Division Galicia which comprised eighty thousand Ukrainians. But most people don't believe that wrongs done during the war can be used to justify doing evil things during peacetime."

He looked at me thoughtfully and asked, "Did the Allies try to change the religion of the Japanese, or did the Americans try to change that of the Iraqis and Afghans?"

"And what was the reaction of the people to the liquidation of their Church?" I countered.

"Some of the clergy continued to operate clandestinely. Priests were ordained secretly, even in the labour camps, and a couple of Bishops were consecrated. Meetings were held in apartments or in the forest and, whenever possible, the sacraments of baptism, marriage and burial were administered. I know of parishioners who have changed Church several times in their life. They may have been baptised as a Roman Catholic in Poland, become part of the Ukrainian Greek Catholic Church in Lviv, switched to Russian Orthodox, and after independence they were attracted to Protestantism."

For those of us from countries where the Church seems immutable, this may sound like disloyalty but in Ukraine it is expedient.

"I know of one case," Viktor continued in a lighter tone, "where it took a woman several years to pluck up the courage to ask the priest why the service had changed from the Ukrainian to Russian language. 'We became Orthodox,' the priest replied flatly, and the matter was never raised between them again."

For many people a church is a place of prayer, and this matters more than the particular branch of Christianity.

Latin Cathedral

Next on the itinerary was the Cathedral of the Assumption of Blessed Virgin Mary, more commonly known as the Latin Cathedral, located in the old city. The exterior is rather nondescript in the context of Lviv's exceptional architecture, but the interior is the most sumptuous of any building in the city and it commands the title of "minor basilica."

Viktor had informed me previously that there were only two non-Orthodox churches allowed to operate in Lviv; both were Roman Catholic, and the Latin Cathedral was one of them. The liturgy is in Polish, even today, and it was and still is the centre of the Polish community in Lviv.

Though our visit was on a Monday morning, communion was in full swing and the church was crowded. A friend had confided to me that entering the church was "like entering a sauna and all moral filth washes away." Thankfully, both temperature and humidity were normal, but it was easy to be moved by the glorious organ music and the richness of the decoration. Every square centimetre is ornately decorated, and no matter where your eyes come to rest there are works of art: sculptures, icons, tombstones, stained glass, and other decorative features.

"Why was the Roman Catholic Church allowed to operate?" I asked as we left the Cathedral and walked towards the rear side.

"Their Church was never forbidden officially in the Soviet Union, but it operated under strict control and was not allowed to communicate with Rome. I don't think they wanted to sever all ties with Rome, but wanted to keep the door open, so to speak. And recent evidence suggests that the Papacy and the Communists occasionally had close relations."

"What do you mean by that?"

His statement then was laden with implications. "The Pope denounced Communism only at the start of World War II despite the execution of several Roman Catholic bishops. They had known of the atrocities for twenty years but they hadn't spoken out. It is now known that the Vatican was conducting secret negotiations with the Kremlin to establish a Roman Catholic Metropolitan on Soviet territory, as either a counter to the Russian Orthodox Church or to replace it. When the Soviets were assured, however, that the Russian Orthodox clergy were totally subservient to their wishes, the alternative plan lost its urgency."

Death, Cemeteries, and Crematoria

We stopped just behind the cathedral, in the shadow of the pretty Boim family church as Viktor continued his narrative. "I always inform visitors that here used to be the main city cemetery, and that in 1783 Holy Roman Emperor Joseph II ordered it and six smaller ones to be moved outside the city, making Lviv the first cemetery-free city centre in Europe. It was here that the concept of the suburban cemetery started. But they never believe me!"

Between the sixteenth and twentieth centuries, Lviv recorded more than fifty epidemics — largely resulting from inadequate sanitation — and the most serious, in 1620, killed two thirds of the population. Centuries later, death and how to handle death was an important question that the Bolsheviks had to face. The Orthodox Church had the answers, of course, but they weren't palatable to the atheists.

The Civil War that followed World War I left hundreds of thousands dead, and though the problem was not so great in winter when the dead bodies froze, more clement weather was accompanied by the threat of disease. Space in cities was also at a premium as urbanisation was proceeding at an ever-increasing pace.

Science provided the answer in cremation. In 1918 in opposition to the violent protests of the Church, funerals were declared to be a state industry and crematoriums were planned for each city. Radical atheists took yet a more extreme approach as is shown by the letter of Central Committee Member, Olminskii in 1924:

> I think that all survivals of religious practice (coffins, funerals...) are nonsense. It is more pleasant for me to think that my body will be used more rationally. It should be sent to a factory without any ritual, and in the factory the fat should be used for technical purposes and the rest for fertiliser.[3]

At the time of Olminskii's death seven years later, there was only one crematorium operating and it is unlikely that his wish was fulfilled.

Progress in mastering the technology was fitful and sometimes macabre. Experiments were usually conducted on dead horses, and frequently the high temperatures required could not be maintained and the combustion was incomplete. Even in the late 1960s, the builders of the Kyiv Crematorium had had to insist that the authorities purchase a British-made *Mason & Dawson* furnace and not the cheaper German furnace that had been used in the concentration camps. Wartime memories were still strong in Kyiv.

Even with the technology mastered, it was not a readily acceptable solution for pious citizens. The fact that Cemetery Directors were among the wealthiest people says a lot about the continued desire of people to bury their loved ones and about the bureaucracy of the process.

The main challenge was to make all the necessary preparations before the body started to decay. Getting the autopsy papers and permission to bury or cremate the body from the local ZAGS office (a local authority department) was just the start of the problems. People needed to be bribed to produce the coffin, burial place, gravediggers, headstone, inscription, and funeral transport in a timely fashion. Dedicated funeral cars did not exist in the Soviet Union (and still don't exist in most of Ukraine), and unmarked vans, used by factories and food concerns, were appropriated for the job. As for communicating the news about the deceased, it was usually by word of mouth since newspaper obituaries were prohibited (with an exception for Party leaders).

Embalming Lenin

A key test of the new policy of cremation was the death of Lenin in 1924, and to most Russians it was unthinkable that he should be cremated. Stalin may have first suggested the idea of embalming the great leader during a Politburo meeting three months before Lenin's death, though it was against the wish of Lenin's wife. When Lenin died, it is thought that Stalin had letters falsified which suggested that the proletariat had demanded embalming, such as one from Kyiv railway workers which pleaded to preserve the body for a thousand years.

The preserving process would prove to be complicated, lucrative, and have lasting consequences. The removal of Lenin's brain for scientific experiment resulted in making cuts through the arteries which would ordinarily be used to pump embalming fluid into the body, and so an alternative technique was needed. Most scientists shied away from the challenge because they understood the dire personal consequences of failure. But two people volunteered eagerly: Professor Vorobiov, a chemist from Kharkiv University in eastern Ukraine, and a colleague, Boris Zbarsky. Vorobiov had already developed a preserving solution of glycerine, alcohol, water, potassium acetate, and quinine chloride, and all he needed was a willing cadaver.

By the time they were authorised to start work, the corpse had turned sallow, the nose was darkening, and the open eyes were sinking into their sockets. Four months later, however, the work was complete, including the installation inside the body of an electric pump to maintain the correct humidity. Initially they presented Lenin dressed in a Red Army military jacket, but his costume was changed just before World War II into his sombre black suit.

Their success and the ongoing need for restorative maintenance every few weeks catapulted Vorobiov into the Soviet elite, and today the embalming institution he established is kept busy with commissions from Russia's new rich.[4]

Golden Rose Synagogue

A short walk from the Latin Cathedral is the Gunpowder Tower, a stumpy, circular building that looks like an enormous Mongolian tent and whose three-metre thick walls date from 1550. Until a hundred years ago, the merchants and gentry stored their fur coats in the tower because the presence of gunpowder ensured that it was vermin-free.

"You see the hole in the middle of the terrace?" Viktor asked as we turned a corner. "Well, that was the site of the Golden Rose Synagogue, but the Germans dynamited it very precisely."

Nearly all of Lviv's one hundred thousand Jews were exterminated at a camp located on Yanovska Street. The Nuremburg Court was presented with graphic accounts of how S.S. Haupsturmfuehrer Gebauer strangled women and children, and how in winter he placed men in barrels of water with their hands and feet tied until they froze to death.[5]

Two gable ends now face each other about twenty metres apart and all that connects the two buildings is a corrugated fence in much need of repair. A black plaque on one of the walls is the only reminder that the synagogue once occupied the derelict site.

Light rain had started to fall so Viktor and I hurried across a remnant of the old city wall and ascended a gentle hill to the 100-year-old Russian Orthodox St. George's Church. The distance from the church porch to the iconostasis is quite short, perhaps only ten metres, and the church can hold no more than a hundred worshipers. On busy days hundreds of worshippers are forced to stand in the yard and listen to the service through speakers. Next door a cinema has been converted into the social club of the church, but there are three brown splashes on the white wall where somebody has thrown pots of paint.

"Occasionally there are outbursts of aggression against the Russian Orthodox Church by nationalists, and St. George's is their only operating church in the city," Viktor explained. "After years of suppression by Moscow, some people feel that the 'shoe is on the other foot.' The Russian Orthodox Church protests, of course. They complain that the local authorities, who are strongly pro-Ukrainian, are preventing them from building a bigger church elsewhere in the city."

KGB Infiltration of the Church

During those years of suppression, the KGB infiltrated deep into the heart of the Russian Orthodox Church as it worked to promote the Kremlin's policies on the international stage. Claims are now surfacing, for example, that three-thousand people within the evangelical community collaborated with the KGB, and that nine of the ten highest church dignitaries were KGB agents.[6][7]

One of the most revealing studies is the work of journalist Alexander Nezhny, who compared official records of the overseas visits of top church officials with KGB records of overseas travel of the same period in order to uncover the code names of the churchmen. According to Nezhny, Philaret of Kyiv, a most senior church leader, had the code name, "Antonov."[8] Philaret is deeply unpopular with some Ukrainians because he prohibited the use of the Ukrainian language during the Soviet period, and he has three children, despite vows of chastity.

New evidence such as this, plus the firsthand experience of Ukrainians, has left many mistrustful of the Moscow Patriarchate which is viewed as irrevocably morally compromised; at best seeking personal material wellbeing and at worst betraying their Church and people. Those implicated might well argue that they collaborated exclusively in order to be able to serve their Church and to protect their dioceses and parishes from closure. Perhaps this is so. But particularly damaging is their continuing refusal to offer a public expression of contrition for their servility to the Communist Party. This has led some people to the ugly conclusion that the moral issues reach far deeper than most imagine or want to imagine.

The rain stopped and weak September sunshine encouraged us to move on to our last stop of the day, the Transfiguration Church. Now rivulets of water were searching for the city's elusive sewers.

"The collapse of the Soviet Union was no doubt hastened by the activities of the underground church in Ukraine," Viktor said as we trod the platinum black cobblestones back into the old city, "After Khrushchev, repression eased a little and the different churches grew tentatively. Small communities of Baptists, Pentecostals, and Adventists appeared and the network of Greek Catholics which had survived underground became stronger. But the real breakthrough came with Brezhnev's decision — whilst on his death bed — to allow limited celebrations of the millennium of Christianity in 1988."

A Religious Revival

The Ukrainian people knew about the momentous changes taking place in countries like Poland and Czechoslovakia, and the Ukrainian religious activists became increasing vocal in advocating for the opening of churches. Perhaps a quarter of a million petitioners turned out on the streets and priests began to perform their duties openly. In 1989 came the heart-stopping news that Ukrainian Greek Catholics could register their communities, and many interpreted this to mean that Church property liquidated by the 1946 Council would be returned.

We walked down Virmenska Street, which houses the Armenian Cathedral founded in 1356. This is one of the oldest churches in the city and, in my view, the most beautiful and spiritual of all Lviv's churches. One hundred metres further is the more recent construction of the Transfiguration Church built by the Trinitarian monks from Spain.

"You remember Kostelnik, the renegade priest who attended the Council in 1946?" Viktor asked as we crossed the church threshold. "He was assassinated on these steps immediately after Divine Liturgy one day in 1948."

From the cafe opposite, the music of Simply Red drifted in through the open church doors and a young woman, no more than 25 years old and wearing a short skirt and high heels, was genuflecting on both knees in front of a picture of Christ on the Cross.

"This was the first church parishioners took control of and returned to the Ukrainian Greek Catholics. This put Gorbachev in a tough spot: he wanted full diplomatic relations with The Vatican, but he didn't want to alienate the Russian Orthodox who supported him. Political indecision followed and the consequences were messy. Some even called it a 'religious war.'"

There were perhaps fifteen hundred churches at stake in the Lviv region, but the jewel in the crown was undoubtedly St. George's Cathedral. Armed with a decree signed by the Lviv authorities, some thirty thousand Ukrainian Greek Catholics converged on the church, and over a period four months they managed to oust the incumbent Russian Orthodox. Today people's views are so coloured by the events that it is difficult to know what to believe, but the stories tell of broken windows, broken bones, tear gas, and kidnapping.

Similar scenes of disenfranchised worshipers taking back their churches were played out across Ukraine. Though the authorities tried to impose some rules — disputed churches held elections or held services on alternating days — the sheer number of Ukrainian Greek Catholics, particularly in western Ukraine, ensured that they recovered the churches that had been taken away by the 1946 ruling.

The turmoil of the time and the subsequent collapse of the Soviet Union ushered in several critical events Ukraine which still dominate the scene today. Schisms appeared (or reappeared in the case of old internal conflicts) within the Russian Orthodox Church, and today it operates as three separate entities. The Orthodox groups are struggling to demonstrate their moral basis and relevance.

The Greek Catholics carry the mantle of martyrdom but struggle to exploit it in eastern Ukraine, and the Roman Catholics carry negative associations of Polish repression. Stealthily, other Churches began to make serious inroads in Ukraine. For the first time people could make individual moral choices and they were particularly attracted by the lack of formality and the charitable giving of the Protestant Churches. It did not go unnoticed that the Protestants were the only ones providing food, shelter, and spiritual support to the mass of people who crowded Kyiv's city centre during the Orange Revolution.

These groups remain poorly networked today. The result is that no one group has become strong enough to dominate at the national level. Ukraine is now a country divided by religion, and more specifically by the *politics* of religion. It may not be the best omen for a country trying to build a sense of nation, but Viktor was sanguine.

"The best way I can sum it up," proffered Viktor, his face shining with hope, "is to use the analogy of a telephone exchange. In the recent past all calls were placed via Rome or Moscow. Getting a line was not easy and all communication was closely monitored. Now we have our own exchange; its capacity is great, and it's open to everybody."

SEX AND THE SOVIETS

"I DON'T WANT SEX, I just want to talk."

"I don't do dirty talk." She put down the receiver abruptly.

So began a series of perhaps a dozen phone conversations before I was eventually put in touch with Larisa and Kseniya. Larisa was a retired prostitute and Kseniya was her 30-year-old daughter and protégé.

The Role of Women

If attitudes to sex can tell us much about a society, Ukraine has experienced extremes with women alternating between a prominent, respected role and a lesser, subservient one. The polarity of views is so sharp.

The pottery from the Trypillyan culture of five-thousand years ago depicts heavily-breasted women carrying children and sowing wheat, which were signs of fertility and of women's central role in society. Moving forward two-and-a-half millennia, archaeologists discovered recently a Scythian burial ground in the Don valley that contained young women buried with weapons. It suggests that Herodotus's tale of the Amazons, a race of women warriors extending from the Black Sea to the Ukrainian steppe, may well have some truth. In the Middle Ages and up the seventeenth century, a strong emphasis was placed on feelings, sensations, desires, and the pleasures of sexual intercourse; and in Ukrainian folklore there is little mention of the physical or mental abuse of women.

Things started to change in the seventeenth century when subservience to the patriarchal Russians placed Ukrainian women under the influence of the *Domostroi*, a guide for men on how to manage domestic and other matters believed to have been written in Novgorod in the fifteenth century. Copies may still be bought from bookshops throughout Kyiv for a few kopeks. Among other things, it describes what sort of whips a man should keep and which is the most appropriate to use on his pregnant wife.

By the second decade of the twentieth century the polarity of attitudes to women had changed yet again, and Russia and the early Soviet Union were among the most sexually liberated societies on earth. A 1923 pamphlet titled *The Sexual Revolution in Russia* discussed homosexuality, sodomy, and various other forms of sexual gratification, states, "Soviet legislation treats these the same as so-called natural intercourse."[1]

This freedom was to last less than a decade. During the following six decades of Communism, the exploration of the erogenous zones was replaced by the exploration of space. Sex became an act performed as a tribute to the motherland, and it was both domesticated and regulated except, of course, if you were a high-ranking official. (Brezhnev, Khrushchev, and even Stalin were all rumoured to have mistresses.)

In yet another reversal, since the fall of Communism Ukraine has been awash with sexual imagery and pornography. There has been an explosion of repressed interest, and "having sex" is seen as a clear expression of having thrown away constraints on personal behaviour. Women are cynically encouraged to celebrate their ability to satisfy a man.

As a sign of the times, a 1990 survey showed Soviet women ranked prostitution eight in a list of the top twenty employment positions, and one-third of high school girls said they would have sex for hard currency.[2] In the following eight years, it is believed that about half a million Ukrainian women were trafficked to Europe or the Middle East for prostitution.[3]

Nowadays, there are believed to be perhaps one-quarter of a million prostitutes in Ukraine. That's a staggering six women in every one hundred women of reproductive age, or, put another way, that's more than all the women of reproductive age in Northeast England.

Why Women Do It

My interview with Kseniya came at a price; though she insisted that I pay her for the time, her mother contributed for free. And so I made a tentative start with Kseniya.

"Why do you do it?"

"It provides a living," she answered matter-of-factly with a penetrating gaze that unsteadied my nerves. "I remember trying to find a job after leaving college. Most times when I applied, the manager wanted sex with me before offering me the job. Ask any girl, she knows, it's a common experience. I told my mother and she agreed I might as well get paid for it. She didn't want me to do it, but she supports me."

I recalled that following the collapse of the Soviet Union the people pushing pornography were much quicker to use the TV and magazines to promote their products than, say, doctors or the church were to use the media to disseminate messages about responsible sex. As a result, oppression was quickly replaced by exploitation and society became permissive overnight without time for proper sex education.

"I don't want to work for next to nothing in a factory," Kseniya continued. "This job gives me some freedom. Whilst British women are busy fighting to go down in the coal mines, our women are still fighting to get out." Her muscles tightened, and she glanced at her mother seated nearby.

Research involving more than six hundred female prostitutes in cities throughout Ukrainian paints an eye-opening picture of Ukraine's prostitutes. Twenty percent of those surveyed said they would not leave the profession even if given a financially comparable alternative, 50 percent of those interviewed had a university education, and 50 percent came from nuclear families where both parents raised them.[4] Ukraine's prostitutes are generally well educated, well brought up, and committed to the job.

Larisa was nodding in agreement with her daughter. "Prostitution made a comfortable life possible for me and helped me bring up Ksyusha as a single mother," she said. "This is even truer today. It's only the older folks who see prostitution as a moral issue."

She gave a tight smile, but appeared unconcerned about the delicacy of the issue as she continued. "Don't think it's about trying to achieve equality with men. It isn't. In Soviet times equality was a falsehood, as it is now. Women just wanted more time with their children, flexible working hours, better childcare, and increased child allowances. We didn't talk about fulfilment or about feminism; those words weren't part of our vocabulary."

I think I understood what she meant. When the Soviet system collapsed after seventy years of so-called equality, there wasn't a single woman in the thirteen-member politburo, and only a handful in the three hundred-member Central Committee. When President Mikhail Gorbachev spoke at a women's conference in 1987 and restated women's role as mother, wife, and the person who raises the children, Soviet women welcomed his respect for the maternal role and the restatement of women's place in society.

"I bet prostitution pays well," I wagered.

"It depends," Kseniya answered. "One effect of the media revealing just how profitable it can be is that the hotels and restaurants are now flooded with girls who will have sex with you."

In general, the Ukrainian (and Russian) media has focused first on successful women in a man's world, invoking stereotypes such as the businesswoman, the model, and the girlfriend of the businessman. Secondly, they give attention to marginal women, such as female prisoners, prostitutes, or "good-time girls" (to whom Kseniya was referring). And following in third position, the media focus on the majority of women in the (less newsworthy) role of the mother, the wife and the friend.

Kseniya continued, "That's why some of us don't mind if the police get tougher. These girls don't have expenses, and in a few nights they make the equivalent of a month's salary. But I have significant expenses. I have a driver to pay and then there are the police, pimps, doctors, and hotel workers. In the end I'm left with only 25 to 50 percent of the price."

As Kseniya's mother informed me later, surges in the number of girls were quite common, particularly in the 1980s when Kyiv started to host international conferences and preparation started for the Olympic Games.

"And what about your clients? Tell me about them," I guided her. My personal curiosity was now as strong as my professional interest.

She shrugged. "Oh, I have a lot of regulars, mostly young men who have something to prove or older men whose marriages are tired and who didn't get to play around before."

In this society, I observed, older men grew up with the ideology of labour and scarcity, not pleasure and abundance. In the 1960s when the West was undergoing a social revolution, there was no equivalent in the Soviet Union. "Free love" and the permissive decade passed them by.

"The young ones are all bravado and older ones appreciate the attention," Kseniya added. "For all the kinds of sex on offer, most men want it straight. I can't see Ukrainian men leading a sexual revolution." She gave her mother a knowing glance. The phone rang and she moved out of earshot. Her almond-scented perfume wafted through the air as she moved.

Her comments jibe with the themes explored in one of the most controversial books in recent years, Oksana Zabuzhko's *Field Studies in Ukrainian Sex*. In spite of the title, the book is not so much about sex as it is about the relationship between the sexes. It is the story of a strong-willed and educated woman searching to find ideal love in modern Ukraine, and failing because her chosen man shows all the neuroses of other men. The sub-text of the book is the stigma of being born in a country built on social lies and one that has never realised its potential. It's about the influence of the weight of history and how it has humiliated Ukrainian men. Unable to find solace in the kitchen or the kindergarten, as many women do, men have sought to take revenge on women. As far as I interpret it, the book is a challenge to modern Ukrainian couples to find role models to replace those of the drunken father and repressed mother.

Masochism

Whilst Kseniya was distracted by the phone call, I rued the idea that perhaps she ought to have had more adventurous clients, given the provenance of the word "masochism."

Leopold von Sacher-Masoch was born in 1836 in Lviv in modern-day western Ukraine on the narrow, cobbled Copernicus Street. He shared his home with his parents and his paternal aunt, Countess Zenobia. History recounts that he had at least five significant relationships, but it was the beatings given to him by the Countess that enraptured him and shaped his persona.

One day whilst playing hide and seek with his sisters, he hid in the closet of the Countess. Moments later the Countess returned to her room with a lover, moved to the sofa and started an adulterous liaison. Alerted to his wife's return, the Countess's husband burst into the room and caught her *in flagrante delicto*. With the Count expressing mild indignation, his wife animatedly punched him in the face, drawing blood, and in the commotion the lover fled. The Count hobbled off to seek medical aid and the boy was discovered by the Countess. Full of anger, she turned on young Leo and beat him mercilessly. Though the pain was great, he recalled later that he was aware of a deep-seated pleasure that he could not forget.

Later in life, Leo kept a fur in an ottoman in his study and stroked it from time to time in order to recall the pleasure of his time with the Countess, in much the same way that the poet Schiller used to keep rotten apples in his desk and inhale the sweet, rancid mustiness to jolt his brain into activity.

Though Sacher-Masoch wrote eighty novels and more than a hundred short stories, he is best known for the 1870 novel, *Venus In Furs*, which is about the masochistic relationship between Wanda von Dunajew (who in real life was his lover, Fanny Pistor), and Severin von Kusiemski, who becomes her slave. This was the novel that Dr. Richard von Krafft-Ebing identified as the origin of the word "masochism."

In spite of his prodigious literary output, Sacher-Masoch's contribution to world literature was marginal, and perhaps it is best to remember him as an early example of an artist who lived his life as art, in much the same way that Freddie Mercury and Andy Warhol sought to do.

Abortion

"And what are your greatest fears?" I asked Kseniya when I had regained her full attention. She curled her feet underneath her. She was lithe and small-breasted.

"My biggest fear is that after having had a few abortions, I won't be able to have a child when the time is right," she replied seriously.

During discussions with a few doctors, I later learned that her experience is all too common. By the time of the break-up of the Soviet Union, perhaps eight million, or a quarter of the world's abortions, were being undertaken by the state, and there were probably four abortions for every live birth. Many girls, I was told, had had more than a dozen abortions.

Larisa gave me her perspective from the 1960s and 1970s. "It was unpleasant but necessary. We knew very little about contraceptives: they were not always available, they cost money and we couldn't rely on them. And if the man doesn't want to be careful, what can a woman do? Oral contraceptives were banned in the 1970s for 'health reasons' and anyway abortion was free."

In spite of the generation she represented, she recalled her experience readily and with no inhibition. She recalled how abortion was not a choice but a necessity — how the lack of men in the workforce forced women to work, and how the shortage of food placed a limit on the number of children a woman could feed. She also spoke about the case of conception outside of marriage and the strong social stigma against illegitimate children. As a result, abortion was a social phenomenon rather than an individual issue, and it became the key tool in birth control.

"It was embarrassing," she continued, "not so much among friends who all shared the same experience, but at work. The doctor would issue a three-day sickness note to the employee which described the reason for the absence. So everyone at work knew. It was during those fifteen minutes with the gynaecologist, however, that I learned the most about my body." She smiled at the naivety of the thought.

Although the Soviet Union was the first place in the world to legalise abortion in 1920, Stalin saw this as a temporary measure. Sixteen years later, in a drive to reassert family values, he reintroduced the ban. It was lifted following his death, and the vacuum aspiration technique was in common usage by 1967, a full ten years before it was adopted in the UK and USA. Clinic waiting room posters dispassionately describe the tool as being useful for "the removal of biological material."

Given the scarcity of resources following World War II and other medical priorities, the Soviets chose not to develop reliable, cheap, and widely available contraceptives. To do so would have been to allow women to take control of their own future, and that would have had profound consequences for population growth and the availability of a labour force. Nowadays, I am struck by the fact that the declining birth rate is often referred to in Russia as a "population crisis," whereas in Ukraine it is most often called a "family crisis," suggesting a small, but fundamental difference in outlook.

"I thought you might have said violence or AIDS were your biggest concerns." I turned to Kseniya for her reaction.

"Well, you have a choice. You either pay the police or pay the thugs for protection. I pay the police and if a client gives me trouble, I try to resist the unpleasantness, but give in if necessary." She hesitated and added, "Later he gets a visit from the police."

"That's the way it is," Larisa added. "As Dostoevsky suggested, 'to be Russian is to comprehend punishment but not justice.'"

"And health issues?" I prompted Kseniya.

HIV AIDS was virtually unknown at the times of the break-up of the Soviet Union but a study in 2005 indicated approximately one quarter of a million people between the ages of 15-49 were living with HIV/AIDS, and the number of reported cases was shown to have increased twenty times in the previous five years[5]

"My mother taught me how to take good care of myself," she said matter-of-factly. "As for AIDS, I get tested regularly. It's like car accidents: they happen every day, but people who drive expensive cars and wear seatbelts are less affected than others."

"But what about the guys? I'm told gonorrhoea and herpes are dozens of times the EU average."

"There's nothing 'average' about this job," quipped Kseniya. The two women looked at each other. "The girls who do the politicians and rich businessmen earn more and they can take greater care of themselves. They're paid just to have sex with those guys, but it's only for a few months and then they're changed. On the bottom rung of the ladder are the girls who work the railway station and the curb side and, of course, the cheap brothels, particularly in south Kyiv. They're the ones at most risk."

Pornography with Ideas

One of the first people to write about the brothels in Ukraine was Alexander Kuprin, who was styled as the Russian Kipling by Vladimir Nabokov. His lurid and overwhelming novel, *Yama* (The Pit), based on the pitiful lives of a handful of prostitutes, has been called "The first and last honest work on the subject of prostitution."

The story is based on Kuprin's experiences in Odesa, Kyiv, and Yamska Street (the inspiration for the title), which runs parallel to the main railway line in Kyiv. The novel describes a world that contrasted sharply with the morality of the Russian intelligentsia, and Kuprin grips the reader from page one with evocative imagery:

> They choose any woman they like and know beforehand that they will never meet refusal. Impatiently they pay their money in advance, and on the public bed, not yet grown cold after the body of their predecessor, aimlessly commit the very greatest and most beautiful of all universal mysteries — the mystery of the conception of new life. And the women with indifferent readiness, with uniform words, with practiced professional movements, satisfy their desires, like machines — only to receive, right after them, during the same night, with the very same words, smiles and gestures, the third, the fourth, the tenth man, not infrequently already biding his turn in the waiting room.[6]

In the same year, Kharkiv-born Mikhail Artsybashev published his controversial novel *Sanin*. It told the story of a powerful and life-loving but amoral man who was bored with religion and politics and pleasured himself by seducing country girls.

Sanin's show of individualism and self-gratification greatly appealed to young people in particular, who experienced an atmosphere of moral despondency in the final years of the Romanovs.

Kornei Chukovsky, who was schooled in Odesa and went on to write the famous children's book, *Doctor Aybolit*, and to translate Charles Dickens and Mark Twain into Russian, was very familiar with the subject matter of Kuprin and Artsybashev. He later commented, "Russian pornography is not plain pornography such as the French and Germans produce, but pornography with ideas."

The period between the publication of these novels and the 1930s was full of ambiguities. It heralded a complete transformation in the sexual landscape based on the idea that sex could be secularized; that it could be separate from the teachings of the church, and that science played a significant part in determining one's sexual orientation.

Though Ukraine (and the rest of Russia) did not have a gay emancipation movement in the same way as say, Germany, wealthy men had gay servants, and male prostitutes worked in bathhouses. Public toilets provided meeting places for like-minded men and the closet door was flung wide open when homosexual acts were decriminalized.

Women's emancipation groups also began to emerge. In western Ukraine they were primarily influenced by nationalist groups and by people who were challenging the Austrian authorities. In eastern Ukraine, emancipation was led by women who were actively working within politics towards a socialist ideology.

The Bolshevik leader Alexandra Kollontai identified what emancipation meant for personal relationships, calling it "A union of affection and comradeship, a union of two equal members of the communist society, both of them free, both of them independent, both of them workers."[7]

She and others proposed that children should be taken away from parents and brought up communally, whilst the parents would be free to move on and mate with different partners. Meanwhile, nudists marched on the streets of Petrograd to celebrate the human body, and in a 1927 legal case, a court recognized the marriage of two women.[8] In Britain, for example, same sex partnerships were only recognized for the first time in 2005.

Increasingly, Stalin moved to resist what he saw as the degeneration of society, and he reasserted family values as a building block of socialism. New laws passed in the early 1930s prohibited homosexuality and attempted to make divorce socially unacceptable by publishing in newspapers the names of those who filed for divorce. After 1944, children born to unmarried couples were registered as fatherless and stigmatized. Naked bodies were no longer allowed in paintings, and the first film screen kiss was not seen until 1956. The first public nudity was shown in the 1978 film, *Little Vera*, a film suffused with the disaffection experienced by many women.

Stalin gave credence to the Marxist view that class was the source of discrimination and prejudice. So by mandating equality and removing class distinctions, he considered that the "woman issue" had been solved and, with it, the need for any discussion about family planning. A woman served the needs of the nation first and, and couples should engage in sexual relations only within the framework of the ideal communist family. Under such utopian conditions, the Soviets reasoned, prostitution could not exist and, in consequence, it could not be made illegal. This led to the bizarre position that the production of church candles was illegal, but prostitution was not.

Prostitution in Soviet Times

I was fascinated to know what Larisa made of all of this, and what it was like to make a living from something that the state said did not exist. She took a breath and narrated her story.

"I had a normal childhood, but my family was poor. When I was seventeen, a girlfriend asked me if I wanted to have sex with some foreign men who were visiting Kharkiv. She told me she had done it already. We joked about it because it would be my first time and I agreed. Only later did I learn that she had been raped and forced to do it. The people responsible told her that unless she cooperated in future and agreed to sex when they asked, they would tell her parents and school, and she would be disgraced. That's how it started."

She made it seem like a nostalgic event, but I suspect the reality had been much different.

"Every few weeks we were invited to a detached guesthouse on Ivanova Street where foreign visitors stayed. They were from the other Soviet republics — mostly Russians but also Azeris, Georgians, or Uzbeks. Government officials ran the house and the visitors were in the city for some sort of official business. They were well dressed, polite, and smelled nice. We usually had a meal, with perhaps five or six men and an equal number of girls. There was always lots of vodka and champagne. Afterwards they might give us small presents; sometimes we took home the leftover food and sometimes we received nothing."

She explained that after a year or so, the man who organised the house left for Kyiv and she and her girlfriend asked him if they could go, too. A few months later, by which time she had had her first abortion and her relationship with her family was in tatters, they joined him in Kyiv.

"You were just a couple of young girls, without jobs or husbands in the capital city," I commented.

"We worked for Dima as we had done in Kharkiv, but we usually had four days a week free, so we turned tricks and built up our own list of clients. Dima took care of us, and because prostitution was not an organized business, there were no real thugs to be afraid of. The only pain in the neck was greedy officials wanting money.

"Perhaps it's hard for you to understand, but in the early days we often didn't receive money for sex. We were perhaps given vouchers for the foreign store or foreign clothes, or perfumes. Sometimes it was just a meal in a good restaurant."

She smiled and continued, "My girlfriend always asked one man to take her shopping before having sex. That's how we bought our groceries!"

I knew that anyone without a job for more than four months in any year could be charged with "leading a parasitical lifestyle," and so I asked her how she got around such problems.

"There were ways around every difficulty," she explained. "If we needed medical help we would pay a doctor. If the police threatened us with some trumped-up charge, we would pay them. If we were arrested for not having a regular job, we'd pay some official to get our name put on the register of a state enterprise, or we became a 'student'. If none of those ideas worked, one could pay a hospital official to register a newborn child in the person's name, so exempting them from work. The solutions were endless."

She paused for a moment, remembering. "Then, in 1978, Ksyusha was born and I had my own child to look after."

Childbirth and Heroines

I didn't ask Larisa about the method used during the birth, but in all likelihood it was developed by doctors from her home city of Kharkiv. The method was parodied by Rachel (played by actress Jennifer Aniston) in the comedy-hit series "Friends."

In 1951, French obstetrician Fernand Lamaze visited a surgery in St. Petersburg where he witnessed a women give pain-free birth to a child using the psycho-prophylactic method. Later he confided that he "wept with joy" on the occasion.[9] He spent the remainder of his life promoting the method whose true name and origins were suppressed by Americans during the cold war, but later became popularly known as the "Lamaze Method." Though best known for its breathing and relaxation techniques, the original method has a wider scope and includes preparing for the experience of birth and the early postpartum period.

The origin of the method was earlier than Lamaze's visit. Following World War II, the medical research facilities in Kharkiv pioneered the search for an improved method of childbirth. It was soon apparent that a drug-based solution was too expensive, so the researchers decided to recondition the thoughts of women, both to remove any potential fear through preparation, and to provide a respectful, professional delivery environment. The research was successful, leading the physician, Nikolaev, to comment that, "If the head is in any way responsible for labour pain, it is not the head of the foetus but that of the mother."[10]

At the world's first conference on the subject in 1949, speakers praised the Soviet achievement and pointed to the failure of Western science, which was seen to offer pain relief only to those who could pay. Within two years, the method developed in Kharkiv was the official method in all Soviet childbirth facilities. In the last half century, it has been used worldwide in hundreds of millions of births. You are possibly among them.

As far as I could tell, Larisa and Kseniya were as close to each other as they could be.

"Is it practical having children in your business?" I asked thoughtfully.

"Well, I'm not going to be a Mother Heroine," Kseniya said, "but I do want children."

"All the girls had many abortions," added Larisa. "There comes a point where you think, perhaps I won't conceive again, or I might miscarry. So you let a pregnancy continue and one day you have a baby. It's not a question of being practical; it's a woman's purpose."

I had heard before about the Mother Heroines of the Soviet Union. In Soviet times, whilst men received a medal for surviving the theatre of war, women were rewarded for surviving the operating theatre. In 1944 Stalin launched Operation Birthrate, under which women who had ten children or more were awarded the "Mother Heroine" medal, and those bearing seven children earned the medal of the "Glory of Motherhood."

"Mother Heroine" was awarded upon the first birthday of the tenth child (provided that nine other children remained alive), and though it seems an improbable feat, the awards were made about 430,000 times until they were abolished in 1991. (Ukraine reintroduced the award in 2004 in an effort to increase the birth rate.)

There is one beguiling film on this subject that rarely fails to make the viewer smile. *Once, 20 Years Ago* written by Ukrainian lyricist, Arkady Inin, is a humorous, gently philosophical film. In 1971, Inin read a letter published in a newspaper from a "Mother Heroine" concerning the challenges and joys of her life, and it formed the basis of the script. It tells the story of a TV personality who decides to gather together his school friends from twenty years earlier. The schoolmates gather in their old schoolroom and the TV personality records each of them talking about their lives and, in particular, what they achieved. Each narrates his or her story of success; of how they achieved their ambition by becoming businessmen, pilots, poets, and musicians, and so on. But when it is the turn of Nadia Kruglova, she admits hesitantly that she became a mother. Her colleagues have no sooner embarked on offering words of consolation and encouragement, when the younger members of Nadia's family appear one by one at the windows of the schoolroom. Within minutes her eleven children are peering through the windows, hands cupped, faces smiling, looking for their mother. The film closes with the TV personality asking each of them what else they are expecting from life, and Nadia answers coyly by pointing to her swollen belly.

Sex Stings

"Tell me where you met clients in those days," I asked Larisa.

"Oh, it varied. It could be an apartment, a hotel, or a taxi. An apartment was the best because it involved paying off fewer people, but it wasn't always practical. If another girl was working in my apartment, I would go a few blocks away to the rooms of a concierge, a friend of mine, who lived on her own. For a few roubles she would go and visit a neighbour."

Kseniya shuffled uneasily in her chair. "Thank goodness this aspect has changed."

Larisa continued, "Hotels were the most problematic, but we worked the Moscow Hotel, the Lybid and, of course, the famous Dnipro Hotel. You had to pay the hotel administration, the doorman, and the dezhurnaya (a concierge who sat next to the lift on every floor of a hotel to monitor and control guests and visitors), and, occasionally, the militia raided the hotels. For foreign clients it was often the only solution since they were suspicious if you suggested leaving the hotel."

Kseniya's phone rang again and she moved to the window ledge to take the call in private as Larisa continued her story.

"We used taxis for clients we picked up from restaurants or theatres. I used a driver I knew and he would wait at a pre-agreed location and I would take the client to the car. In summer he would park somewhere discrete, mostly near the river, and smoke outside, all the time on the lookout for trouble. In winter he would just drive around whilst we had sex in the back."

Perhaps I've read too many books or seen too many films, but I just had to ask if Larissa ever spied on the men she had sex with.

"Only once do I recall something comical happening to a girlfriend," she said as crease lines appeared on her face. "She was in middle of it — it was a new client — when the door burst open, a man entered, switched on the lights, and took some pictures. Their faces must have shown such surprise." Remembering this, she rocked with laugher. "Needless to say, she never saw that client again."

Most commonly, it seems, this sort of client was working for an embassy or was a politician, and the photos were taken as a future "insurance policy." The information sat in a file somewhere until the important man needed to be coerced in some way. Genuine examples are difficult to come by, but one case involved a plain, vulnerable but intelligent Ukrainian girl, Nora Korzhenko. It is narrated in her book, *I Spied for Stalin*,[11] and in her husband's response, a book called *A Spy Called Swallow*.[12] The books tell the story of Soviet spy, Nora Korzhenko, who in 1942 was assigned to seduce British Embassy naval attaché, John Murray and to encourage him to work for the Soviet Union. The young and impressionable Korzhenko (code named "Swallow") fails to complete her assignment and the two fall in love and flee Moscow for a new life together in England.

The now familiar shrill ring of Kseniya's pink mobile phone broke into the conversation, and again she moved to the far side of the room to take the call. For the first time in over an hour, I was aware of the approaching dusk and the noise of the traffic on the street.

"What do you think," I asked Larisa, "is a working girl's life better now than it was?"

"There's only one thing that's better and that's contraception. Now she can decide when she wants a baby." She smiled at her daughter.

"I've got to run, Sergei's waiting downstairs," Kseniya said excitedly.

There was urgency and gaiety in her voice. She shouldn't keep a good client waiting, I thought.

"He wants to go to a film." She glanced towards me. "Don't forget to pay my mother." She kissed her and headed for the door.

"That's an expensive film if he's paying the rate I am," I joked.

"No, this is free time. Sergei is her boyfriend."

"How does that work? Does he approve of her work?" I knew I would have difficulty sharing my partner, even if she did buy the groceries.

"You know, if he learns the first time they meet, he'll walk away. But Ukrainians are very natural about sex. The idea of romantic love that I see in Western films, the tortuous tears and not calling even when you want to, doesn't appeal to us. It's too complex and it ignores biology. If they're attracted to each other they'll make love, but if either finds the relationship unsatisfactory, they'll go their own way. The worst thing is holding on to someone who doesn't want to be held on to."

AT THE COAL FACE

I ENTERED THE BAR a few minutes early and was greeted by broken linoleum, nicotine-stained wallpaper, and glaucous windows. It was not my choice of establishment, but a typical working class bar that served vodka and beer from six in the morning. I had agreed to meet three miners, a father and son, and a retired miner who was now part of the editorial team for a miners' newspaper. Benches lined the perimeter of the room, but there were no chairs at the metal tables, which stood chest high and were supported by welded piping. I ordered a beer at the bar and took it to a free table.

The barman would have been hung drawn and quartered in any miners' club back home for serving the short measure that he gave me, only slightly more than two-thirds of a glass. But in Ukraine I'd grown to accept it and I certainly wasn't going to argue. Ukrainian friends smile and joke when I complain about beer measures; they just don't seem to understand the gravity of the matter.

As I waited for the miners to arrive and the froth to settle, I couldn't help but contemplate that this town was once the industrial heartland of the Soviet Union. It provided the coal to smelt the iron ore, and to produce the metal that was used in the tanks, missiles, aircraft, ships, and submarines that threatened the West for so many years. Yet, this town was built by a stocky, and by all accounts, amiable Welshman called John Hughes.

The Welshman who Built Donetsk

At the end of the nineteenth century the Donetsk region was a melting pot of cultures. Coal had been discovered nearby in 1721 and the first railroad was built in 1865 to connect the grain producing areas to the seaport of Odesa. Like elsewhere in Europe, railroad construction signalled the industrial boom, and the emancipation of the serfs stimulated the development of industry by releasing labour from the land. The region of Donetsk became a locus where locals with Russian, Ukrainian, Jewish, Greek, or German backgrounds did business with visiting British, French, and Belgium entrepreneurs.

In 1866, the son of Viktor Kochubey — State Chancellor of Nicholas I and important estate owner in Ukraine — was given permission to develop a steel plant adjacent to the coal fields. But he failed to raise the money necessary and sold the rights to John Hughes. Hughes formed two agreements with the Tsar: (1) to establish the New Russian Society of Coal, Iron Forming and Railing Production; and (2) a Railway Society Agreement to build a branch line to connect to the Kharkiv-Azov line.

For the construction of the metallurgical works, Hughes chose a site just south of the coal deposits yet close to iron ore, limestone, water, and labour. In 1870 he brought to eastern Ukraine eight shiploads of equipment and about a hundred mostly-Welsh ironworkers and miners to build the steelworks and a town. Working through the severe winter with temperatures below -20° Celsius they constructed the furnace in just eight months and produced their first cast iron in January 1872. Immodestly, he named the company town Hughesovka, after himself.

Within twenty years, four out of five workers were newcomers from Moscow. They set the example for much of the industrial development in eastern Ukraine. Led by the political parties and the trade unions, the language of the town was Russian, and Ukrainian peasants arriving from the rural areas were obliged to conform. By the end of the century, 42 percent of the 425,000 industrial workers in

Ukraine had been born elsewhere,[1] and today industrial Ukraine is still almost predominantly Russian-speaking.

Mineral resources do exist in western Ukraine, but the deposits are smaller and more difficult to extract. Importantly, from Stalin's time, western Ukraine was seen as a potential theatre of war — a no man's land that could be razed if necessary — and so strategic investments were mostly confined to the east.

Hughesovka ceased to be a "company town" and was given the status of a real town in 1917. For Hughes it had been an immensely successful venture and he had repatriated millions of pounds in profit. Within fifty years the Donbas had been transformed from a frontier land and fugitive's paradise into the principal coal mining and iron and steel producing area of the Russian Empire. Vladimir Lenin, the leader of Russian Bolsheviks, described the Donbas as not merely "an indispensable area," but "a region, without which the entire construction of socialism would just be a piece of wishful thinking."[2]

The name of the town was changed to Stalino in 1924 (no prizes for guessing who approved the change), and it changed again in 1961 when it was called Donetsk. Coal production in the Donbas increased steadily from 250,000 tons in the 1870s to more than a hundred million tons in the 1970s before starting to decline in the twilight years of the Soviet Union.

So it happened that a Welshman established the town that powered the Soviet Union.

In Their Fathers' Footsteps

The door to the bar swung open and the three miners entered, each a different height but dressed similarly in trainers, jeans, high-necked sweater and leather jacket.

Ivan, the retired miner, voiced the mantra of hardened drinkers. "Beer without vodka is like throwing money to the wind." After I gave him some money and he went off to the bar, I exchanged introductions with Vladimir and his son Roman. The father was an imposing figure in his late forties, though he looked much older. The band of his helmet was still barely visible on his high forehead, and his bushy drooping moustache, bulbous nose, and piercing eyes suggested a Cossack ancestry. Roman was clearly his father's son, but distinguished by a large scar across his left cheek that was barely healed. I enquired about its origin.

"In the tunnels the vertical struts supporting the roof are bolted to horizontal beams on the walls," he said without emotion, apparently unmoved by the incident. "Occasionally the pressure builds up and the weaker bolts shoot out like bullets. I was hit and knocked unconscious. It was my fifth trip down the mine."

Ivan returned with a round of beers, a large bottle of vodka, shot glasses, and a platter of salted vegetables. We toasted our health with a cold swig of beer. "Why do you do it, risk your lives each day?" I asked.

Vladimir fixed me in his gaze. A blue vein beneath his left eye appeared prominent and he blinked almost continuously. "I used to know. I followed in my father's footsteps and went to work down the mine because it was a dignified job. We were the highest paid workers, we were given apartments, people respected us, we retired ten years before other professions, and we had a good pension. As Stalin said, 'Coal is the bread of industry.' There were accidents, of course, but we all looked out for each other and there was camaraderie."

He recalled stories from his life down the pits and those his father had told him. The relatives of these men literally lived together, fought together, and died together. In World War II, the 383rd Miners' Rifle Division was created. It was given the name "Shakhterskaya" (which means miners) and was originally comprised completely of miners from the Donetsk region.

"Now we do it for the money, though we barely scrape a living," Vladimir continued. "I didn't want Roman to go down the pits, but he insisted. It was either a life of crime or this. This is what we know." Nodding in the direction of the pit cemetery, he added sadly, "My father and six relatives lie buried over there."

Stakhanovites

Judging by their stories, the life of the miner had been in decline for fifty years. But it had not always been so. The pride, dignity, and respect to which Vladimir referred, had been palpable between 1930 and 1950 and most evident in the "Stakhanovite" movement. Alexey Stakhanov, a Ukrainian, came to prominence in August 1935 when he was "discovered" by a party worker. It was reported that Stakhanov, who worked at the mine in Kadiyivka in the Donbas, had mined a record of 102 tons, or fourteen times his quota during his six hour shift. Earlier that year he had attended technical college and he attributed his success to what he had learnt there.

The authorities seized on the success of this ordinary, illiterate, clean-shaven and handsome worker and held him up as a peoples' hero. His images appeared in newspapers and on posters, and others were encouraged to copy his achievement. As emulators began to appear in industries ranging from textile, railroad, engineering, and automobile production, Stakhanov beat his previous record and produced a remarkable 227 tons in a single shift. The propaganda value was not lost on Stalin, and in November he convened the 1st All-Union Stakhanovite Conference in The Kremlin. Several thousand "Stakhanovites" attended the productivity fest and the resolution of the Conference declared:

> The Stakhanovite movement means organizing labour in a new fashion, rationalizing technologic processes, correct division of labour, liberating qualified workers from secondary spadework, improving work place, providing rapid growth for labour productivity and securing significant increase of workers' salaries.[3]

To Western ears this must have sounded like a retreat from Communism: "To each according to his needs" appeared to have been replaced by "For each according to what he produces." But for ordinary Soviet citizens it was meant to show the lifestyle of the new Soviet man or woman: hard working, prepared to learn and help others, clean living, and sharing the good life with their family. For his part, Stakhanov was feted in Moscow. Stalin gave him a new car and Stakhanov bought his wife silk lingerie and French perfume, all of which was captured on newsreels and newsprint to be seen and read throughout the Soviet Union.

In December 1935, as Stakhanov fever swept through Moscow, he appeared on the cover of *TIME* magazine, and its somewhat contemptuous lead article explained that what Stakhanov did was:

> To organize a gang of three miners with such teamwork that Stakhanov, the skilled pneumatic driller, was able to spend all his time drilling out coal, while the others did the propping and panting. By this means the three got out enough coal in a six-hour shift to raise their per man output about five-fold of what it had been when it was a case of no teamwork and every coalminer for himself.[4]

Despite the artificiality of the movement, the productivity gains were real, and it was just the sort of event to remind the West of the Soviet's ability to propagandise and motivate. So much so that during the Second 5-Year Plan (1933–1937) coal production reportedly increased by more than 80 percent.

Even in the 1980s, when productivity gains were negligible and *Homo Sovieticus* was convinced that a workers' utopia existed only at the bottom of a bottle of vodka, Stakhonov was still being upheld as a role model. But it was to have little effect. An official report in 1982 found that 30 percent of workers surveyed were absent for personal reasons, either to go shopping or visit the doctor.[5] Stakhanov, who had been elevated to Deputy of the Supreme Soviet of the USSR, died in 1998 a lonely disillusioned man.

The Women Tractor Drivers

Labour heroes were not confined to men. The most celebrated and highly decorated female labour hero in Soviet history is Pasha Angelina, an ethnic Greek and founder of the first all-female tractor brigade.

Born in 1912 in the Donetsk region, she commenced work as a coal carrier at the age of nine. During the collectivisation in the 1920s, she transferred to a farm where, in spite of opposition from her male colleagues, she learnt to drive a tractor. Bereft of a man's strength, they argued, the women would not be able to start the newly arrived American-built Fordson tractors. This was true, since in practice it took at least five men and more women to hand-crank these machines. But following Stalin's call for the increased participation of women in the labour effort, and with the support of the collective administrator, Angelina introduced a training course for other aspiring female tractor drivers in 1933.

By the end of spring they were ready for their first outing to a real field, and Angelina recalled, "We were in a buoyant mood. All the way to the red ploughman kolkhoz we sang Ukrainian songs and kept laughing at the slightest excuse."[6]

Life was about to change for the estimated one-and-a-half-million male tractor drivers in the Soviet Union. Word spread of the girls' escapades, and when Angelina initiated a competition for the best woman tractor driver, two hundred and fifty of the best women's brigades from across the Soviet Union competed for the honour. Whereas a 15-horsepower male-driven tractor ploughed an average 1,015 acres, the best all-female brigade managed to plough an average 1,838 acres.

Angelina was elected to the Supreme Soviet of the USSR in 1937. Unlike Stakhanov, she was literate, but nonetheless had a complete lack of a formal education. On starting her new role she recalled with more than a modicum of innocence:

> I remember my first batch of mail. One voter needed my advice. Another wanted his invention recognised. A third was asking for my help in securing a building for a village club. A fourth was complaining about some district office. As a deputy I was responsible for the outcome of every one of those requests. Now I can only smile when I remember how lost I felt during the first

week. I even sat down to write a letter to the Supreme Soviet Presidium asking for instructions or some kind of written manual.[7]

Pit Life a Generation Ago

As Ivan broke the seal on the vodka and poured the shot glasses, I noticed his heavily calloused, discoloured hands and thick stubby nails. We had another round of toasts to those who had given their lives.

"What was life like in the pits in the late 1960s when you started?" I asked him quizzically. He wiped his mouth with his cuff.

"Better than now and that's the tragedy. We were paid on time, the food was edible, and we had holidays at sanatoria in Crimea. Despite our struggle for better conditions, things haven't really changed. The mines have deteriorated as they've grown older, and as we mine deeper there's more methane in the air.

"We used to rely on rats to let us know if there was methane in the air. Sometimes the coal looks wet or there's a hissing sound, both of which are signs of methane. Nowadays the rats are gone and the detectors are either turned off or don't work. It was safer back then." He eyed my modest frame and seemed to be saying, "You wouldn't survive long, son."

Vladimir spoke now, his mood sombre. "Miners live to be just forty years old on average. We pay with our blood. We pay with our health. It's just plain physical labour. We work the coal seams with our hands. Either we don't have the technology or the equipment is broken. We don't want luxuries, we just want to have a normal life and to know our children's life will be better. Our only pleasure is a glass or two of beer after the shift."

He took a deep draught to empty his glass. "And we wait for our lungs to give out, or our heart to tell us to stop." The beer and vodka mixture seemed to be doing nothing for his mood.

In the 1960s there emerged several signs of the Donetsk region's demise from its previously central economic role. Foremost of which was the discovery of the huge oil and gas fields in Siberia that resulted in a shift of investment towards the east and a lowering of the demand for coal. From the mid-1970s, though miners were still celebrated as heroes of the Soviet Union, these changes resulted in declining salaries and unsafe working conditions. These fed the growing perception among miners that they were being exploited.

The discovery of oil and gas in Siberia (and to a lesser extent in Ukraine) is a fascinating and largely untold tale that is worth a digression before we continue with the miners' stories.

A Short Digression Deeper Underground

The view developed by Russian and Ukrainian scientists concerning the origin of coal and oil is completely different from the view most Westerners hold. It is so different, in fact, that the Western scientists and energy companies have largely dismissed their theories. But if proved correct — and the evidence is growing — then Western geologists (and the energy multinationals who employ them) are missing two generations of accumulated knowledge in the search for energy resources, and the former Soviet republics have a mind-blowing strategic advantage in the search for new reserves.

Most of us were educated to believe that coal and oil are "fossil fuels" that are formed from the deposition of organic matter. I certainly recall my teacher showing a picture of a swampy carboniferous landscape, inhabited by dinosaur-like creatures, and being told material from decaying animals and plants formed layers that became sedimentary rock. These were heated and put under pressure and, according to the school curricula, coal and oil were formed. The fossils imbedded in the pieces of coal we passed from classmate to classmate were the final proof needed by young, impressionable minds.

But the school children of the Soviet republics were taught a different curriculum. At the end of World War II, it was becoming evident to the Soviets that the extraction cost of coal was increasing and alternative sources of energy were needed. At the same time capitalist countries were increasingly exploiting oil and gas reserves in the Middle East and elsewhere, and they were edging out the Soviets.

These factors encouraged the Soviet political leadership to look for new energy reserves within their own vast backyard and to review the theories on which exploration was based.

The scientist Vladimir Vernadsky, founder of the National Academy of Science of Ukraine and the founding father of biogeochemistry, provided some of the inspiration for the explorers. Vernadsky established the idea that the earth has three layers in it: the geosphere (abiotic, inanimate matter), the biosphere (biotic, biological life), and the noosphere (cognition, intelligence). Whereas Western geologists see the biosphere as being the source of hydrocarbons, the Soviets began to see the source as being located in the geosphere.

Nikolai Kudryavtsev enunciated an alternative theory to the "fossil fuel" idea at the All-Union Petroleum Geology Conference in 1951. In fact, he turned the old theory on its head. Rather than being formed as a result of deposition from above, he postulated that coal and oil were formed by eruption from below and that the process was not biological at all. He called it the Russian-Ukrainian theory of deep, abiotic petroleum origins.

The Academician Vladimir Porfir'yev immediately took a lead in developing these ideas, which were supported by fellow Ukrainians Emmanuil Chekaliuk, Grygori Dolenko, and Vladilen Krayushkin. Over the course of the next forty years, their work transformed the energy landscape of the Soviet Union.

They undermined the theory of a biological origin for coal and oil by asking questions for which there are no satisfactory answers. For example, why can't conventional geology explain that some oil is found at depths of thirty thousand feet when there is no fossil evidence at even half this depth? What is the biological process by which oil is formed from organic matter? Why have no actual fossils ever been found in petroleum? How can conventional geology explain a fifty-foot coal seam that would require six thousand feet of organic matter to produce it? Chekaliuk was so confident that the biological theory was wrong that he said:

Any notion which might suggest that hydrocarbon molecules spontaneously evolve in the regimes of temperature and pressure characterized by the near-surface of the earth, which are the regimes of methane creation and hydrocarbon destruction, does not even deserve consideration.[8]

More importantly, the Ukrainian scientists demonstrated the abiotic theory in practice, and they did so in spectacular style. They argued that because oil is formed deep in the earth, and under conditions of very high temperatures and pressures like that required for diamonds, they needed to perform tectonic and structural analyses of old rock basins, not recent sedimentary basins. So, they choose to look in Siberia and in the Dnipro-Donetsk basin and, as we know now, they made spectacular finds.

Following the collapse of the Soviet Union, Vladilen Krayushkin, the leader of the project to explore the Dnipro-Donetsk basin, made a presentation at the conference in the USA. He described to the audience the oil discoveries made in Ukraine and then said:

The eleven major and one giant oil and gas fields here described have been discovered in a region which forty years ago had been condemned as possessing no potential for petroleum production. The drilling which resulted in these discoveries was extended purposely deep into the crystalline basement rock, and it is in that basement where the greatest part of the reserves exist. These reserves are comparable to those of the North Slope of Alaska.[9]

Vladimir Porfir'yev played a lead role in developing this theory and produced more than nine hundred articles and monographs; yet his work remains largely unknown or disbelieved in the West. The most profound and politically challenging aspect of the theory is that, if correct, the amount of coal and oil available is limited only by the amount of oil and coal-forming constituents that were present at the time of the planet's formation and by man's ability to find it and extract it. In other words, *it is a hoax that the world is running out of oil.*

"The Coca Cola Life"

With replenished glasses and pledges to our spouses renewed, I wanted to ask the miners about their political awakening. Despite some sporadic outbursts of public discontent against the Soviet authorities, the Donbas community remained more loyal to the communist ideal than other parts of the Soviet Union. Arguably, the main reason the Soviet Union survived for so long was the absence of pressure from the working class for drastic change.

From the late 1980s onwards, and coinciding with the start of President Mikhail Gorbachev's reforms, the workers gradually shed their fear of repression and held numerous major strikes. The strike of 1989 was the first large-scale, anti-establishment protest in post-World War II Soviet history. The strike started in July with a single pit stopping work, but within a short time half a million miners from 173 of the 226 Donbas collieries were on strike.

"What changed in 1989 to make you turn against the system?" I asked.

"In the first years of perestroika we began to see on television that another life was possible," Ivan answered. "We called it 'the Coca Cola life.' Yet we suffered food and consumer goods shortages, endless queues, widespread lawlessness, and frustrated expectations. We could not pretend not to see this other life, so we started to demand basic rights." He then reeled off a list of their demands: travel time to the coal face to be included in working hours, a minimum wage, a review of the soap allowance, recognition of illnesses as being work-related, reduced cost for kindergartens, special allowances for working with the pneumatic drill or heavy machinery, family holidays, and so on.

"And the official trade unions supported you?" I asked, already half knowing the answer.

"The official unions were a waste of time and still are. They're pansies, bought off by management. If a union official steps out of line and supports the workers, he'll be replaced or they'll bring in others and our views will be splintered. We've never trusted the Unions."

Once the strikes had begun, the miners started to elect their own strike committees — thus avoiding the issue of management-controlled unions — and these subsequently formed the basis for the Independent Union of Miners. In order to calm the situation, Mikhail Gorbachev made a promise to meet some of the strikers' demands and they returned to work still unsure how far they could push their newly found freedom of expression.

"Did you believe Gorbachev's promises in 1989?"

"Partly," replied Ivan. "We aren't political animals and we wanted to believe it, but a year later nothing had changed and so we went on strike again during the 28th Party Congress. I personally thought our audacious move would result in physical reprisals, but this time Gorbachev sent Congress Party member Boris Yeltsin to us. Like Gorby, he didn't honour his promises and we were forced to strike again in 1991. It was a year none of us will ever forget."

The strikes of 1991 were not particularly well supported, but if everyone had gone on strike the miners would have plunged the country into darkness. Many of them were loyal to the idea of the brotherhood of the union and they didn't want that to happen.

Ivan huffed, reflecting on the contemporary problem of being held hostage by Russia over gas supplies, something unthinkable when the Soviet Union intact. "We subsidised the rest of the Soviet Union through cheap coal for fifty years. They took our resources and now the bastards in Russia are holding us to hostage over gas prices."

In May 1991, Gorbachev abolished the Ministry of Coal and conceded that the republics could control their mines, thus removing the ability of central planners to coordinate the Soviet economy. It was a massive concession to Ukraine and a turning point often missed by Western commentators. The Soviet miners — the backbone of the industrial behemoth — had just played an instrumental role in the break-up of the Soviet Union. On December 25, 1991, Gorbachev resigned from office and the Soviet Union was officially dissolved.

The Year without Meat

By 1993, the situation was even more critical. Retail price inflation in Ukraine reached its record level of 10,000 percent a year and the average real wage decreased by about 80 percent from its 1990 level. Ukraine no longer had paper money but issued coupons instead, and the abacus, for so long the tool of check-out clerks and market stall holders, finally became redundant because it could not cope with all the zeros.

Other than the toasts, Roman hadn't said a word for thirty minutes. His eyes were glazed. Stubble covered his jaw, dark circles ringed his eyes, and a gaunt, haunted expression inhabited his face.

"So again you went on strike in 1993. Was it the low point?" I suggested knowing that many referred to 1993 as simply "the year without meat."

Before Roman could answer, his father replied, "It was just a bad year amongst many. We were on our knees. Our wives could take no more. Some of the men took their own lives. We had sold everything that we could. We were willing to stay out as long as it took. We hadn't been paid for seven months; not pensioners, workers, or the disabled. But we had widespread support from local management, the unions, and other industrialists, so we demanded regional independence for Donbas."

This overtly political demand — indicating a desire to separate — strained the relationship between the miners and the rest of the Ukrainian population.

Roman jumped in. "We wouldn't touch politics unless forced to. We raised political issues because we could see that Kyiv was just assuming the role of oppressor that had been held by Moscow. We were becoming Kyiv's bitch." He paused, and then glanced at his father before continuing. "Anyway, many countries have a federal structure and they have a better life than we do, so I don't know what all the fuss was about."

As it happened, within a couple of weeks President Kuchma capitulated, agreed to limited demands, and was eventually forced to call new elections. For the next five years the situation in Ukraine was precarious as the nation struggled to control inflation, clans fought to the death over property rights, and ordinary families struggled to survive. Roman explained how every day for nearly two years he and his father and mother ate only a small piece of sausage, a piece of onion, a piece of cucumber, and a hard-boiled egg. This was the "Tormozhki," a paper bag food ration provided by the mine for miners to eat during their break. The family's life savings disappeared in a matter of months. The accumulated wealth of all the generations of his family had been eaten away by something called "inflation" (a concept unfamiliar to those who grew up in the Soviet Union).

Ivan said that disabled miners or miners who had serious work-related health problems were paid 30 percent of their salary plus their pension. But in 1999 a commission came to visit the pensioners and judged that most people's illnesses had disappeared. In a cynical ploy to stop paying the allowance, hundreds of amputees were judged to be recovered fully, as if their limbs had grown back.

The New Pit Owners

One of the most remarkable effects of the collapse of the management structure of the mines was the subsequent concentration of the properties in the hands of a few men. I was interested to hear if the miners had tried to control their mine, to determine their own destiny.

"Yes. But it was a lost cause," Ivan said. He pulled his pack of cigarettes out of his left jacket pocket and his lighter from his right. "We were raised to be uninterested in politics. We don't understand ownership rules and share structures. We could trust no one who advised us. We were still living from hand to mouth, we were in debt, and we gave what little rights we had in return for a salary. Besides, these guys were killing each other without remorse."

It was, perhaps, the one time when being at the coal face was the safest place to be. The most high profile assassination was that of Yevhen Shcherban, a leading Donbas businessman and a member of the Ukrainian Parliament who was killed together with his wife and son. Other local businessmen and a handful of gas traders also died. Ukraine's Prime Minister Pavlo Lazarenko and his Dnipropetrovsk-based gas-trading monopoly were reportedly behind the assassinations.

One of the beneficiaries of this power struggle was Viktor Yanukovych, a miner's son, who at the time was the main political rival of Victor Yushchenko. Yanukovych became Prime Minister of Ukraine in 2002 and again in 2007. When he was five years old, his parents died and he was placed in an orphanage. In 1967, while still a teenager, he was convicted of robbery; three years later he was jailed for severely beating someone. By the mid-1970s he had become the director of the transportation department of a mining company and was accused of large-scale theft of state property. Mysteriously, all police records of this case (and all the others) have gone missing.

By the turn of the millennium, the regional economy had returned to a recovery path. The centralisation of control and power amongst people like Yanukovych brought some welcome stability, and he proved to be a popular leader in eastern Ukraine. In the years since, the Donbas has increased its share of the national gross domestic product, the unemployment level has been below the national average, and real wages have grown above the national average. Now the average mine worker earns five to eight hundred dollars per month, nearly twice the national average. Though things have improved, Ivan explained how the stability came at the price of what he called "lawless capitalism."

"The new shareholders just squeeze profits from the unsafe mines. The national government subsidise the mines and so it isn't in the shareholders interests to improve the working conditions. That would result in a reduction in government support. So, the money goes into their pockets and they kick back to their friends in the Ministries, who offer them more the next year. It's a perpetual circle. They say they don't have money for improvements to working conditions or to salaries, but they do. Just look at the new management dining room or the Directors' offices, or the cars they drive." He sneered as he added, "No one takes responsibility and, unfortunately, it takes an accident like Zasyadko to bring it to attention."

This cocktail of money, politics and safety makes the coal mining issue one of the most intractable yet urgent problems in Ukraine today. According to the World Bank, approximately two-thirds of Ukraine's two hundred or so large mines should be closed. In addition, there are a staggering six thousand small, unregulated and illegal mines—some employing women and children.

How can it be, I've asked friends dozen of times when faced with uncomfortable facts almost impossible to comprehend. "Values are different here," they invariably reply, and their body language says, "Now let's talk about something more pleasant."

The Zasyadko Disaster

The four of us had been standing, drinking, and talking for a couple of hours now, and though I had tried to drink less than the others, the peculiar chemistry of vodka and beer was beginning to take its toll. Both Vladimir and Ivan jumped down my neck for suggesting the Zasyadko disaster was the worse accident in Ukraine's history.

Vladimir's sonorous voice filled the cavernous bar. "To describe it as the worst in the country's history is pretty meaningless. Ukraine is younger than my son. There were much worse accidents in the time of the Soviet Union. I'm not playing down the disaster, just commenting on the ignorance behind the comment."

Ivan slurred the words but revealed the view — widely held in this region — that "Ukraine" is a modern concept. Indeed, surveys have shown that if the locals could vote for a person of their choosing to be Ukrainian president many would vote for Vladimir Putin.

In November 2007, a methane explosion ripped through the Zasyadko mine killing nearly one hundred miners. Overnight the figure of the blackened-faced miner having just emerged from the coalface into fresh air became the most televised image of the Donbas.

"What went wrong?" I asked soberly, knowing that ten thousand people work at the mine and approximately four hundred and fifty had been underground at the time. (Since the collapse of the Soviet Union, more than 4,700 miners have been killed in Ukraine.)

Barely concealing his contempt, Vladimir responded. "Well, the talk is that the methane level was above eight percent — a methane level above six percent is considered dangerous — and management ordered the detection system to be switched off so that work could proceed to meet the quota. Also the ventilation equipment in the shaft had not been working for two days prior to the explosion."

I said I had heard that within hours of the explosion a spokesman for the mine stated, "The Safety Watchdog had reported that miners were working in accordance with regulations."

"Bullshit!" said the miners in unison as they shook their heads. "The rules are broken all the time because otherwise the system won't work," Vladimir said. "Whatever our fear, we cannot refuse to go down, even if the methane rate exceeds the limit."

Miners are paid based on the volume of coal they produce, giving an incentive to continue to work in adverse conditions. I knew it was a naive question, but I asked, "And what about safety training?"

"The chances of getting out are very low," Roman said. "The respirator provides forty-five minutes of air, but the walk to the shaft in total darkness and in oppressive heat may take much longer. Will the route be blocked? Will we be injured? Will we know which way to go, away from danger? We always wonder about these things."

"Most of us have already decided what to do," interjected his father. "Over the years you occasionally have the conversation with the voice inside your head. Some will just sit there and try to find some peace; others will fight towards the shaft until they give their last breath. We all carry a talisman of one form or another."

It was a sobering thought. I lifted my slumped shoulders and took a breath of smoke-filled air. Unable to find a positive thread after this depressing conversation, we made small talk about football as we finished off a bottle.

Football: a Local Distraction

Rinat Akhmetov, reputedly Ukraine's richest man and owner of FC Shakhtar, the local football club, had recently bought a new football player. It was the topical conversation of the time in this football-crazy city. The club was formed in 1936 and initially named after Stakhanov and given the logo of a jackhammer.

To some, Akhmetov is a man who supports the community. To others he is clever for getting so rich. To still others he is the paymaster, and it's best not to be asking too many questions. Me? I can't help but remember that he is an owner of the local mines. Safety equipment is defective or nonexistent, yet he paid US$28 million dollars for his new team member. But I shrug my shoulders. Values are different here. Now let's talk about something more pleasant.

BITS, BYTES, TRITS, AND TRYTES

KYIV IS AN OLD CITY. It was probably founded in the fifth century, a full six hundred years before we find the first reference to the city we call now Moscow. Nikolai Gogol, who was fascinated by architecture and history (having at one time studied ancient architecture), suggested that each city should have a street that showcased its history through various architectural styles. In an essay in 1835 he wrote, "This street would become in a certain sense a history of the development of taste and anyone too lazy to leaf through weighty tomes would only have to stroll along it in order to find out everything."[1]

If there is such a street in Kyiv, it is Volodymyrska. The line that Volodymyrska follows passes through the site of Prince Vladimir's ancient city. By the beginning of his reign in 980 the city was already known as one of the richest and largest in Europe. Initially a pagan ruler (he had more than eight hundred concubines and numerous wives), Prince Vladimir converted to Christianity in 987 and proceeded to baptise the whole of Kyivan Rus. Though little remains of his city — the houses were made of wood and the streets lined with wooden blocks — Volodymyrska evolved as a microcosm of architectural styles covering one thousand years of history.

I walked up Iriniska and turned left onto Volodymyrska en route to the Academy of Science where I was going to attend an evening lecture on the history of computing. The Academy has an important place in the history of computing, but this is only partially recognised by Ukrainians since much of the work was conducted in secret, and across numerous locations. It is even less well appreciated by the rest of the world.

There are numerous heroes of computing who were either Ukrainian born or worked extensively in Ukraine, the most significant being Sergei Lebedev. I was hoping to learn more about him and his talented, under-recognised colleagues.

The heat of the summer's day was declining and the imposing buildings cast long shadows across the street. The pavements were busy with workers making their way home as exhaust fumes drifted lazily from the stationary traffic. Cafe-less, Volodymyrska is a street of mostly official buildings, many of which are associated with the Academy or with St. Vladimir's University, located nearby.

Number 45, on the left, is an imposing building built in 1892. It has a highly ornate brown and white façade and at ground floor, life-size figures in the form of atlases and caryatids support the first floor balconies. Since 1947 it has been the House of Scientists. A little further ahead, and almost opposite the Academy of Sciences, is building number 53, which was begun in 1914 but only completed in 1927. It had been designed as St. Olga's Girls' Grammar School, but was surplus to the revolutionaries' requirements and given to the Academy.

I crossed the street and entered number 54, the Academy of Sciences, built by Beretti in 1850. The plain, pale green façade is almost windowless and dominated by seven-meter-high white columns. Prior to the Bolshevik Revolution the building had been used as a dormitory for the pupils of Funderley Girl's Grammar School, but afterwards it was given to the Academy.

Discovering Bits and Bytes

Already late, I made my way quickly to the lecture room and took my seat in the audience of perhaps seventy people, apparently a mixture of academics and students. The format was two sessions separated by a short break. Igor, a small man in his late forties, threw himself headlong into an evangelical introduction.

"Today we are once again trying to promote Ukrainian computer technology to the rest of the world, but with one significant difference. In the 1950s and 1960s, we were invited as equals. Now, however, we are trying to get in by any means available, driven by our wish to be part of a wider technology revolution."

He pushed a button and a slide appeared on the white screen. The slender, nervous, scholar appeared ill at ease behind the podium, but his mastery of the subject was not in doubt. "Our predecessors faced enormous challenges: bureaucracy, lack of resources, indifference, war, and corruption. Yet our experts rose above all this. Personal ambition and the desire to contribute to technological progress propelled Ukrainian computer specialists to be amongst the very best in the world. Though, sadly, most of them are not recognised today in the wider world."

The audience had settled down by now.

"Our evolution of computing followed a different path from that of the US or Western Europe. The initial Soviet approach — with some justification — was that technology transfer from outside was prohibited or strictly controlled. As a result, our computing developed without the benefit of the cross-fertilisation of ideas between countries and we had to build every component, every board, every box, and every machine from scratch. We couldn't just copy. Like the process of evolution on an island, we evolved species of computers that did not develop elsewhere, and like island species they had adaptations perfectly suited for the environment. They may not have been the most beautiful of species — though the builders would no doubt disagree with me on this point — but they were amongst the fastest, most efficient and diverse machines. As a testament to these facts, by the 1960s there were over three hundred types of computer systems in the Soviet Union."

He talked at some length of the extraordinary brilliance of one of Ukraine's pioneers, Sergei Lebedev, who reigned over the field of computer science in the Soviet Union. Lebedev is credited with developing the first programmable computer in continental Europe. From 1946–1951, he headed the Kyiv Electrotechnical Institute of the

Ukrainian Academy of Sciences. His wife had been reluctant to move to Kyiv from Moscow where she was a musician with the prestigious Moscow Orchestra, and the family made the decision to relocate only after drawing papers from a hat. But once in Kyiv, they were given a residence in a prestigious block reserved for scientists (15 Kostyolna Street), built by the architect who designed the neo-classical style Ukrainian Parliament building, Volodymyr Zabolotny.

If not for the war, Lebedev would have completed his computer even earlier, and his wife recalled the dark wartime evenings when her husband would sit in the bathroom, lit by an oil lamp, and scribble the 1s and 0s of the binary operations. The basic elements were complete by 1948, and two years later his "Small Electronic Calculating Machine" (called MESM) was operational. Many of the original design documents are kept at the National Academy of Sciences and scribbled on the front cover are the words, "To be kept forever."[2]

At the time there were only two similar working machines in the world, both in England: Maurice Wilkes' EDSAC, and a machine called the Manchester BABY developed by Frederick Williams and Tom Kilburn. In fact, Lebedev's machine was superior because it performed several calculations simultaneously (what we now call "parallel processing"), whereas the EDSAC and BABY employed a sequential method of calculation. By reading US journals the Ukrainians had learned of the world's first computer, ENIAC, completed in 1946, but it was not programmable.

Lebedev referred to MESM as "small" because he was already considering the development of its big brother which was subsequently called, somewhat uninspiringly, "Big Electronic Calculating Machine" (or BESM), which would be capable of ten thousand operations per second.

To a contemporary observer, MESM would have appeared far from small. It was a monster with thousands of small twinkling lights that filled the wing of a former Orthodox Monastery. Floor-to-ceiling cabinets lined the edge of the room and a console some three metres wide and two metres high was located in the centre of the room. MESM required more than 170 square metres' space, equivalent to the living space of four families. It had about 6,000 vacuum tubes (a big improvement on ENIAC's reputed 18,000 tubes), and the heat generated was so great that the ceiling was removed in order to increase the room volume. MESM could perform approximately three thousand operations per second.

Igor's description of the computer being built in a monastery and being operated by engineers with rolled-up sleeves intrigued me, so I decided to make a visit to the monastery as soon as time permitted.

From the day that MESM was operational, a succession of people from the military, the scientific community, and from state planning departments travelled to Kyiv bringing mathematical problems to be solved. The computer was involved in answering some of the most pressing questions of the day concerning quality control, electricity transmission, dam construction, space flights, and rocket technology. The challenge of designing programmes to solve these questions led directly to the foundation of the Soviet programming school.

Rivalling the Americans

At this time, the US publicly derided the state of computing in the Soviet Union without knowing the true state of advancement. The Soviets knew, however, that the Americans had made a number of incorrect assumptions, the main one being that the Soviet's lack of a serious interest in computer technology before the war would delay progress. In reality, the Soviet Union kept a credible pace with the West until the 1970s and even managed to surpass it for short periods of time.

Following his success with MESM, Lebedev moved to Moscow where he became the director of the newly established Institute of Precise Mechanics and Computer Technology and where he worked until his death. The Institute is now named after him. Soon after relocating, Lebedev was elected to the Soviet Academy of Sciences and he shared his electoral banquet with another recent appointee, a nuclear physicist called Andrei Sakharov. As we know now, Sakharov would become a Nobel Prize winner and a world-renowned dissident.

Election to the Academy was regarded as the highest honour for a scientist. Lebedev benefited from an award of five thousand roubles per month, plus a chauffeur, in addition to his existing salary which was probably more than six thousand roubles per month.[3] (At that time an average skilled worker in Moscow earned approximately eight hundred roubles per month.)

At the Institute, Lebedev worked first with vacuum tube computers and then with super high-speed computers based on semiconductors, followed by computers based on integrated circuits. It is believed that he led the development of fifteen models of computers. The fastest computer in Europe, BESM-1, was operational in 1953.

The last of the line, the semiconductor-based BESM-6, had a production run of three hundred and fifty machines and was completed in 1966. It was the workhorse of computer centres established throughout the Soviet Union and a part of the computer suite that controlled the joint US-USSR Apollo-Soyuz space mission in 1975. The Soviet scientists later boasted that they completed the mission's data processing thirty minutes ahead of their American counterparts.[4] Lebedev also played a key role as the chief computer designer for the Soviet Union's anti-missile defence system, but this work was shrouded in even greater secrecy and may never become public knowledge.

I found out later that, in 1992, the Senior Curator of Computing and Information Technology at the National Museum of Science and Industry in London had travelled to Siberia to negotiate the purchase of the last working version of the legendary BESM-6 computer. He wrote an article of this exploit that began, "Russia's BESM class of supercomputers, designed more than 40 years ago, may give the lie to US declared technological supremacy during the Cold War years."[5] In the article, he argued that the West needed to upgrade its view of the Soviet's achievements. I don't know if the curator ever got the machine working in its new home in London or if the cash-strapped capitalists of Siberia had sold them scrap metal.

Networks Across the Soviet Union

Igor took a sip of water, clarified a few points, and then continued by explaining the story of Mikhail Sulim, a Ukrainian colleague of Lebedev, whom Lebedev referred to as "The Godfather of the Soviet Computer Industry."

The 18-year-old Sulim distinguished himself in the fierce battles near Ponyry during World War II and was one of those who pushed through to Berlin in 1945. Following demobilisation he completed his studies at the Electro-Technical Department of Kyiv Polytechnic Institute.

By 1953, Lebedev was working on the development of second-generation machines, BESM-2 and a state-of-the-art but smaller M-20 project (the "20" referred to the computer speed that was anticipated to be twenty thousand instructions per second). Recognising Sulim as both a gifted technician and a savvy politician, he appointed him as deputy for the M-20 project. Project delays and infighting threatened to derail the production of the M-20, but four years later the machine was running and the State Committee declared it as the "fastest machine in the world."

But Sulim's real aptitude was for getting the system to do things. In 1957 when President Khrushchev established Regional Economic Councils in an attempt to reduce the inefficiencies of centralisation, Sulim accepted eagerly a council position with responsibility to control the factories producing the various computer components.

Within six years he was Deputy Minister of the Ministry of Radio Industry and, as such, was responsible for building new production plants, ensuring targets were met, and that resources flowed to where they were needed. This was a vital period in Soviet computing. Computer demand was growing strongly and production had to be increased, standardised, and quality-assured. Sulim was instrumental in building this fabric of factories and institutions and in establishing the basis for a Union-wide computer industry.

Both Lebedev and Sulim agreed avidly that if the Soviet Union could collaborate with the leading European firms they could improve the quality of mass-produced computers. The lack of consistent quality was a key constraint on their ability to develop their indigenous technologies. But the late 1960s were a turning point. Despite opposition from the scientists, political voices won over the Soviet leadership and the decision was made to abandon the path of indigenous growth and instead to copy Western technologies and, in particular, the IBM360 system.

Using the island evolution analogy which I referred to earlier, deciding to clone the IBM models was like introducing grey squirrels into a population of healthy red squirrels. The aggressive greys consumed more and more of the resources needed by the reds, whose numbers declined. Soviet-built systems ceased to be improved or repaired and the demand for entrepreneurship and inventiveness disappeared. A clear result was that the technology gap between the Soviet Union and the West increased with the Soviets falling behind.

The reasons for the change of strategy are poorly documented, but it appears the political leadership was concerned about the growing cost of computer projects, the relative weakening position of Soviet computing power, and a growing faith in the ability of espionage to provide the necessary information and material.

Lebedev sought a meeting with Premier Alexey Kosygin to warn him that the Soviet's computing capability would decline if they pursued the path of cloning, but a meeting was rejected. Sulim was so disappointed that he resigned.

Hacking and Pirating

We stopped for a short break and immediately a group of students surrounded Igor on the small stage. I turned to a few students nearby and struck up a conversation.

"How do you feel when you hear this history?"

A pretty student in a pale blue dress answered, saying, "Both proud and sad." She seemed rather bulimic and overly bronzed. "Much of Ukraine's computer talent is being wasted nowadays. Many, including my brother, have left to take up lucrative positions in other countries. Ukrainians will work very hard for success if they are properly rewarded, but no computer professionals are working today for the glory of Ukraine."

Ironically, under the Soviet system highly qualified people were better rewarded then than they are now. "Being a scientist has lost its prestige and now most young people want to be in business," she added.

"That's right," suggested a young man wearing gold-rimmed glasses, "there is some good work being done in computer research as shown by the development of the 'Kolchuga' radar system."

Former President Bush would not have been pleased by the young man's response. A few years ago Ukraine broke United Nations sanctions and sold the technology to Iraq. It is leading-edge work that uses clever computing algorithms to detect Stealth Bombers.

"Ukraine does have a bad reputation abroad," the girl said with a grimace. "Foreigners just read the headlines and form an instant negative opinion."

"Is it surprising?" I quizzed, my palms facing upwards as I explained the results of a recent survey. Statistics indicate that at least 30 percent of students are involved in computer crime and that 70 percent of all computer crime is committed by people below the age of thirty. More than 90 percent of the software in use in Ukraine is pirated and the inference is that many of the most respected companies and institutions are using illegal software. You just need to visit any market in Ukraine to see how easily and cheaply even the most recent releases can be obtained.

In a high profile case a few years earlier, a Ukrainian man called Maxim Kovalchuk was arrested as he ate ice cream whilst holidaying in Thailand. He was taken to California to face trial and up to twenty years in jail. (The United States does not have an extradition treaty with Ukraine and so the FBI waited until he left the country.)

Kovalchuk was accused of selling perhaps US$50 million of pirated software on the Internet for about five percent of its face value. But as Ukrainians are eager to point out, he didn't do anything special; he just copied and sold software that could be bought at any marketplace in Kyiv. The idea of intellectual property rights has still to catch on big-time in Ukraine.

Closer to home, a student from the prestigious Odesa State University established a "School of Civil Hackers" at which he taught three hundred students a year how to hack computers. When arrested, he described his mission as, "to give knowledge and to inculcate a sense of responsibility for application of these skills to be good or bad." And in his defence he offered, "Hacking is not always a crime, like a knife is not always dangerous. Everything depends on a person."[6]

Four conditions create this environment of growing computer crime: ability, motivation caused by unemployment or low salaries, opportunity, and the lack of imposition of Ukrainian laws.

"What about consultancy work and the trend towards outsourcing?" I asked, already aware that even for those who are employed, the rewards can be limited: commercialisation is everything, and the majority of work being undertaken is funded by Western companies who have patent rights over any inventions.

"Yes, European companies are outsourcing to Ukrainian companies." the girl student replied. "A typical programmer in Ukraine is not a programmer by education; he is more of a scientist, perhaps a physicist, or a mathematician. They approach problems differently and European companies like that because they are creative."

Creativity combined with access can also be problem, and it is estimated that one in five of Ukraine's hackers are bank employees. But the girl's point strikes me as being correct; outsourcing could establish Ukraine as a high-tech centre in Eastern Europe.

Also, I wanted to listen to their views about the prospects offered by the Internet, but the girl's lack of optimism surprised me. "Internet use is very low," she said as she curled her long hair round her index finger, "perhaps only ten percent, and many of those people only use it a few times per month, perhaps in a cafe. Computer ownership is also just a few percent and the majority of users are based in Kyiv."

A young man who so far had said very little interjected. "Because of the headache of installing fixed landlines for telephones, most people now prefer to own a mobile phone. Ironically, this has discouraged telecom operators from expanding the fixed line network. So, we're stuck with a dilapidated Soviet network and that means that widespread Internet use is still many years away. Activities like shopping online just aren't developing. This is one case where the free market doesn't supply the answer."

The "Information Age"

People returned to their seats, conversations faded, and Igor continued by telling us about Viktor Glushkov, the third pioneer of Ukrainian computing.

We learned that Glushkov foresaw the collapse of Soviet competitiveness and fought assiduously to stop it, but he was prevented by the short-sightedness of Soviet leaders. Glushkov predicted, correctly as it turned out, that without an efficient means of sharing information the Soviet bureaucracy would cease to function. But efficient communication was not in the interests of local and regional fiefdoms, so his work was thwarted at all levels. In part, one of the reasons why the Soviet Union collapsed was because of the small-mindedness of middle- and high-level bureaucrats.

Glushkov, who started his career as a mathematician, was another protégé of Lebedev and the founding father of information technology in the Soviet Union. He was the first person to solve Hilbert's "generalized fifth problem" (though it took him three years), and this immediately placed him among the top-ranking mathematicians in the Soviet Union. But his main interest was cybernetics, which he defined as the science of complex control systems and information processing. His 1964 book, *Theory of Digital*

Computers, established much of the groundwork for the development of personal computers, or PCs as we know them today.

He anticipated the development of the "Information Age" when computing technology was still in its infancy. This led him in the 1960s to propose a complex, large-scale project to implement a management system (called OGAS) for the Soviet economy that would link more than two hundred regional centres and ten thousand local centres. His goal was to computerise the workplace of government, administrators, and institutions; something we now take for granted.

His vision was clear. It was a twenty-year project that would cost more than the space and nuclear programmes combined (more than 20 billion roubles) and would require the development of new skills in image recognition technology, computer-aided design software, paperless technologies, and enterprise management software. Premier Alexey Kosygin supported him, but others within the Soviet system openly ridiculed him and they saw, probably rightly, that such a system would strip away their control which was based on bureaucratic tyranny. In the end, cybernetics contradicted some long-cherished Soviet management methods.

When the issue to either go ahead with the project or to stop it was discussed by the Politburo, it was rejected. In response, a disillusioned Glushkov remarked, "The problems in our economy are such that, by the end of the 1970s, we will have to go back to the OGAS project. Otherwise, our economy will collapse."[7]

Not long afterwards Glushkov was incapacitated by astrocytome and confined to home, where he lamented how the Soviet computing industry had become so military-oriented as the technology matured, and how the Soviet leadership never understood the value of computing for society. Or perhaps they were afraid of the personal empowerment that it would bring.

By now it was clear, even to the most obdurate listener, that Ukraine has a rich history of technology pioneers working within the Soviet Union. But it's worth a small digression to introduce two men with Ukrainian roots who changed the world.

World's First Mobile Phone Call

Marty Cooper is hardly a household name, but he has been called "the most influential person no one has ever heard of."[8] He grew up in Chicago, the son of Ukrainian immigrants. On April 3, 1973, he made the world's first "official" mobile phone call — on a one-kilogram device he developed when working at Motorola — whilst hosting a press conference to introduce the phone at the Hilton Hotel on the Avenue of the Americas in New York. The idea had come to him just three years earlier when cellular phones were unwieldy devices built into car dashboards and attached to a box of equipment (a two-way radio and a power supply) in the car's boot. He became a zealot for products being portable, and though not everyone shared his vision — many in Motorola thought there were products with greater potential — today over half the world's population has a mobile phone.

The Process of Inventing

Jacob Rabinow was born in Kharkiv and moved to Siberia and China before settling in the 1920s in New York, where his mother had an established corset shop. His formative influences were a love of machines and the novels of Jules Verne, which he had read repeatedly during their arduous travels. Rabinow became one of America's most prolific inventors, filing more than two hundred and thirty patents. His best known inventions are the computer disk (1954) and the scanner (1960). When he first produced a disk file, the common reaction was "Why bother providing so much capacity? Who needs it?" So he sold the foreign copyrights to Remington Rand for US$15,000. When asked about the process of inventing, he replied:

> If you invent something when everybody wants it, it is too late; it's been thought of by everybody else. If you invent too early, nobody wants it because it is too early. If you invent very late, after the need has passed, then it is just a mental exercise. I assure you that it is very hard to invent just at the right time.[9]

The Ternary Computer

Igor brought his very interesting presentation to a close and took questions. His jerky mannerisms and awkward stance appeared to convey a troubled intellect as he answered them one by one. One of the students I had spoken to earlier asked, "What needs to be done to return Ukrainian computing to a leading worldwide position?"

"I doubt it can be done," he replied. "The gap between the technology pioneers and Ukraine is too great. We need a government that is willing to establish the right conditions, and here I'm thinking about things like the development of technology parks. Also, in order to regain credibility, we need greater recognition of the Ukrainian pioneering spirit."

He paused and took a breath. "My personal hope is that one day the work of fellow countryman Nikolay Brusentsov will be recognised and adopted by the rest of the world. He invented a working ternary computer. Today there is nothing stopping the semiconductor industry from making trinary-based chips, except lack of demand. One day trits and trytes may replace bits and bytes."

I offered to buy the students a beer and we walked along a poplar tree-lined avenue to Taras Shevchenko Boulevard where we found an Internet Cafe. By now it was 9 p.m. and the cobbled streets were mostly quiet. The students were mostly from well-to-do families and they talked casually about life in Kyiv and their hopes for the future. Sustained by local beer, we eventually found a reference to Brusentsov, the creator of the Ternary Computer. Like other pioneers he was born into a poor family in rural Ukraine, saw fierce action in the war, and then supported himself through his studies. In 1956, he was appointed to direct the development of a small computer for use in university laboratories, which he named "Setun," after a small river near to Moscow University.

Then, as today, all computers were based on a binary system whereby the processor uses 1s and 0s (so called "flip-flop" positions of a switch) to make calculations. But Brusentsov was not impressed, and he reasoned that if he used a balanced ternary system[10] using *three* elements — 1s, 0s and 1s (so called "flip-flop-flap" positions of a switch) — storing numbers would require less space than in a binary system. Other advantages would follow from this: circuit boards would be smaller, lighter, consume less power and be more reliable; connections would require less cabling; and most importantly, computers would be quicker and cheaper.

Brusentsov completed the project in record time and the first model of Setun was demonstrated at a National Exhibition in Moscow in 1958. He had realised all the benefits he had outlined and the machine could be programmed in one-tenth the time of a binary machine. Following the exhibition there were many requests from foreign companies to purchase a Setun even at the high price of 27,500 roubles, but the Soviet Union refused all requests. In total, fifty Setun machines were built, but I don't know of any examples that survive today.

"Imagine," said the girl student in a voice barely concealing excitement, "we've found the invention that could one day change the world and put Ukraine back in the list of technology leaders."

"Do you think it's patented already?" asked her friend.

A Visit to a Monastery

A couple of weeks later I decided to search for the legendary MESM computer — the first programmable computer in continental Europe and the first in the world to operate parallel processing of instructions. Recalling Igor's description of the location of the machine, I visited the Panteleiman Monastery in Feofania.

The restored monastery is an imposing monument painted brick red and white with five black domes. Located about fifteen kilometres to the southwest of the city, it overlooks the Dnipro River and is the largest building in Kyiv's suburbs. Surrounded by mighty oaks and enjoying panoramic vistas, it is a pleasant respite from the traffic and bustle of Kyiv.

The area was first mentioned in the late fifteenth century when there were already several religious building occupying the site. The new monastery dates only from 1914, and the locals called it Panteleimon Monastery in honour of the great martyr. Soon after, the Bolsheviks confiscated the monastery complex and the outbuildings were given first to an orphanage and later, in the 1930s, to Kyiv Psychiatric Hospital. One man, who attached himself to me as I wandered around, said that as many as seven hundred inpatients of the Hospital were shot by Nazi firing squads after Hitler ordered the extermination of "all the mentally deficient and physically handicapped people" in the occupied territories.

After the war, though much of it was in ruins, the site was given over to the Academy of Science so that scientific work could be conducted with the utmost secrecy. In those days simply getting to Feofania on unsurfaced roads was a minor challenge. One nun I encountered recalled that the Academy had used the buildings for "the storage of books." Another nun confirmed that the Academy had built several new two-storey buildings some distance from the church that are today used as their sleeping quarters. I strolled around for quite some time, both inside and outside the buildings, looking for some sort of clue as to the exact location of the room in which MESM had been housed.

Finally it dawned on me that if I were caught, I would have had difficulty. "That's right madam, we've apprehended your husband in a nun's bedroom." The policeman's voice played out in my head. "His rather feeble excuse is that he was looking for a top secret program to build a computer. We're not sure whether he needs a prison or a hospital."

TOURING CRIMEA

DEPENDING ON TO WHOM you listen, Crimea is either a haemorrhoid hanging from the bottom of Ukraine, or a diamond in the Black Sea, and to stumble upon its treasure is a serendipitous event.

Those who prefer the medical analogy insist that First Secretary Nikita Khrushchev cannot be forgiven for ceding Crimea from Russia to Ukraine in 1955. The Russians paid with blood, so the argument goes, and Crimea was given away as an act of generosity by a pro-Ukrainian leader. Khrushchev in turn paid a price; he was ousted, and lived out his life as an ordinary pensioner. He was denied a state funeral, and suffered the indignity of not being buried in the Kremlin wall.

Khrushchev's Gift

On the journey from the railway station of Simferopol, the capital of Crimea, our tour guide Eugene explained to my wife, Irena, and I the background to Khrushchev's apparent generosity.

"Some say Khrushchev's act was a cynical gesture, since immediately prior to his undertaking he visited Crimea and he saw firsthand the adverse effects of the ethnic cleansing. There were no functioning farms, for example, and the region was a burden on Russia, not an asset. Its value to Russia was less than zero."

He explained how during World War II the Crimean Tartars incurred the full extent of Stalin's wrath. On the pretext that some Tartars had collaborated with the German forces, in May 1944, a month-long operation began to relocate the entire Tartar population. More than thirty-two thousand members of the police and security forces went from house to house and demanded the occupants leave within fives minutes. They were taken to rail junctions and crammed into rail carriages to begin their eastward journey. Thousands died of suffocation or starvation during the journey and perhaps 40 percent of the survivors died in the first two years of resettlement, mostly woman and children.[1] According to information of the security forces by November 1944, there were one hundred and fifty-one thousand Crimean Tatars working in the mines, factories, and farms of Uzbekistan and another forty-two thousand in other republics.[2]

With his eyes fixed firmly on the winding road, the driver narrated a particularly chilling episode of the deportation. "Having completed the relocation operation, the security forces realised that they had overlooked an entire village close to the coast. The bureaucrats recording the deportees' details and those arranging the rail transport had already been reassigned, and so the security forces took the villagers to sea in boats and threw them overboard."

Soon after, Soviet historians set about rewriting Crimean history with a more Russian complexion, and Stalin ordered thousands of Russians and Ukrainians to be resettled in Crimea, where they were given the Tartar property in perpetuity.

More recently, and often with much publicity, nearly two hundred thousand Tartars have returned to Crimea. But they are treated as second-class citizens, caught in a Catch-22 situation; without somewhere to live they cannot register legally, and without registration they cannot buy a house or get a job. The television coverage invariably shows pictures of the Crimean authorities bulldozing illegally built dwellings of the Tartars whilst police armed with batons hold back the angry and frustrated settlers. The Tartars feel like foreigners in their own land.

It was early morning, but the sun was already burning away the cool shadows as we crossed the Angarskiy Pass in the Yaila Mountains on our descent to the resort towns of Alushta and Yalta. I had contacted the 50-year-old, bearded, stout-framed Ukrainian several

weeks before and he had agreed to act as our guide for our holiday.
"What should I expect?" I had asked Eugene whilst making
preparations for the visit.

The plan was to explore Crimea in his blue Ford every other day
and to relax around our base town of Simeiz on the intervening days.
"Come here if you want to see an early example of
globalization," he answered somewhat obliquely.

The sound of Chris Rea's gruff voice and crisp guitar emanated
from the car's speakers. Irena looked at me, a small smile curling on
her lips as we watched eagerly for our first glimpse of the Black Sea.

"You realise," said Eugene, nodding his head towards the trolley
bus we were overtaking, "that the journey from Simferopol to Yalta is
the longest trolleybus ride in the world. The line was easier and
cheaper to build than extending the railway through the mountains."

The eighty-five kilometre journey costs two dollars by trolleybus,
and may take over two hours, but time is hardly a consideration since
the views along the serpentine route are breathtaking. Careening first
one way, and then the other, you descend towards the sea shore, one
minute in dense forest alongside a babbling mountain stream, the next
emerging into sunlight and panoramic views of mountain ranges.

Simeiz: Lured by a Diva

The town of Simeiz nestles on the lower slopes of the mountains
where two rocky beaches, separated by the imposing forty-five metre
high rock, allow access to the sea. Some say the "Diva Rock," as it is
known locally, resembles the bust of a woman with long flowing hair.
The name Simeiz is believed to derive from the Greek word
"Simeon," meaning "sign," and the Byzantine word "Iz," meaning
"destiny." So, it is literally translated as "Sign of Destiny." It has been
compared with a poor man's Kalkan (Turkey) or Lindos (Greece), but
the mountain backdrop exceeds anything they can offer. It is, simply,
spectacular.

In 1828, Count Ivan Maltsov, founder of the famous Russian
glassware factory, was impressed by the Diva Rock, and he decided to

go swimming in its shadow. Whilst bathing he lost the gold wedding ring given to him by his wife (who was the mother of Alexander Pushkin by an earlier marriage). Distraught at being unable to find the ring, his bathing companion, a Russian diplomat, suggested to Maltsov that he should buy the area and so even if the ring was never found he would remain its owner. Appeased by the idea, Maltsov bought eighty acres, and several generations of his family built the European-style resort which would become the home of Leo Tolstoy and the playground of many notable artists and military men.

Simeiz won first place at the International Contest of Resorts in 1913, but only in the last ten years have new buildings started to appear, and so Simeiz retains an air of nineteenth century chic, albeit much decayed.

The Ancient City of Chersonesos

Two days later, when the shadows were cool but the morning sun was rising, Eugene arrived to discuss the day's itinerary.

The road westwards from Yalta to Sevastopol has been compared with driving southwards from San Francisco. It is one of those routes where you can feel the hand of a creator at work. Around every corner there are new perspectives on the Black Sea as the mountains plunge into the blue-green bays along the coast.

Within a few kilometres, Eugene stopped the car and opened the bonnet to inspect the engine whilst we stretched our legs and looked down to the sea and towards Mikhail Gorbachev's dacha. It was here in 1991 that Gorbachev was held on house arrest whilst the news media was told that he was receiving medical treatment. Meanwhile the military coup took place in Moscow. Today, it is the residence of the President of Ukraine but, now as then, parking is prohibited, and within minutes a police car arrived and moved us on. Eugene rapidly repaired the fictitious problem and closed the bonnet.

The ancient city of Chersonesos lies just a few kilometres outside Sevastopol. It was probably founded by Greeks from the ancient city of Heraclea Pontica (now in Turkey) during the Peloponnesian wars in the year 421 BC. Eugene had arranged for us to meet a teacher who lived in a cottage on the edge of the site, and she gave us a lively lecture and refreshing iced tea.

"Just think," she concluded, "the legend of Jason and the Argonauts and their heroic quest for the Golden Fleece was played in these parts. Commercial, political, or religious forces have waged a continuous struggle for control of Crimea, mostly for its natural resources. It's no coincidence that Istanbul, which guards the entrance to the Black Sea, became one of the richest cities on earth."

Excavation of Chersonesos was started in 1827, and ever since it has been regarded as one of the most important archaeological sites in Europe. Located on the Heraclean headland that juts into the translucent blue-green water, we explored the rectangular city and its original theatre, bath houses, and temples. The city thrived by trading wine and slaves for half a millennium before it was overrun by the Romans.

Christianity probably arrived about 100 AD with St. Clement, author of the epistle to the Corinthians, but his preaching and miracles failed to enamour him to his hosts, who attached him to an anchor and threw him into the sea. Today, the columns and portico of an early Christian church built at the time of the founding of Istanbul in the fourth century stand next to the sea.

The city was visited in 868 AD by Cyril (who was later canonised as St. Cyril), who contrived the Cyrillic alphabet on which modern Russian, Ukrainian, and other Slavonic languages are based. The area prospered under Byzantine rule for another half-millennium until the arrival of Islam when power migrated eastwards to the Crimean cities of Sudak and Feodosiya.

"Two thousand years of history, and look now," said Eugene, pointing to the incongruous view of crumbling Byzantine walls set against the background of the rusting, idle, modern-day warships of Sevastopol in the far distance.

The Siege of Sevastopol

Lunch was a bowl of cold soup, known as okroshka, and a fish shashlik in a harbour-side restaurant in Sevastopol followed by a brief walk on the promenade. The sun was now high and only mad dogs and Englishmen ventured out.

After World War II, the entire city centre of Sevastopol was rebuilt as it was before the war, complete with statues which attest to the military history of the city — a lunging soldier with jacket billowing, an eagle on top of a high column, an eternal flame.

There are hundreds of stories about Crimea in World War II, but one that moves me concerns a young Ukrainian woman called Ludmila Pavlyuchenko. When the Germans invaded, she and her husband were vacationing in Odesa. Unable to return home to Kyiv, they signed up as snipers with the Red Army in Odesa and, later, after it fell, in Sevastopol.

During the two hundred and fifty-day siege of Sevastopol, nearly one quarter of a million well-armed Germans could gain control of the city for only four days, despite being supported by the massive fire power of a huge artillery siege train, the Luftwaffe's crack air force, and a flotilla of fast attack boats. One in three Germans would not return home.

Using a bolt-action Moisan Nagant rifle with a five-hundred metre range, Pavlyuchenko is credited with killing more than three hundred Nazi soldiers, or an average of nearly three each day. She engaged with one unfortunate German sniper for more than eight hours before dispatching him. In his notebook he had recorded more than four hundred kills of Soviet soldiers.

At the end of the war, having seen her husband killed next to her, and having been wounded four times, Pavlyuchenko was invited by First Lady Eleanor Roosevelt to tour the USA as part of the relief effort. And she became the first Soviet citizen to meet a US President.

Panorama of the Crimean War

We drove down Historic Boulevard, past the statue of Leo Tolstoy, and parked close to the imposing circular museum. Built of Inkerman stone, the museum houses the panorama of the Crimean war. Niches high in the exterior walls house twelve marble busts of prominent people from the war, and a long queue showed us the way to the entrance portal.

Inside the more than one-hundred metre long, four-metre high canvas painted in 1954 (after the original 1905 version was partly destroyed by a German bomb in World War II), is a life-size depiction of a battle scene. In the foreground are models of people, equipment, and buildings. These blend with the canvas to create the impression that you are experiencing firsthand the battle that took place on June 6, 1855 when the Russians defenders repelled the British and French assault on the centre of Sevastopol. Leo Tolstoy recorded his own experience of the war in his *Tales of Sevastopol*.

> You see the sharp curved knife pierce the white healthy flesh; you hear the wounded man suddenly come to with a frightful bloodcurdling scream and a volley of oaths and you see the field doctor throw the amputated limb into a corner... You will see war not as a splendid array of troops in excellent formation, with music and beating of drums, fluttering colours and generals on prancing steeds, but war in its true aspect — blood, suffering and death.[3]

The more you take in the 360-degree vista, the more detail you see: soldiers fighting, others loading canon, a lone sniper, a field hospital, some engaged in their domestic duties of cooking, cleaning, and feeding. All set against a yellow-pink featureless sky, raging fires, and smoldering buildings. You can almost smell the action.

"Come on," said Irena, sensing we'd overstayed. She pulled her hair out of its sloppy bun and shook it free. "We can only take so much sadness, and Eugene has promised to show us something that few people have ever seen."

Secret Submarine Facility 825

Not far from Sevastopol is the town of Balaklava and its beautiful bay. In the 1950s, concerned about nuclear attack, Stalin ordered the construction of three kilometres of tunnels for a submarine dock and repair yard that had to be hewn out of the soft rock near the entrance of the bay.

In the dying dry heat of the late afternoon sun, and on a flat sea, we left the bay in a rowboat worked by an elderly local in his sixties, and approached the entrance of the submarine facility — known to a select few as Facility 825. Metal doors had once protected the entrance, but the only reminder was rusted hinges and steel masonry that partially blocked the entrance. The rower's strokes were infrequent and shallow, and seawater dripping from the blades was the only noise as we floated through a narrow gap.

Once inside, having adjusted to the lack of light and the sudden temperature drop, we began to understand the enormity of the engineering operation. The huge cigar-shaped tube was like a water-filled metro station, only bigger. We clambered up a metal ladder onto a walkway, lit the torch that Eugene carried in his car, and for the next hour explored the workshop areas. Now stripped of all moveable equipment, only rusted gantries and pipe work remained. Finally the dank smell and the spookiness caused by the shadows and the scurrying rats drove us back to the boat.

"Did you notice that the restaurants on the waterfront are called 'Tavernas' in Balaklava?" Eugene said. "This only occurs in this town of Crimea and reflects the strong Greek influence in the area."

We chose a taverna, and as twilight approached we spent a couple of joyous hours sampling grilled fresh fish, oily white wine, and Eugene's company before Chris Rea serenaded us back to Simeiz.

Bakhchiserai and the "Fountain of Tears"

A couple of days later, Eugene returned to take us into the mountains to the Tartar capital of Bakhchiserai. We left the coastal road and, using little-used minor roads, climbed through the mountains to the plateau country with its distinctive rock-walled canyons. On each side of the road, escarpments had been eroded into fantastic shapes by centuries of wind and rain.

The air was fresh and sweet, and the vernal abundance of spring was still evident. Though the word "meadow" is so quintessentially English, I realised that I had never really seen a true meadow in England. Constellations of mountain peonies, Adonis flowers, and sweetly-scented violets produced a carpet of chrome yellow, cobalt blue, and carmine red; colours much used by the Post-Impressionists.

Bakhchiserai, or the "Garden Palace," was built in 1532 by Sahib I Giray as the capital of the Crimean Khanate and the centre of political and cultural life of the Crimean Tatar people. It is a unique example of architecture, and though the palace complex has changed over the years — it was restored by Catherine II, and Alexander, I as well as being occupied by German forces in World War II — a number of original rooms and features remain.

The Palace is best known for its "Fountain of Tears," located in a tranquil inner courtyard built by Iranian sculptor Omer. Just as the "Mona Lisa" by Leonardo da Vinci disappointed me with its size, but captivated me with its beauty, so did the fountain.

There are several beautiful legends as to why the fountain was built, but the most famous (and fallacious) is immortalised in Pushkin's 1823 poem in which he provides a counterpoint between the beauty of the location and the misery of its three main inhabitants. According to the poem, a ruthless Khan captured and fell in love with Maria, the daughter of a Polish Prince whom the Khan had murdered in battle. He did everything he could to turn her heart towards him, and even neglected his favourite wife, Zarema. But Maria could not love the man who had killed her father and soon she died. The Khan was mad with grief, and when he learnt that Zarema had taken to visiting Maria, he assumed she was implicated in Maria's death, so he drowned her and declared war on her homeland of Georgia. Returning home, still in grief, he ordered the creation of a fountain over Maria's grave from which the water would drip as an eternal symbol of tears of sadness.

"The Soviets tried to change the name of Bakhchiserai to Puszkinsk," explained Eugene, "until they realised that they couldn't erase Pushkin's poem from the face of the earth."

Today, Bakhchiserai is a unique glimpse into a vanished way of life and one quite remote from European culture. It was sad to observe, therefore, that not a single Tartar worked there.

Sacred Caves and Mountains

"We'll have lunch in the newly built village of Khodzha-Sala," Eugene announced. "It is being built by Tartars who have returned from deportation."

The village was a scattering of partly-built houses on the side of a narrow valley just beyond a small artificial lake. We sat on a raised bed-like platform covered with a carpet and shaded from the midday sun. Lunch was a fragrant rice dish called "plov," fried pork parcels called, "chiburik," and mint tea that was served by a woman bowed with arthritis and wearing a rainbow coloured dress. The toilet was a pair of ski-like wooden planks above a hole in the ground. Life for the Tartars was clearly hard.

A hundred metres away was an old Soviet helicopter whose pilot offered to take us "Vietnam style" (legs hanging out of the doors) to the plateau above the valley to see a cave town. Both pilot and machine had seen better days, so we declined politely.

There are fourteen cave settlements of significant size in Crimea, and the most famous is Mangup-Kale. "There is nothing in any part of Europe to surpass the tremendous grandeur of the place," wrote English traveller Edward Daniel Clarke in the eighteenth century.[4]

We parked the car on the meadow and Irena collected a variety of orchids: the red hellebore, the lesser butterfly, the monkey orchid, and an abundance of poppies. Heady aromas wafted on the gentle southern breeze.

The ascent was a rocky incline of perhaps three hundred metres, but Irena displayed the same confidence with which she tackles ice-covered pavements in winter.

The ancient town extends for a kilometre along an escarpment that offers breathtaking views of the landscape. In all directions plateaus of meringue-like limestone sit on top of wooded slopes of oak, ash, rowan, and grey-green sagebrush. The town was excavated in Soviet times and the artefacts were sent to museums in Kyiv, Moscow, and St. Petersburg. So all that is left are the dwellings, churches, and a series of staircases cut inside tunnels that provide access to the plateau. The paths were deeply scoured by cartwheels between the third and sixth centuries as first the Goths, then the Alans, and finally the Khazars occupied the city.

But the greatest pleasure was to explore the fortifications and to begin to understand the structure of their society perched on this high plateau exposed to nature.

On the return journey, Eugene dropped us off on the top of Ai-Petri (meaning Sacred Rock) a twelve-hundred-metre peak that forms the back drop to the thirty kilometres of coastline around Simeiz. The mountain is the weathered remains of a coral reef formed millions of years ago. From the peak, looking down on isolated scudding clouds and the motionless mirror of the sea, I felt acutely the power and grandeur of nature and of my own fleeting existence. Inhale, silence. Exhale, solace.

At the small Tartar hamlet on the plateau, we ate a delicious meal of lamb shashlik and lavash bread, whilst watching the sun deepen in colour as it moved to the horizon. Irena went to buy tickets for the cable car — her hair tumbling around her in waves, burnished silver and gold — and I wandered off to the toilet. It was a wooden shack no further than ten metres from the thousand-metre precipice, and the shack door faced the magnificent view of the coastline. You might say it was an unforgettable relief.

The nearly four kilometre descent by cable car is one of the longest in Europe, and as the sun sets, the rock colours change every few seconds. The thistles, heather, and wormwood give way to stunted birch, oaks, and maples, and then to more delicate laurel, magnolia, orchards, and vineyards. In the distance lays the landscaped park and palace of Livadia with its distinctive tree tops of cedar, laurel, and pine.

Livadia and the Tsars

The next day from Simeiz to Livadia, we took a mashrutka (a minibus that acts as a local bus service) along the old coast road now abandoned by major traffic. At designated stops, you clamber into the back of the bus and pass your money, via the other passengers, to the driver who returns any change by the same means.

Livadia is a serene and majestic Florence Renaissance-style mansion nestled on a cliff outside of Yalta. Once the refuge of the Russian Tsars, it was originally designed by Ippolito Monighetti and gardener Clement Hekkel for Alexander II between 1862 and 1866. The mansion became a carefree retreat from the oppressive court of St. Petersburg, and during the Tsar's residence it became the centre of Russian political and social life. Yalta and the surrounding area benefited greatly, particularly with the building of theatres, hotels, shops, and roads.

In 1867, a group of American guests to Livadia arrived at Yalta on the steam ship, "Quaker City." Mark Twain, one of the ship's passengers, referred to the Tsar's hospitality in his book *Innocent's Abroad*, saying, "We have been in no country yet where we have been so kindly received and where we have felt that to be Americans was a sufficient visa for our passports."[5]

Alexander II was assassinated in 1881 and Alexander III died at Livadia in 1894 at the age of 49. He left the house to his son Nicholas and his young bride, the Hessian princess Aleksandra. The young couple considered their sojourns to Livadia as an opportunity to renew their strength, and Nicholas could often be found chasing butterflies in the garden with his children. They commissioned Yalta architect Nikolai Krasnov to rebuild a good proportion of the estate, and though Krasnov is little known outside Crimea, he designed some of the great local houses and estates including Koreis, Harax, Djulber, and Ai-Todor, as well as planning the restoration of Bakhchiserai. In Yalta he was responsible for designing just about everything, including the famous promenade that is "the" place to stroll and be seen on a summer's evening. Nicholas II was overjoyed with the extensive remake of the house. Airy and sunny Italian and Arabian courtyards were built on the ground floor, and the impressive White Hall was designed for grand dining. It was the room in which Churchill, Roosevelt, and Stalin met during the Yalta Conference in 1945, and from where they declared the post-war division of Europe.

Nicholas II abdicated in March 1917, and his request to be allowed to live in Livadia with his family was rejected. The family members were executed in July 1918 in Yekaterinburg, and Krasnov fled Ukraine to live out his life in impoverished surroundings in Belgrade.

Bourgeois Olives and Massandra Wines

A few kilometres further are the Nikita Botanical Gardens, previously owned by the Smirnov family (of Vodka fame) and nowadays an oasis of tranquillity.

As we were examining the rugged gnarled trunk of an olive tree, a woman gardener wearing flip-flops and a large kerchief explained that the olive was regarded by the Soviet Union as a "bourgeois" fruit and its cultivation was discouraged. "Nikita is one of the few places it grows in Ukraine," she said.

This fact no doubt explains why Ukrainians use sunflower oil as a salad dressing and greedily devour olives whenever the opportunity arises.

With the sun setting, we made our way to a wine tasting at Crimea's oldest winery, Massandra, built just outside Yalta in 1894 by Prince Lev Golitsyn, the father of Russian wine making. It is claimed the subtropical microclimate and sparse soil infuse the grapes with fresh, vibrant flavours from which Massandra produces a range of sweet and fortified wines including Sherry, Madeira, Port, Marsala, Tokay, and Muscat.

A hundred or so tasters poured out of minibuses from hotels, taking seats at long refectory tables. In front of each of us were nine wine glasses, each containing a sample of wine. The lecturer appeared and she introduced the first wine, a white Muscat, by recounting that it was a wine favoured by Queen Elizabeth II, who had it shipped to her secretly during Soviet times.

Encouraging us to hold the glass in the correct way prior to sipping the wine, she looked up from her lectern, and her jaw dropped open. Row upon row of tasters had empty, or near empty, glasses in front of them. Unaware of the etiquette of the occasion, many had drunk the samples whilst waiting.

Champagne for the Proletariat

Wine making in Crimea is thousands of years old, as proved by the wine remnants that have been found in Greek amphora from Chersonesos. By the middle of the seventeenth century, the Cossacks of Tsimlanskoe (nowadays, the label name of one of Ukraine's cheap sweet sparkling champagne wines) had mastered the manufacture of sparkling wines as evidenced by Pushkin's reference in *Eugene Onegin*. Though this significantly predates the efforts of the French monk Dom Perignon, the first documented sparkling wine production in Ukraine was recorded in Sudak in 1799. Soon after, all along the Crimean coast, rich merchants and aristocracy were producing sparkling wines.

The Crimean War temporarily halted progress by destroying vines, wineries, and precious research notes, but after the war Golitsyn took up the challenge of improving wine quality. He experimented with hundreds of grape varieties before selecting the Pinot Franc, Pinot Gris, Aligote, and Chardonnay grapes for his champagne, which are more climate tolerant than those preferred by French vintners.

Golitsyn constructed wine cellars that extend deep into the Koba-Kaya mountain in Novy Svet, one of Crimea's most idyllic towns, The winery still produces eleven types of champagne and is open to the public, though even on a summer's day you'd be advised to carry a sweater with you if you wish to linger in the cellars where the temperature is a constant 11° Celsius.

Golitsyn's champagne "Coronation" was served at the coronation of Tsar Nicholas II and won the Grand Prix in Paris in 1890. At the celebratory dinner hosted by Count Chandon (of Moet & Chandon fame), the Count unwittingly mistook Golitsyn's champagne for the very best of his own, thereby establishing Novy Svet as one of the world's best champagnes.

At some time in the 1920s, Stalin was offered a glass of champagne and liked it. He resolved to make readily available for special occasions a proletarian version of the bourgeois drink, and he ordered oenologist Anton Frolov-Bagreev to lead the research. In 1934, the oenologist unveiled a production method involving the use of the Aligote grape and fermentation in large tanks, rather than in a bottle. This enabled mass production at low cost. In this method, the wine passes through a series of enclosed pressure and temperature-controlled storage tanks, with yeast and sugar being added in predetermined amounts at each stage, a process that enabled sparkling wine to be bottled in less than four weeks. Nowadays, whilst most former Soviet republics are busy discarding any associations with the word "Soviet," the Ukrainians still love their "Sovetskoye Shampanskoye" brand. It represents dependability and prices from as low as three dollars a bottle.

The tasting at Massandra concluded with a tour of their magnificent cellars, excavated into the mountain face, which contain upwards of one million bottles that include an unbroken collection of vintages back to the nineteenth century. A few years ago, a bottle of Sherry de le Frontera from the Massandra cellars was sold at a Sotheby's auction for a world record price of US$50,000.

Karadag and the Luminous Black Sea

For our last tour with Eugene we decided to travel eastwards to the city of Sudak, but because of the distance and bad roads, we would make the trip over two days, spending one night sleeping on a beach.

By mid-afternoon, exhausted by the lurching and twisting of the car's motion, and drunk with the breathtaking vistas of hazy-blue mountains in the distance, we reached a region called Karadag, where we decided to stop for the day.

Karadag is an indescribably beautiful Jurassic landscape of rocks weathered into fantastic shapes, the result of an extinct volcano which thousands of years ago spewed lava and debris into the sea. A popular summer job for students to earn money is to collect the amethyst, onyx, cornelian, agate, jasper and many other crystals and minerals that can be found on the local beaches.

"Sudak has been controlled by the Greeks, the Genoese, the Ottomans, the Turks and the Russians," Eugene said as we grilled fish on a barbeque on the beach.

"I'll never forget Bakhchiserai," continued Irena. "A Tartar Khan of Mongolian origin formed alliances with the Cossacks and Ottomans and married a Georgian. He loved a Polish princess and they lived in a palace decorated by Italians and Iranians. And a Russian poet who based his work on the oriental tales of the Englishman Byron immortalised the place."

"As I said, Crimea is a microcosm of the world affairs."

That evening we undressed on the beach, lit only by the light of the moon, and entered the warm sea. It murmured gently on the ebb and cackled on the flow as small pebbles tumbled seaward. We waded out to waist level. Looking seaward the gentle waves had a strange luminous quality and the sea phosphoresced as a result of millions of plankton suspended in the water. This is an infrequent occurrence at best, limited to just a short period of the year on Crimea's southern coast.

Who could not agree, I thought, that Crimea is a diamond in the Black Sea?

WHIRLYBIRDS AND WITCHES

"I WASN'T AFRAID of being killed in combat. But I was afraid of capture," said Pavel, a salt-and-pepper-haired man with empathetic eyes and a trace of dark stubble. He was a retired helicopter pilot whose medal for valour on the breast of his military uniform glistened in the sunlight of the spring morning. He was one of the fortunate ones; most of the medals were awarded posthumously.

We were standing outside the National Aviation Museum in the Kyiv suburb of Zhuliany. I was in the company of a group of students from the National Aviation University, and we were on a tour of the museum. Pavel was our guide.

Afghanistan and Conscription

The Soviet Union invaded Afghanistan in 1979 in order to prevent a communist state from breaking from their orbit, just as they had done in 1956 in Poland and Hungary and in Czechoslovakia in 1968. Throughout Soviet history, any potential uprising in the Central Asian republics (Tajikistan, Kazakhstan, Uzbekistan, and Kyrgyzstan) had been crushed with ease, so entering Afghanistan must have seemed like old hat to the military planners. But this time it was to be different. Though the Soviets were reasonably well trained and equipped, this was a guerrilla war, and conventional tactics would not work. It was to be the Soviet Union's Vietnam.

"Was the war worth fighting?" asked one of the students, a young man in his late teens.

"My country thought so." Pavel replied. "Soldiers are taught to fight and I was sent there to fight a war."

Whatever he had witnessed had not changed his loyalty.

"You know, no one wins a war. Both sides kill each other until the politicians are forced to sort it out. When you are in the combat zone, the politics go away and it becomes personal. When you've been shot at and seen your comrades fall, it becomes a personal fight. We were young and we didn't have a wider perspective. To us, Afghanistan wasn't a prize, it was just a mortuary."

I was recalling that Ukrainians were deeply affected by the 10-year unwinnable war. Most families had a son, cousin, or nephew who faced the prospect of being drafted or had already been killed in the war. My Ukrainian friends confided to me how their families had paid their doctors to certify their male offspring as mad or deaf in order to avoid compulsory service. Others hid with friends and relatives when the Recruiting Officers were known to be in the neighbourhood; often they would call in the middle of the night.

Matrosov Assignments

"What role did you play?" quizzed another student, his jeans and tee shirt in marked contrast to Pavel's uniform.

"We were involved in reconnaissance, search and destroy, deploying and lifting troops, and Matrosov assignments."

I imagined a row of Hind helicopters, noses dipped, hovering and throwing up whirlpools of dry dust and could almost hear the dreaded "whoop, whoop" of their blades as they hacked into the hot air with 192 missiles under the stub wings, seconds from being released. For many crouching, crying Afghan woman and children in their mud brick shelters, these were their last sights and sounds.

"We hated Matrosov assignments because we were sitting ducks," Pavel said with obvious emotion. "We flew beside the jets that were taking off or landing at Kabul airport and we released flares to distract any incoming shoulder-launched heat-seeking missiles. The tactic was to sacrifice the Hind if that meant the jet aircraft carrying people or supplies could be saved. During the war 333 helicopters were brought down."

The students shifted uneasily to look at each other, and my vocabulary was enhanced with a few new expletives.

Alexandr Matrosov was a young Ukrainian soldier who threw his body over the muzzle of a German machine gun and took all the bullets in order to let his comrades break through. He was a hero of World War II and was posthumously awarded the highest honorary title of Hero of the Soviet Union.

"Let's go inside and look at the museum and then we'll go to the concourse," Pavel suggested. Indoors there were hundreds of aviation exhibits and outdoors nearly forty aircraft on display. "The names and contributions of Sikorsky and Antonov are particularly well known," he explained as he led us through the first part of the museum, "but during the period 1910 to 1914 Kyiv was home to men of broad ambition who built and flew nearly forty different aircraft."

Photographs and aviation paraphernalia filled glass cabinets and Pavel traced the story of the early aviators. Shortly after the beginning of the twentieth century, Kyiv established a special place in the history of aviation because of a combination of forward thinking academic institutions, a lack of any bureaucratic interference, and wealthy, fearless hobbyists who were gripped by a passion for this new gentlemen's pastime.

The locus of the aviators' attention was Kyiv Polytechnic Institute where, less than four years after the Wright brothers made the world's first flight a special interest group was established by Nickolai Delone, Professor of Engineering Mechanics. He designed one of the world's most enduring glider designs and in 1909 published a booklet titled *How to build an inexpensive and light glider and learn to fly it,* which was the first practical guide to flying. It was a fellow professor, Alexander Kudashev, who was the first man to fly in the Russian Empire. In 1910, he powered his pine-framed biplane "Kudashev-1" off the ground and flew it for nearly two hundred metres.

Early flyers also included airplane and flying boat designers, ace pilots, parachute designers, engine designers, and the men who would first establish the rules of air combat. They came together to form the Kyiv Aeronautics Society, issued their own magazine, and owned their own airfield in Kurenyovka where they organized exhibitions and competitions and gave flight demonstrations.

The Karpeka family, whose home I had come across whilst walking down Volodymyrska Street in central Kyiv, was typical of their breed. The family lived on the second floor of the building at the junction with Tolskogo Street. Their eldest son built one of Kyiv's first airplanes in the communal courtyard, no doubt to the amazement of their neighbours. Even a motor car would have been an uncommon sight on the streets of Kyiv in 1910.

Dogfights and Aircraft Spin

As we shifted from exhibit to exhibit, Pavel revealed his enthusiasm and depth of knowledge, often engaging us with stories of glory, like those of Evgraf Kruten or Konstantin Artseulov whom one of the students wittily nicknamed "the Ace of Spin."

Evgraf Kruten was born in Kyiv in 1892 and graduated from aviation school in 1914. In World War I he led the first nighttime sorties to locate enemy positions, a novel use for aircraft at the time. Through his dogfight experiences with enemy aircraft he began to develop techniques for mid-air combat, engaging enemy aircraft singly or in groups, and attacking from behind cloud cover or using the sun to hide his aircraft's approach. Before long he was teaching his fellow pilots their first lessons in the strategies of aerial combat.

In the spirit of the age he is remembered as a gentleman. On one occasion following the successful attack on an aircraft, he flew over the German airfield from where it had departed and dropped a message to the pilot's family. In it he apologised for his adversary's death, but reflected that the alternative outcome was not acceptable to him. Today, amongst the small circle of aviators, Kruten is regarded as one of the fathers of the strategy of aerial combat.

Artseulov's story likewise combines bravery with innovation. One of the more invincible enemies of the early aviators was aircraft spin — the spiral descent of the aircraft that caused speed loss and stalling — which inevitably resulted in a crash. Artseulov, the commander of a group of Nieuports based in Sevastopol, watched more than half a dozen of his colleagues die in such spins before he deliberately put his own Nieuport-XXI into such a situation. He reasoned correctly that the spin could be corrected if the pilot pushed the stick away from his body. This was contrary to the intuition of earlier pilots who had pulled the stick towards them in an attempt to raise the nose of the airplane. Pulling on the stick has the effect of reducing the aircraft speed and only aggravates the problem. Artseulov's experiment caused a sensation and, by overcoming the unknown, he gave confidence to thousands of pilots.

First Airmail Services

We left the museum and went out into the spring sunshine. On the concourse stood a comical array of aircraft that looked like they could have come from a child's toy box. No two were the same. We stopped first by a small, sleek, chocolate brown and silver-coloured Anatra Anasol biplane.

Between 1909 and 1918, Artur Anatra, a prominent Odesa businessman of Italian descent, established the Anatra Aircraft Works and built more than seventeen hundred aircraft. His parents and grandparents had made their fortune by exporting wheat from the Ukrainian steppe to the Mediterranean lands. When the Bolshevik Revolution started, Anatra envisaged there would be difficult economic times ahead, and though Odesa was less affected than say, Petrograd or Moscow, he recognized the need to diversify. So, in 1918 he pioneered one of the world's first airmail services and the first in Russia. His Anasol aircraft offered a five-hour delivery time to Ekaterinoslav at a cost of one rouble per item.[1] Later that same year he started an airborne "taxi" service that has only recently been copied (using helicopters) in our traffic-congested megacities. His passenger service operated between the city centre and the suburb of Fountains, and though they are only a few kilometres apart, road conditions between them were often poor. The advertising of the service stated reassuringly, "This service will use five of Anatra's best airplanes and the flight itself will take two to three minutes."[2]

Sikorsky's Aircraft

The ten or so helicopters on the concourse, all roughly the same size, appeared to be the most homogenous group. Standing next to a Sikorsky, Pavel injected fresh energy into his voice. As a helicopter pilot he owed his lifestyle to the man who designed and built this machine.

"Do any of you know of another high technology transportation company that has been a world leader for ninety years?" Pavel challenged the students. He looked around for dissenting voices and, hearing none, began to narrate the story of one of the world's most famous designers.

Sikorsky was born in Kyiv in 1889 in a small three-story house at 15 Yaroslaviv Val, not too far from the famous Golden Gates of Kyiv. His father was a professor of psychology at Kyiv University, but it was his mother who inspired him by telling him stories about the flying machines of Leonardo da Vinci. Initially it looked at though the young Sikorsky might pursue a career in the navy, but after he graduated from St. Petersburg Naval College he returned to Kyiv to study engineering at Kyiv Polytechnic Institute.

Still living with his parents, he built his first helicopter in the yard of their house in 1909. It was underpowered, but after some tweaking he managed to get it to lift its own weight but not that of a man. It was the Russian Empire's first helicopter to get off the ground, but it suffered from excessive vibration. Seeing no immediate solution, Sikorsky switched his energies to building aircraft.

Initially, he collaborated with others but found the experience unproductive, and so he concentrated on his own ideas, producing twenty-five versions of aircraft and two helicopters in the next twenty years. He did all his own flight testing, and there are stories about his antics whilst in flight. On one occasion it was said that, to extinguish a fire, he walked to the edge of a wing wearing a greatcoat, leather gloves, and helmet. On numerous other occasions he was seen standing on a wing drinking a hot cup of coffee. His S-5 model, which was built and tested at the Kyiv Aviation Society's airfield at Kurenivka, set four new records, and the S-6 achieved a world record for flight speed with two people on board. Within a few years, after tireless experimentation, he designed and built the world's first two-engine aircraft, a momentous achievement that established the blueprint for just about every modern aircraft.

"Who knows what inspired Sikorsky to use two or more engines?" Pavel asked. He had the complete attention of the students.

"More power," answered one.

"Reliability," shouted another.

Pavel smiled and said, "Actually, it was the mosquito. Sikorsky witnessed an accident and realised that the engine air intake was blocked with dead mosquitoes and this led to the idea. "And in what year do you think an airplane was fitted with a toilet?" he added.

Smiles and frowns appeared across the students' faces, and the consensus was sometime in the 1930s or 1940s.

"Well, it was 1914. Sikorsky's luxurious aircraft, which he called 'the Grand' — also disingenuously called 'The St. Petersburg Duck' by the foreign press — was a four-ton aircraft that boasted a cabin with four wicker chairs, a sofa, a heating system, and a toilet. Emperor Nicholas II disbelieved the press reports and went to see it for himself, after which he presented Sikorsky with a timepiece as a reward for his achievement."

War and revolution drove Sikorsky from his homeland in 1918 and, after spending a few uninspiring months in England and France, he chose to settle in New York. Life was difficult for the penniless and non-English speaking émigré, and Sikorsky survived only by teaching. Later, using money from friends and, in particular, from the composer Sergei Rachmaninoff, he established the Sikorsky Aero Engineering Corporation in 1923.

Within a year Sikorsky had built the world's first all-metal aircraft. (He also designed it so that it was capable of flying on just one engine if the other failed.) Numerous other models followed quickly and were eagerly deployed by the fledgling Pan-American Airways, which was then opening up cities in the interior of the USA and in central and southern America. Most successful were the S-38 and S-42 aircraft. They pioneered commercial flights across the Atlantic and the Pacific Oceans, breaking numerous world records. These flying boats were ideal for reaching places with no man-made airstrip; the world would have to wait a few more years for the invention of the tarmac runway.

Prototype of all Hypersonic Jets

Back in the country of Sikorsky's birth, the interwar period was a fertile time for design ideas and for two other great aircraft designers, Konstantin Kalinin and Yosef Neman. Both would meet their death as a result of Stalin's purge.

It is one of the ironies of the time that many of those who were purged by Stalin were working on ideas and innovations that would have been invaluable to the Soviet Union had they been allowed to develop. But most of them were lost in the secret police archives. Meanwhile, Stalin and his successors spent ceaseless energy trying to acquire these same ideas and innovations by plundering the nations defeated in World War II or, during the Cold War, from other countries through spying and espionage.

Kalinin's story, in particular, is worth recounting. He served in the air force of the Ukrainian People's Republic in 1919 and then graduated in aircraft design at the Kyiv Polytechnic Institute. A man of exceptional talent, he was immediately made head of the Kharkiv Aircraft Design Bureau where he worked closely with Yosef Neman, who was arrested on false charges in 1938 and sent to the gulag where he died.

Kalinin's best designs were his "K" series models (the "K" denoting his surname just as "S" denotes Sikorsky's models), which were common on internal routes in the Soviet Union. His two-tailed K-7 aircraft was a schoolboy's dream, at least on paper. With huge elliptical wings and powered by seven engines, it was capable of intercontinental flight of five thousand kilometres. But in 1933, on only its second flight, it crashed after a crack appeared in the rear, killing nearly everyone on board.

Undaunted, Kalinin pressed ahead with further innovative designs. The K-12 design, also known as "Firebird," was garishly painted with feather patterns to look like a bird. A surprising characteristic of the aircraft is that it had no tail and, to the aeronautically challenged observer, it looked as though it had been in an accident even before takeoff. In 1958 the British magazine *Air Pictorial* featured a rare photograph of the K-12 with a caption that read, "This craft was a prototype of all modern hypersonic jets."[3]

The plane was successfully tested, but Kalinin did not live to see it built commercially because he was arrested in April 1938. Whilst in prison he produced detailed notes and drawings for a tailless delta-winged aircraft he designated K-15. Although he did not have sufficient knowledge to make it fly (nor the freedom to do so), it was clearly a forebearer of the US Stealth bomber and other hypersonic aircraft. The Soviet secret police dutifully filed the notes and drawings in a folder and placed them on a shelf in a storage room where they gathered dust for nearly fifty years.

Shortly after the war, using documents that had been seized from captured Germans, Stalin ordered research to be conducted on hypersonic flight. The resulting design was almost indistinguishable from the one that Kalinin had penned whilst in prison some ten years before. Though the date of Kalinin's death is unknown, he is believed to have died from torture sometime in mid-1938.

Sikorsky's Helicopters

Back in America, the successful but modest Sikorsky turned his attention once more to the challenge that had occupied him as a boy; to build a helicopter.

In September 1939 he revealed the VS-300, a skeleton of tubes with a completely open pilot seat that used a single three-blade rotor. Development progress was slow, but Sikorsky piloted the VS-300 to achieve a one hour and thirty-two minute flight record. In 1942, using the lessons learnt, he put a modified design (the R-4) into mass production. Though a few of these machines saw action in World War II, many were sceptical about their ability. It was only in the 1950s after the experience gained in the Korean War that they became universally accepted by the air forces and commercial fleets.

"You know," extolled Pavel, "Sikorsky was a deeply religious man, and his helicopter inventions always gave him greater pleasure than his aircraft. Whilst both machines can be forces for destruction, the helicopter has more humanitarian uses, and this comforted Sikorsky greatly. He died at 83 after having received hundreds of awards and honours."

On the concourse, a few metres from the Sikorsky, stood a menacing and lethal looking Hind, Pavel's best friend. He gave us the dummie's guide of how to fly it.

"The pilot uses three controls to fly the helicopter. You see the cyclic control stick? Well, that tilts the rotor disc. To turn, the pilot pushes it left or right. The lever to the left connects to that plate on top and changes the pitch of the rotor blades. This enables the helicopter to climb or descend. Those foot pedals connect to the tail rotor blades, and you work those together with the cyclic to make left or right turns."

"You said you'd show us how to bring down a helicopter," reminded one of the students, whose graffiti-daubed jeans didn't bode well for him making rank of Major anytime soon.

"That's right, take a look. The Hind has only three weak areas: the turbine intakes, the tail rotor assembly, and the oil tank located beneath the red star on the fuselage, just about here." He pointed to the spot.

"So, just aim at the red star!" hollered one of the girl students.

It was an opportune moment to declare a break.

About a third of the students in our group were women, and women probably make up some 50 percent of all volunteers and probably 10 percent of total military personnel. Ukrainian women have played a prominent part in twentieth century aviation history — and it is a brave man who says otherwise — but the full extent of their involvement has only become apparent in recent years. Two examples, in particular, that deserve telling are the stories of women's long distance flight and the so-called "Night Witches."

Women's Long Distance Flight

Valentina Grizodubova, who was born in Kharkiv, was to become the first woman to be decorated as Hero of the Soviet Union after she completed a momentous long distance flight. Her father, rather irresponsibly, took two-year-old baby Valentina on a maiden flight with him in an untested machine he had built, because there was no one else with whom he could leave the child. Undaunted by the experience, Valentina followed her father's footsteps and went on to become the country's first woman instructor, teaching hundreds of men to fly at Tula Institute.

Valentina's co-pilot, Polina Osipenko, shared a similar ambition but had a very different upbringing. Osipenko was head of a chicken farm near Kyiv when she fell in love with a military pilot working at the Kacha Flight School. She enrolled at the school and started out by working in the canteen making breakfast for the pilots, but before long had inveigled her way into the pilot training programme. She excelled at training and was transferred to Kharkiv where she married Alexander Osipenko, who later became a famous general and Hero of the Soviet Union.

Over the next three years, in flying with fellow navigator and pilot, Russian-born Maria Raskova, Grizodubova and Osipenko set several new women's distance world records and were awarded The Order of Lenin. (Nowadays, it seems somewhat quaint to be awarded a medal for making a four-hour flight, but then it had all sorts of implications for military supremacy.) The three women enjoyed working together, and with Stalin's support — it is thought that Raskova may have been his mistress — they embarked on a flight across the Soviet Union.

Despite deteriorating weather they took off on September 24, 1938 in an aircraft named "Rodina" ("Motherland"). It was a monoplane ANT-37 with a glazed forward navigator's cabin where Raskova was seated, and a pilots' cabin for the other two girls located behind.

Almost immediately the visibility deteriorated and they were forced to fly at a high altitude. The crew began to suffer from hypothermia as the air temperature reached -37° Celsius and, to add to their problems, the radio equipment failed and Raskova had to rely on the stars to determine the aircraft's location.

Some twenty-five hours after takeoff, as they approached the Sea of Okhotsk the instruments warned of low fuel; the result of a mistake by the fuelling crew to completely fill the tanks. Knowing that a crash was inevitable, and fearing that the aircraft nose would be crushed on impact, Commander Grizodubova ordered Raskova to bail out of the forward cabin. Raskova would spend ten harrowing days before she was found in the cold, black bear-infested Taiga with only two chocolate bars for food. Meanwhile, "Rodina" crash landed in a marsh and the pilots waited to be rescued.

Some fifty aircraft took part in the search, and not long before she died, 80-year-old Valentina Grizodubova recalled how sixteen of the rescuers had died needlessly. When the pilot of a small Douglas aircraft was overjoyed at having located "Rodina," he decided to show off and do an acrobatic stunt of looping the aircraft. In the process he crashed into a lumbering Tupolev bomber, bringing down both planes.

By foot, canoe, river launch, train, and open-top car, the three girls made it back to Moscow where they were Stalin's guests of honour at an enormous reception. The entire country was lifted by the achievements of the aviators. Soon the Federation Aeronautique Internationale confirmed that the distance covered of 6,450 kilometres was a new world record, beating that of Britain's Elizabeth Lyon.

Stalin awarded them the highest honour and his official endorsement of their achievement opened the publishing floodgates. Soon after there appeared dozens of posters, books, and stamps depicting women pilots, mechanics, and parachutists, thus ending forever the Soviet notion that aviation was the exclusive domain of men.

A few months later, Polina Osipenko was killed in an aircraft accident. In what seems to be an unusual act of humility towards a Ukrainian peasant, Stalin was a pallbearer at the funeral.

The "Night Witches"

Neither Soviet historians nor Western historians have paid much attention to the extraordinary role of women in the Soviet war effort.[+] In addition to those serving in the Air Force, more than eight hundred thousand women saw active service on the battlefield serving as nurses, snipers, gunners, paratroopers, and tank crews. Eighty-eight women received the highest decoration, Hero of the Soviet Union, and twenty-four of those (eighteen pilots and six navigators) were from a single regiment, the 588th Night Bomber Regiment of the all-female Aviation Group 122, which was led by Raskova. The Germans nicknamed them the "Nachthexen" or "Night Witches."

All the women were volunteers, and the three-year training programme was compressed into a much shorter but physically taxing period of six months. Women performed every task, with pilots hauling bombs and ammunition cans, and ground crew performing maintenance and repairs in the open in all kinds of weather. They suffered greatly from frostbite, sunburn, hunger, fatigue, and, perhaps most of all, loss of friends. Nearly one in three Night Witches died fighting.

They achieved their notoriety in part because they flew the Polikarpov 2, irreverently called "the sewing machine" by male pilots. The open-cockpit wood and canvas biplane, which was armed with four small bomb racks, was an anachronism capable of only very slow speed. On the plus side, it had high manoeuvrability and was often difficult to detect because it could fly low and its canvas body absorbed radar.

The main task of the Night Witches was harassment bombing of German storage depots and encampments in occupied Ukraine where soldiers were trying to rest. They used the psychological effect of terror and insecurity, invoking constant restlessness in the Germans. Sometimes they would approach their target, switch off their engine, and then glide over the target before dropping their bombs. On other occasions they would fly in a formation of three, with two of them drawing the attention of the searchlights and the flak whilst the third went to the target and dropped her payload. When enemy fighters appeared, the unarmed Polikarpovs tried only evasion, flying perhaps below the tree line or turning sharply. Since the stall speed of the German fighters was above the maximum speed of the Polikarpovs, if the fighters missed hitting the little plane on one run, they were forced to circle back and give the little chap a breathing space before lining up for another try. Night after night, the Night Witches would fight against a better equipped and better trained and prepared enemy.

Among the more prominent Ukrainian women of the 588th were Natasha Myeklin, Evgenia Rudneva, and Vera Bjelik. All three of them were under the age of twenty-three when they joined the regiment in 1942, and by the end of the following year, Rudneva and Bjelik had been killed in action. In that short time they had flown 980, 645, and 813 missions respectively, and statistics show that the regiment flew nearly twenty-four thousand sorties and dropped three thousand tons of bombs.

Air Commander Johannes Steinhoff, who had more than a hundred victories to his credit, recalled, "We simply couldn't grasp that the Soviet airmen that caused us the greatest trouble were in fact women. These women feared nothing. They came night after night in their very slow biplanes, and for some periods they wouldn't give us any sleep at all."[5]

The "Ace of Aces" and the Big Birds

Moving on, we stopped next to the World War II fighter aircraft collection where Pavel called everyone to gather around. "This Yak was the most popular Soviet fighter," he said. "It was similar to the aircraft that was flown by Ukrainian Ivan Kozhedub, one of my childhood heroes and the so-called 'Ace of Aces.' He flew on three hundred and thirty combat missions and shot down sixty-two enemy aircraft — that's more kills than any other Allied Air Force pilot.

"There is a story that, whilst flying over Berlin with just one other airplane, they came across a group of forty enemy aircraft. They decided to attack despite being massively outnumbered. Climbing above and behind the FW-190s, they drove a wedge between the aircraft and panicked the Germans into dropping their bombs. Regrettably, on another occasion, he was also forced to shoot down two American P-51 Mustangs after they mistakenly took him for the enemy." On saying that, Pavel sighed and turned his palms upwards. These things happen during wartime.

As the tour was drawing to a close, we walked across the shimmering tarmac and gathered together in the shadow of the undercarriage of an Antonov; the AH-26. The Antonovs are the big birds of the collection, visible from any part of outdoor museum, and they look rather like a mother duck surrounded by siblings. If Kyiv is the mother of all Rus cities, Antonov is the mother of all aircraft.

"Antonov is our flagship company," Pavel explained. "Today, Ukraine is one of just nine countries worldwide that is designing and building both transport and civil aircraft. "Oleg Antonov established the Design Bureau, which was tasked with developing an agricultural aircraft. That's the small aircraft you see over there." He pointed to one of the siblings. "From its inception, the Bureau was characterized by its speed of development and an inclination to think big. For many years it played a cat-and-mouse game with the Americans to build the biggest aircraft. To date, Antonov has produced more than twenty-two thousand aircraft and broken dozens of world records."

For the remainder of the tour, Pavel discussed the modern history of Antonov, which reminded me of my childhood memories of the 1965 Paris Air Show. The AH-22, or "Antheus," was demonstrated at the show and was indisputably the biggest aircraft in the world at that time. It was also the world's first wide-body aircraft and the first to lift more than one hundred tons. It stirred the Americans to respond, and within three years the USA introduced the Lockheed Galaxy.

Antonov died in 1984 just before seeing the commercial debut of the answer to the Galaxy: the AH-124 or "Ruslan." This is currently the world's largest commercially available aircraft, and it is used for transporting super-heavy cargoes such as turbines, railroad engines, helicopters, and space capsules. According to the *Guinness Book of World Records*, the highest single load ever transported by air — a Siemens power generator weighing 135 ton — was carried in an AH-124.

To almost everyone there seemed no logic to building an even bigger aircraft except, that is, to the Soviets themselves. So, in 1989, following rumours of its development, the AH-225 or "Myria" (meaning dream or inspiration), appeared at the Paris Air Show with a Buran Space Shuttle sitting on its back. Capable of lifting 275 tons, its diverse cargoes have varied from eighty new cars to 216,000 prepared meals as part of a humanitarian aid programme.

"The people at the air show weren't sure whether to be impressed or horrified at this feat of engineering!" exclaimed Pavel.

Yes, I thought, that could be an epitaph on Soviet technology in general, recalling a bakelite wind-up shaver I had bought in the Soviet Union twenty-five years earlier. My youthful chin suffered greatly from its cruelty.

"But of all military technologies," Pavel summed up his tour, "aviation does have the redeeming element that so comforted Sikorsky. It is the technology that can most clearly be used for both 'good' purposes and civilian purposes. And in the race with the USA, it was a Ukrainian manufacturer who had the final word."

ZOOS, SCIENCE, AND EVOLUTION

I CROSSED SUMSKAYA, A cobbled avenue and the main street of Kharkiv, and entered Park Shevchenko. Kharkiv is known locally as "the city of parks" and there are more than one hundred within the city boundary. Immediately ahead of me stood the imposing bronze statue of Taras Shevchenko, the national poet of Ukraine, surrounded by sixteen other figures.

A Stroll in Park Shevchenko

Shevchenko was a serf, but he spoke eloquently and simply of the suppression of the poor and incited others to rise against Tsarist suppression. Though the government had banned the display of effigies of Shevchenko, public support for "the people's hero" among the poor was such that it was a losing battle. The first statue of Shevchenko to appear in Ukraine was in the park on Alchevskaya Street in 1899, adjacent to the house of the founder of the first all-female Sunday school. Its author was the Kharkivite and prominent sculptor and professor of the St. Petersburg Academy of Arts, Vladimir Beklemishev.

In March 1935, to the sounds of trumpets and the *Internationale* (the anthem of the Soviet Union prior to 1944), thousands witnessed the unveiling in Shevchenko Park of the great landmark of the son of the Ukrainian people. Yanka Kupala, the national poet of Belarus, recited poetry he had dedicated to the national poet of Ukraine. The composition stands eleven metres high. A six-metre figure of Shevchenko stands on a pedestal, its furrowed head bent slightly forward, its right fist clenched in anger and indignation — an image that projects resoluteness and power. The sixteen near-natural-size figures surrounding the pedestal symbolise the evolution of the people's struggle against oppression, from rebellious figures of Shevchenko's own works to participants in the First Russian Revolution in 1905–1907 and including participants in the October Revolution: a coal-miner, a collective farmer, and a woman-student — symbols that glorify free labour and the youth of Ukraine.

Seen from a short distance, the harmony, coordination, and unity of the statue is nothing short of breathtaking. The best Leningrad founders cast the statures of the monument; Ukrainian as well as Russian craftsman worked together on the erection of a pedestal. Due to a collaborative effort of many artists, sculptors, and builders, the monument was completed within one year. Actors from a local theatre were enrolled as models for the figures.

In my travels across Ukraine, I have lost count of, but never tire of seeing, the thousands of statues dedicated to famous historical figures. No place is bereft of a reminder of the past; even the smallest village will have a statue dedicated to those who perished in World War II. In the cities, provinces, and rural areas these statues provide a visual and emotive connection with the past that is mostly absent in Western Europe outside of city centres.

Continuing through the park, I walked past the misleadingly named *Singing Fountain* towards the zoo, which is located on the far edge and bounded on its other sides by the Kharkiv State University and the cobbled Freedom Square. This square, previously called Dzerzhinsky Square after Felix Dzerzhinsky, the founder of the Bolshevik secret police, is the third largest city-centre square in Europe.

Kharkiv Zoo and Veterinary Pathology

It was early March. The weather was cool and the trees were still bare. Dirty snow still lay in the hollows. I had agreed to meet Sergei outside the zoo entrance, a twenty-metre wide turquoise-painted wall with gate that was built by architect Shirshova in the 1930s. Unlike most of the zoo, it had survived World War II intact. A bright red banner suspended between pillars at either end of the wall announces "Zoopark," and models of two white polar bears sit on top of the wall together with four black panthers.

We had talked previously only on the telephone after the zoo director recommended that I meet him. He was a tall slim man with a full crop of grey hair, and he stood erect, wearing a suit and tie beneath an overcoat. We approach warily, exchanged greetings, and walked towards the ticket kiosk located next to the entrance.

As with so many kiosks in the former Soviet Union, whether you are buying a journal, bread, or cigarettes, you are required to bend down to a small window the size of a cornflake packet, located at waist height, and to crane your neck upwards towards the salesperson. Long ago I stopped asking why the kiosks are designed like this after a saleswoman informed me curtly that when chair manufacturers make chairs with longer legs she would raise the height of the window. The entrance price was just two dollars for adults, but stuck next to the schedule of prices was a handwritten note informing visitors that entrance was free to those bringing either five kilograms of acorns or carrots.

"This year the acorn crop has failed and the wild pigs are left without food," Sergei informed me on seeing me trying to make sense of the note.

"And the carrots? I asked.

"Oh, they're probably for the staff," he replied as I handed him his ticket.

"I get into the zoo free of charge because of my past work. But you can afford it and they need your money."

I never tire of visiting zoos, partly because they bring into focus a number of interesting paradoxes. They are designed by adults but are most popular with children. They are justified by scientific endeavour but viewed by the great majority as entertainment. And whilst they are dedicated to good, they are increasingly subject to ethical objections. A zoo in modern times can be a contentious subject, and a zoo with no money and poor conditions for the animals is especially so.

At the end of the nineteenth century, the study of veterinary pathology in the Russian Empire was way ahead of the English-speaking world, particularly in the practical aspects of the science. Students spent a large part of their time doing autopsies whilst their overseas colleagues were only doing the theory. This position was lost steadily during the Soviet era, but nevertheless a diploma from the Institute is prestigious; and according to the Institute's website they have trained more than thirty-two thousand zoo engineers who have worked in nearly eighty countries.

"Tell me about your work," I suggested as we strolled down the avenue of bare sycamore trees that led to a large colourful map showing the zoo layout.

"I studied at the Kharkiv Zooveterinary Institute in the 1960s. It's the oldest higher school of veterinary medicine in Ukraine, and it was founded more than one hundred and fifty years ago. My speciality is veterinary pathology."

"And that means?"

"I specialize in the diagnosis of veterinary diseases through the examination of animal tissue and body fluids."

We stopped to review the map showing the layout for the zoo. Wooden boxes, empty except for a layer of ice at the base, suggested that once upon a time they had contained brochures.

"That's right," informed Sergei, "years ago the zoo published a guidebook containing a map. In a country where people had little exposure to the outside world and virtually no access to travel, the guidebook served as a travel guide for a journey to distant lands. For children it was a magic carpet to imaginary places."

He pondered for a moment. "That is really what Kharkiv Zoo is about; it's part journey and part education."

The Early History of Zoos

The Soviet Planners recognised early on the importance of access to open areas and green spaces and had continued or strengthened the approach established under the Tsars.

A few privately owned formal gardens in French style or Italian baroque style appeared from the 1700s onwards, but public parks such as Lviv's beautiful Stryi Park (Ukraine's first park) only appeared from 1877 onwards. Kharkiv Zoo was established in 1896, Askania Zoo in 1898, and five others, including Kyiv, were established after 1900. These parks and zoos were oases in the quickly growing cities where apartments rather than houses were the predominant living accommodation.

Parks and zoos were neglected in the early years following the Bolshevik Revolution, but in 1926 a law was passed to protect this legacy and a planning hierarchy of green spaces was established. The most local or communal space is the "dvor," or yard playground, located adjacent to virtually every apartment block. Next are public parks and botanical gardens located within city boundaries; then forest parks located on the city fringes that provide an area for picnicking, swimming, mushroom picking, hiking, and cross-country skiing; and finally, national parks and nature preserves that are large areas set aside for recreation and conservation.

We agreed on a route around the zoo and Sergei continued to offer his ideas. "Odd though it may seem, the zoo is one of the few cultural establishments that survived the Soviet period relatively unchanged. There were some extreme cases in which individual animals were regards as "bourgeois" and so were not allowed, but generally the authorities encouraged zoos."

I toyed with the idea for a few moments, wondering if perhaps the penguin, with its dinner jacket-like attire, was considered "bourgeois."

"Theatres were forced to change their repertoires, circus clowns were forced to change their acts, and galleries and museums were forced to change their exhibits, but zoos exist today in very much the same way they did a hundred years ago."

"But is the zoo concept still relevant today, particularly when the conditions for the animals are so poor?" I pressed.

He was a quiet-spoken man, but now he spoke with an authoritative voice. "You can't expect to understand our culture without having endured our history." He chose carefully a verb that suggested prolonged pain and hardship.

"The Anglo Saxon countries exploited the world when it suited them, and now they assume a mask of responsibility. You now ask all the less developed countries not to do what you did. But you offer no support other than words to help us change. Isn't that hypocrisy?"

His eyes scrupulously avoided me. "Let me teach you some zoo history," he snapped. And as we walked he revealed his story.

Zoos appeared relatively late in Eastern Europe. Vienna's Tiergarten Schönbrunn, established in 1752, was the world's first zoo. It preceded by more than one hundred and forty years Ukraine's first zoo, established at Kharkiv. The founder was Professor Alexander von Brandt who held the Chair of Zoology at the University of Kharkiv.

The initial idea was to construct an aquarium, but by the time the organising committee had agreed on the location in the University garden, the idea had broadened to include a birdhouse and a section for hoofed animals. In 1903 visitors could see twenty breeds of chickens, geese, and ducks, seventeen species of mammals, and several dozen fish species housed in giant tanks.

Revolution and World War I were not kind to any of Ukraine's zoos. The first few years of Kyiv Zoo, for example, were precarious to say the least. Funded by private donations, the "Nature Lover's Society of Kyiv" established the zoo in 1908. Overeager to get started, they purchased the animals before a zoo site had been agreed upon and, with the arrival of winter and average temperatures of -5° Celsius, they were forced to shelter them in the food department of Kyiv railway station.

The following year the animals, whose numbers had increased by procreation and new purchases, were temporarily relocated to the University Botanical Garden. This was another less than optimal location, and the animals began to disrupt the work of the University and to consume the botanical garden's exhibits. In 1913, four years after the collection was started, a permanent home was found, and for the first time the animals were provided with heating for the winter months. But World War I took a heavy toll and, by 1919 when Lenin signed a decree nationalising the zoos, they were all very run-down.

Kharkiv became the capital of Ukraine, and the 1920s was one of the heydays of the zoo, with annual ticket sales regularly exceeding three hundred thousand tickets. The zoo flourished as a result of animal donations from Hamburg Zoo, the opening of a zoo museum, and numerous exhibitions. The zoo exhibited the living animals and the museum exhibited the dead, preserved animals. Together they increased awareness among the proletariat about nature, man's place in it, and, importantly, they also offered insights into the opportunities for improved agriculture and animal husbandry. Together they formed part of a continuum where the main beneficiaries were seen as both science and education.

The Zoo as a Symbol of Hope

On the afternoon of Sunday, June 22, 1941, visitors heard over the zoo's loudspeaker system that war had been announced. The city mobilised quickly and when men left their jobs at the zoo to join the army, women replaced them. Initially there was no threat of occupation, but as the months passed and the Germans advanced, it became inevitable. As the Red Army prepared to leave the city, pits were dug and food supplies were buried for the animals. The Director of the zoo agreed to remain in the city in order to try to save the animals.

Under the occupation, and through the winter of 1941, the city's population suffered greatly and many animals starved. The following year brought some fresh food supplies, and despite the difficulties, the zoo remained open to the public. Tickets and information booklets were issued in both the German and Russian languages and contemporary records show that a quarter of a million tickets were sold in 1942 and that the zoo made a small profit.

But the attendance and financial figures hide the terrible suffering of Kharkiv; the city was occupied by the German Army three times and was recaptured each time. Residents witnessed heavy bombing in 1943, and German aerial photographs taken at that time show that the city centre and zoo were badly damaged. More than 180,000 Soviets died in the defence of the city.

During their final withdrawal, the Germans routed what remained of the city and destroyed decades of records concerning the city administration and all the zoo records, which included information about the animals' upkeep, diet, medical records, autopsies, and research materials.

On the fifth day of liberation of the city on August 28, 1943, the Executive Committee of the Board of Directors of the zoo announced they would open the following day. The site was cleared of debris and an inventory of animals was prepared.

A report listed the animals that had been killed. It included lions, 9; wild dogs, 6; polar bear, 1; brown bears, 2; elephants, 2; leopard, 1; tiger, 1; monkeys, 26; pigs, 12; crocodiles, 5; zebra, 1; camels, 4; antelope, 1; llama, 1; reindeer, 17; buffalo, 3; donkeys, 2; eagles, 2; horses, 22; wild ducks and geese, 567; plus others.

No doubt many of the animals were killed for food; survivors of the war confirmed that they wouldn't have lived without elephant meat. Starting from one hundred and fifteen animal species at the start of the war, the roll call of animal species that survived is brief: bears, 4; monkeys, 5; and wolf, 1.

Some of those that survived had escaped from the zoo. The Macaque monkeys, for example, escaped from their cage and hid in a nearby building. Police cornered one of the animals and shot it, but the others escaped and found refuge in the attic of a residential house where it's believed they spent the winter. The following year when the Red Army liberated the city, they were caught and returned to the zoo.

Sergei narrated the history with little emotion, and then carefully folded the documents he had shown me and put them back into his bag. Many of the cages around were in bad condition with no signs and spartan interiors. I couldn't help but mention it.

He turned toward me, purposefully. "What you see as an animal rights issue, we see as part of our history. We survived the war and the zoo remained open. It is a symbol of our resilience, determination, and continuity with the past. To close it now would be too symbolic and an injustice to those who died. The condition of the animals may not be ideal, but neither is the condition of our society. Whilst our people suffer, particularly the elderly, we can only move at the speed that our resources allow."

I realised then that he was making the point that the zoo is a place that allows us to review aspects of our history, identity, uniqueness, and role.

"Look at what happened to Belgrade Zoo, to Kabul Zoo, to Kuwait Zoo, and most recently, to Baghdad Zoo."

He was referring to the NATO air strikes on Belgrade, the heavy toll of civil war in Afghanistan, the killing spree by Hussein's soldiers in Kuwait Zoo, and to the looting of zoo animals during the coalition attack on Baghdad.

"None of these zoos was in a good condition. The do-gooders had an ideal opportunity to close them down. But no, they gave limited aid to make them workable. They're all still working and no doubt the conditions are lamentable. The point is," he added as he stabbed his finger in the air, "the zoo is a strong symbol of hope."

We rounded a corner then, coming within sight of the elephant house whose occupiers had provided sustenance to Kharkiv's starving citizens, Sergei's conversation turned to the challenge of funding the zoo.

"With the fall of the Soviet Union, the maintenance of green spaces including the zoo stopped, and so they deteriorated. The state institution that provided us with cheaply sourced animals is located in Russia, and they stopped offering animals to Ukraine. Slowly, money is once again being spent on the parks."

I understood that a challenge for the local authorities is how to balance competing priorities.

"Our politicians have widely different views as to how to view our cultural history," Sergei continued. "For example, what architecture should be protected and what should be demolished? I hear that Kyiv Zoo is under pressure to relocate outside the city to Vyshgorod because property speculators want to build a new supermarket and elite residences on the site. The challenge of the post-Soviet period is that values collide."

It was clear from his expression that Sergei's own values were biased to the old ways.

"Government funding is barely enough to pay the staff wages," he said. "Hay and cereals are about the only animal food that is in abundance. Every staff member brings apples or berries from home for the animals. At times of difficulty, particularly during a hard winter when temperatures can fall to below -20° Celsius, the zoo borrows money and pays it back however it can."

Donations and sponsorship are increasingly important. A few years ago the local people came together to buy an elephant when the old one died. Perhaps there is a lingering sense of gratitude to the species. The elephant, Tandi, could be seen in the distance pacing his enclosure with a companion, Aung Naing, recently arrived from Emmen Zoo. The keeper was forking forage into a high-level food hopper.

Limonov: A Young Scoundrel

We turned a corner and headed up a gentle slope towards the camel enclosure. It looked empty and barren but I caught a glimpse of activity inside and, as we approached closer, a strong smell.

I was reminded of the book, *The Young Scoundrel*, by Eduard Limonov. He was born Edward Savenko, but one of his best friends nicknamed him "Limonov" (which means "Lemon") because of the yellowish parlour of his skin.

Eduard Limonov is the bad-boy of Ukrainian modern literature whose memoir trilogy, *Ours Was A Great Epoch*, documents his real life transformation from an adolescent hooligan to a bohemian writer in the city of Kharkiv in the 1960s. His second book, *A Young Scoundrel*, is a story of his fight against the odds, against the system, even against his friends. It's angry, it's disrespectful, and he is a writer the Soviets tried hard to repress. Nowadays, 65-year-old Limonov heads up the banned National Bolshevik Party of Russia.

Limonov and his friends, referred to in his books as the "SS unit," spend a lot of time in their playground, Kharkiv Zoo, which they broke into at their pleasure. On one occasion two of the gang decide to ride the camels. Limonov describes it, thus:

> Fima and Lyonka, with the help of their 'SS' unit, managed to herd the camels against the massive fence of black iron, and from there Fima, and then Lyonka, too, had managed to belly-flop onto the bald, discoloured backs of the beasts. The lunatic Lyonka had quickly failed. The former sergeant jumped, screaming, from the fence — but the beast shied, and Lyonka landed on the gravel which, in the minds of the Kharkiv zoologists, represented the surface of the camel's native desert.[1]

The book describes how Lyonka manages to climb onto his one-hump camel, but the animal tries to scrape him off against the metal railings:

> "Lyonchik, the camel doesn't want you! Get off, or he'll chew you up!"
>
> "No fucking way! I'm a man and he's a beast! Man is the crown of creation! He must submit!"
>
> The camel suddenly falls on its front feet and onto its side. Not expecting such a devious move, Lyonka flies off the beast, hands extended, and slams into the gravel.

Lysenko and the Manipulation of Science

By now we had reached the hippo enclosure where we decided to head for the cafe located adjacent to it.

"Did Lysenko have any affect on the zoo?" I queried as we took our coffee and sat outside.

"Very much so. He had a profound effect and numerous Kharkiv institutions lost good people. It was an enormous task to catch up with the West. We had no cadre of experienced teachers, no books, no research knowledge. The position was just recovering when I started to study and so I lived through exciting times."

Lysenko's name had come up in a number of discussions I had had in Kharkiv, largely because the city has a strong reputation for science education. I was already aware of the man and his actions.

Limonov's phrase, "Man is the crown of creation," is a slogan that played well in the Soviet Union, the first country with a government policy and large scale public support for science. Indeed, it was through science (and technology) that it hoped to win the race with Western capitalism. It is surprising, therefore, that one man, Trofim Lysenko, who promoted a mixture of legitimate and bogus science that got out of hand, oversaw the destruction of classical genetics and created what some call the biggest scandal of twentieth century science.

For forty years Lysenko suppressed the development of the science of genetics and hundreds of dissenting scientists were murdered or imprisoned. Under Lysenko, science was used to show what the State wanted it to show and was guided by ideology rather than by theory and experimentation. Today, his experimentation is largely viewed as fraudulent.

Lysenko came from a peasant family that lived near to the city of Poltava. He graduated from the Kyiv Agricultural Institute in 1925 and rose to prominence when the Soviet newspaper, *Pravda,* reported (with some sensation) that he had grown a winter crop of peas.

The discovery became known as "vernalisation," a technique that allowed winter crops to be obtained from summer planting by soaking and chilling the germinated seed for a fixed period of time. In 1930, following several bouts of famine, the Ukrainian Commissariat of Agriculture ordered extensive use of the technique in the hope of raising productivity.

Lysenko's humble peasant background suited the authorities who wanted to elevate common people in the Soviet hierarchy, and he was seen as someone who could motivate peasants to return to farming, following the unpopular collectivisation reforms. He was viewed as a popular "barefoot biologist," finding practical solutions and supporting socialist construction at a time when other geneticists were busy speculating about the brain size of chimpanzees. This found resonance with Stalin, and in 1929 he made a famous speech praising application and practice and denouncing those who merely theorised.

Lysenko experimented with changing the environmental conditions of crops in order to "teach" them to accept a new growth pattern, and this led him to believe that he could control crop development. He appalled many scientists by espousing the idea that, "In order to obtain a certain result, you must want to obtain precisely that result; if you want to obtain a certain result, you will obtain it."[2]

During his experiments he invariably used small samples and failed to use control groups, often reporting only his successes. So, it was just a small step for him to develop a full-blown — but ultimately grossly misguided — evolutionary theory that rejected the existence of genes.

Lysenko's philosophy was based on the work of Lamark and Michurin. He believed that evolution occurs because organisms can inherit characteristics that have been acquired through learning by their ancestors. So, for example, a giraffe can have a longer neck if it learns or wants to stretch higher for food in a tree. The idea that wilfulness could be applied to nature was appealing to those who stressed that Soviet man could transform the world in whatever way he chose to do so, but the philosophy was at odds with that of Mendel and Darwin. In natural selection, Darwin argues that animals cannot "will" themselves to evolve; they either have genes that help them survive or they do not. Similarly, those who survive are not cleverer or superior; they survive because they are fit to survive.

The complete dismissal of the ideas of Mendel and Darwin was a hard pill for many scientists to swallow, and, through the 1930s and early 1940s, many Soviet scientists did not easily kow-tow to Lysenko. The verbal fighting was bitter and no amount of conferences could reconcile the increasingly polarised viewpoints of the Lysenkoists and the Mendelian geneticists.

One of the most outspoken critics of Lysenko was Nikolai Vavilov. He had lost his position as President of the Lenin Academy of Agricultural Sciences, but he continued to challenge Lysenko. Vavilov was arrested in 1941, stood trial, and was found guilty of "sabotage in agriculture" and spying for England. He died in prison of malnutrition two years later, a fate he shared with hundreds of other scientists.

By 1940, Lysenko was Director of the Institute of Genetics within the USSR's Academy of Sciences and, following a speech he made in 1948, all scientific dissent from his theories was formally outlawed and supporters were declared "enemies of the people." Their books were removed from library shelves, texts were changed, institutions were closed and scientific journals ceased to be published. Stalin had read Lysenko's speech beforehand, giving it his support and annotating each page with his own thoughts. Thereafter, dissenting scientists were left with unpalatable options: confessing their errors or facing dismissal, imprisonment, and possible death. But Lysenko still did not forget those who had opposed him over the previous twenty years. According to biologist Nikolai Vorontsov, "That fall, in all universities, in all institutions, three thousand biologists lost their jobs and all possibility of research — *three thousand.*"[3]

Stalin died in 1953, but Lysenko continued in his position with the support of President Nikita Khrushchev. By 1964, a number of respected scientists such as Andrey Sakharov were speaking out openly against Lysenko, and when Khrushchev was dismissed, the Academy of Sciences removed Lysenko's immunity to criticism. The floodgates opened to a torrent of devastating critique. The abandonment of Darwin's ideas had led Soviet genetics down the wrong path for forty years.

Sergei had been pensive for a few minutes now, and he looked at me thoughtfully and said something that struck me as quite profound. "I see parallels today with the creationist movement in the United States that has prevented the teaching of Darwinian evolution in many schools. The world should read its history. The abandonment of an idea that is beyond refute will be very costly."

Smuggling Animals

The cafe was becoming busier as visitors came in for lunch; a young couple in love, a mother who appeared to be looking after friends' children as well as her own. Our drained coffee cups stood on the plastic table, but before leaving I wanted to ask Sergei about a new trend.

"I hear that rich Kharkivites are starting to keep exotic pets at home. That should be good for a vet, what do you think?"

"Yes, it's true. I don't think they have a deep knowledge of or love for the animals, just too much money and an ignorance of the needs of the animals. Their mentality is, 'they haven't attacked my children, so they are harmless'. My colleagues have treated rare birds, monkeys, crocodiles, snakes, and even wild cats which are kept as pets. I know of one family that has three lion cubs."

He informed me that on the black market a cub can be bought for two thousand dollars. But the price is rising rapidly following the introduction of a law placing restrictions on keeping wild animals at home. Animals are being stolen to order from under-resourced zoos who are either complicit in the transaction or who don't have the security systems necessary to prevent a break-in. Not so long ago a female lion cub was discovered missing from Kharkiv Zoo by two night watchmen. The lock on her cage had been sawn through. The challenge is how to implement the law because rich people simply bribe any nosy inspectors.

He picked up his coffee cup and shook out the remaining dregs.

Perhaps he sees the dregs as inspectors, I thought, as they splattered on the ground.

"I have colleagues who are vets with the customs unit in the Eastern division of Ukraine. They regularly intercept animals that are being smuggled into the country. A few years ago Kharkiv Zoo received sixteen hundred Horsfields tortoises that were intercepted whilst being smuggled on the train from Tashkent to Kharkiv. More commonly it's birds of prey or reptiles, and sometime plants such as soaproot from Tajikistan and Uzbekistan. Viper venom can cost a thousand dollars per gram, but as you can imagine, it's easy to conceal."

Whilst I pondered the uses of viper venom to anyone except a viper, Sergei continued. "Such stories don't surprise me anymore. Over the years I've seen visitors commonly ignore warning signs and fences to cavort with the animals."

As we stood up to leave he pointed to the hippo enclosure and the fetid, brown water in the pool. "Just recently a young woman jumped over the fence in order to swim with Masha, the three-ton resident. Masha was frolicking with her offspring and took offence to the intrusion. So she sat on the woman." He looked at me to gauge my reaction. "She sat on the woman — for a very long time."

We parted soon afterwards, but a month later Sergei called me. "Switch on the news," he said.

The newsman was reporting how a visitor to Kyiv Zoo clambered down into the enclosure of four adult lions. He shouted to the families watching, 'If God exists, he will save me.' Moments later a lioness went straight for the man, knocked him down, and severed his carotid artery.

"As my University lecturer used to say," Sergei recalled with resignation, "'if lions could talk, hunters wouldn't be heroes.'"

THE CHIEF DESIGNER

"Comrades," he said, "I have a plan to overtake the US in the space race. You will land on the sun."

"But Comrade Brezhnev," they protested, "we'll burn up!"

"Don't take me for a fool," he replied. "You'll land at night!"

I was socialising with friends, and the vodka was starting to loosen behaviours. We were talking about political leaders and, as so often happens, the discussion turned to jokes. Leonid Brezhnev, who was born in southern Ukraine and was General Secretary from 1964–1982, presided over a period of relative stability and the slow, sombre start of the economic decline. He is often depicted as a simple-minded buffoon with a delusion of grandeur, his dark suit enlivened by a selection of some of the one hundred and fourteen medals he received.

"Didn't you know it was compulsory for us to learn astronomy at school?" asked the student who told the joke.

"You're joking, right?" I replied with some incredulity. Astronomy seemed to be as relevant as including heraldry or organic farming in the students' curriculum. But it was true.

Odesa: City of Humour

The next day my head was spinning like a Sputnik, but I was sufficiently wired into the previous night's conversation to book tickets for a visit to Odesa. I'd been considering it for some time because there were other topics I wanted to research whilst in the city. I made contact with an associate of the Odesa Observatory, called Stanislav, and he agreed to talk to me about the role played by Ukrainians in the space race.

Odesa is built on a terrace fifty metres high that descends by steep crags to the Black Sea. Ancient Greeks used the port as a trading point with the hinterland, but it was only established as a city proper in 1794 by a French governor in the service of the Russian empire, and with the help of Greek and Italian settlers. As the terminus for the first railway line in Russia — built primarily for the export of wheat — the city grew quickly into Ukraine's largest city, whose streets were alive with more than a dozen languages.

According to the Encyclopaedia Britannica published in 1902:

> The general aspect of Odesa is that of a wealthy west European city. Its chief embankment, bordered by handsome houses, forms a fine promenade; a superb flight of steps descends to the sea from its central square, which is adorned with a statue of Richelieu. The central parts of the city have broad streets and squares, bordered with fine buildings and mansions in the Italian style, and with good shops.[1]

Though modern Odesa has seen better days, there is enough shabby chic discernable in the architecture to see its past glory, and much needed restoration provides the feel of a colourful, cosmopolitan seaport complete with promenade.

I walked down Engels Street towards Park Shevchenko where the Observatory is located, and where I had agreed to meet Stanislav. Sunshine, birds singing gaily, and a view of the Black Sea held the promise of a perfect summer's day.

We exchanged greetings and strolled along the linden tree-lined path. The park was quiet at this time of morning. We started to talk about the observatory and why it had been built in the park.

"Yes, it's quite unusual to have a city centre site," Stanislav began, tugging downwards on his grey goatee beard. "It's very convenient to go to the Opera House in the early evening and then walk to the observatory to work during the night."

Perhaps he was mocking me, but Ukrainians do call Odesa "the city of humour."

Ukrainians Led Space Development

"It was all to do with the astro-climate of Odesa: clear nights, no pollution, no wind, and low rainfall. One hundred years ago this was a highly favourable location. Today, less so, but the observatory is still one of only two sites worldwide for the study of variable stars, and it has one of the largest libraries of space photographs in the world."

"Is it true that Ukrainians were important to the Soviet space development programmes?" I asked. I was only really aware of Yuri Gagarin and a mongrel dog that went into space.

"Ukrainians have dominated just about every field. The world's first exhibition dedicated to interplanetary space travel took place in Kyiv in 1925 and had as its foundation the work of Nikolai Fedorov. He is considered by many to be the father of human space flight. He was born locally and studied at the Richelieu Lyceum in Odesa. His theory of 'cosmism' was a real force in pre-revolutionary Russia."

The science fiction theme of leaving our terrestrial cradle and colonising other worlds can be directly attributed to Fedorov. He had some apparently crazy ideas — articulated more than one hundred years ago — such as shifting the world's energy base from fossil fuels to solar energy, viewing the Earth as an ecosystem that must be maintained rather than exploited, and replacing human body parts with artificial organs.

"The challenge was to put theory into practice," continued Stanislav. "And this started by Ukrainians such as Nicolai Kibalchich, who came up with the idea of using the energy of a slow-burning explosive and using multiple combustion chambers — the first step in the history of space flight — and Yuri Kondratyuk, who described the idea of using the gravitational slingshot to break away from the earth. You may know that it was this rocket flight strategy that is referred to as the 'Kondratyuk's loop,' and it was adopted by the Americans to put a man on the moon."

I was starting to understand why several Ukrainian friends have rows of science fiction books on their shelves. They really did grow up surrounded by these ideas. We sat on a bench close to the observatory. Our only companions were a group of sparrows that hopped close to our feet, perhaps expecting breakfast. Stanislav spoke with enthusiasm, switching between Russian, English, and French when a particular word or phrase seemed to dictate a change.

"Other Ukrainians provided practical solutions to the challenges of space travel. Three names really stand out as titans of the twentieth century: Sergei Korolev, Vladimir Chelomei, and Valentin Glushko. They were all like-minded in their quest to travel space, but their deep passions and rivalries were also their undoing. That's what makes it such a fascinating story."

As I was to learn, each of them had their own patrons in the Kremlin, each was imprisoned or badly treated by Stalin, and each believed in the superiority of his own ideas. What struck me as particularly noteworthy — and Stanislav emphasised keenly — was that although all three men were grossly mistreated by the system, they continued to work relentlessly for their own ambition and the Soviet ambition; rarely did the two goals deviate. It was a perfect recipe for drama, but it was a drama that unfolded in the major space cities deep in the Soviet heartland. Ukraine was just too close to the border of the Soviet Union with Europe to be the location for such a sensitive industry.

Korolev: the "Chief Designer"

"Shall we concentrate on Korolev?" Stanislav looked towards me for some sort of agreement and continued. "His name was kept secret from the citizens of the Soviet Union until his death in 1966, because the authorities and President Khruschev, in particular, were concerned that the CIA would assassinate him. As the 'Chief Designer' he delivered what is possibly Communism's greatest public triumph — putting a man in space."

He tugged his beard again — a mildly annoying affectation — but it indicated key moments in the story.

"In the end, hard work killed him, and in his honour he has a crater on the moon, a crater on Mars, and an asteroid named after him."

And I should add that a city and dozens of streets also bear his name.

"To add to the loss," he continued, "It was the USA who put the first man on the moon. But had it not been for Korolev's untimely death, and internal rivalries between him and the others, perhaps the Soviet Union would have claimed this honour.

As we strolled through the park, Stanislav narrated Korolev's story. At home there were family problems, so he grew up as a lonely boy, a sceptic, a cynic, and a pessimist who took the gloomiest view of the future. Fascinated by the military seaplanes stationed in Odesa, he joined the hydroplane squadron and had his first flying lesson. He was so driven by ambition that before the age of twenty he designed his first glider, and soon the famous aircraft designer, Andrei Tupolev, was advising his work. Indeed, it is awesome to realise that the young Korolev had planned a moon landing in detail, even before the Wright brothers took flight.

His enthusiasm fit the spirit of the age; through science the Soviet Union planned to build a communist utopia that would overpower the West. In the early 1930s, the government established a Jet Propulsion Research Institute and this brought together the three Ukrainians, Korolev, Glushko and Chelomei.

Korolev lit the fuse on the first Soviet rocket in 1933. It used liquid oxygen to burn gelled petroleum in a large casing, and though it was crude in design it established the principles that led Korolev to declare publicly, "Our rockets must now conquer space!"

A few years later a rocket-powered airplane designed by Korolev caught the attention of the Kremlin leadership. Stalin viewed such innovation with deep suspicion — particularly when he didn't appreciate the potential of the innovation — and in a ruthless purge many leading lights of Soviet rocketry were arrested on trumped-up charges of misuse of state funds. Korolev was among them, and he learned later that Glushko, a specialist in rocket propulsion (who later would be referred to as the "Father of Soviet Rockets"), had denounced him. It would result in a lifelong animosity between the two men.

Glushko, born in Odesa in 1908, was a student worker at the observatory. He spent much of his life in the shadow of Korolev and only became Chief Designer after his death. He was a man of incredible talent but also of enormous ego; after becoming an honorary citizen of Odesa he erected a statue of himself in the city.

Following his arrest, Korolev was tortured into "confessing," then sentenced to ten years' hard labour in the notorious Kolyma gulag, a surface gold mine in Siberia. He probably would have died there if not for the intervention of aircraft designer Tupolev, who asked that Korolev be transferred in order to assist him in his work.

At the end of World War II, discharged by special government decree and his prior convictions dismissed, Korolev travelled to Germany to learn about the V-2 (silent flying bomb) technology of Werner von Braun, the leading German rocket scientist of his day. Von Braun had already been transferred to the USA (where he would eventually lead the US space program), and Stalin, realising the potential of the technology, had to settle for rocket designs and plans looted in Berlin.

Korolev and Glushko were given the task to reproduce the V-2 under the guidance of Vladimir Chelomei. Working day and night in a run-down leaking factory on the outskirts of Moscow, and growing their vegetables in the factory yard, Korolev launched the rocket a year or so later.

How Sputnik Came About

With the dawn of the cold war, both America and the Soviet Union wanted rockets powerful enough to deliver the ultimate weapon.

When Khruschev came to power, he told Korolev to build a nuclear missile that could reach America, and Korolev readily agreed. A rocket capable of carrying a five-ton warhead five thousand miles, he reasoned, could also be adapted to go into space.

After several failures, Korolev demonstrated the R-7 in 1957 by firing it from a secret location in Kazakhstan to Kamchatka. In his memoirs, Khruschev recalls seeing the rocket for the first time, together with other members of the Politburo, and being in absolute awe of the beast. The R-7 was thirty-four metres long, three metres in diameter, and weighed two hundred and eighty metric tons. It had five main engines fuelled by a lethal mix of kerosene and oxygen. It was the world's first intercontinental ballistic missile.

Korolev immediately turned his attention to his real objective and asked Khrushchev for permission to launch a satellite. Once the leader was satisfied that the military programme would not be adversely affected, Khrushchev gave his go-ahead. Few at the time realised that this spur-of-the-moment decision, made in order to placate Korolev who was restricted in travel and had no public recognition, would upset the world superpower balance within a matter of months.

Neither the Soviets nor the Americans knew details of the other's progress towards achieving a space flight, so time was of the essence. Within months, Korolev had designed and personally assembled a small ball-shaped satellite — not much bigger than a baseball — with a transmitter and batteries.

On October 4, 1957, Sputnik became the first manmade object to reach orbit. Though Sputnik was not visible from Earth, the casing of the R-7 booster travelling behind it could be seen. Korolev dearly wanted the world to hear the "beep, beep, beep" of his satellite. The signal, which continued for twenty-two days, could be picked up on an ordinary radio and millions around the world tuned into it. If the irritating "beep" wasn't bad enough for the Americans, they also had to recognise that it was flying directly over North America and, thus, American sky had been violated.

We stopped by a fountain. Stanislav was elated and he groomed his beard; evidently the story was a source of pride and joy for him.

As we know now, Korolev's tiny sphere shook America's assumptions of its own superiority and sent some hard-to-believe messages. If the Soviet Union could deliver missiles to America, then winning a war with them would be practically impossible.

"Why," I asked, "was the event seen initially as not being newsworthy?"

I'd obtained a copy of *Pravda* for the day following the launch, and the news barely made it on to the front page. It was just a couple of paragraphs at the bottom of the page.

"I guess it seemed a natural progression," he answered nonchalantly. "The Soviet Union had opened the world's first nuclear power plant, the Soviet MiG fighter aircraft had set world records, and the Soviet Tupolev-104 was the most efficient airliner of its class. So Sputnik did not surprise our leadership."

The American technology and education system was not unrivalled, after all. A centrally planned economy could be a better model for delivering huge projects, and there was a risk that third-world leaders, after seeing this success, would gravitate to the Soviet model rather than the capitalist model.

"Suddenly, our leadership understood that space was good propaganda," Stanislav reasoned.

Dogs in Space

What followed were the steps needed to put a man in space. The rocket developers had taken a well-deserved holiday, but Khruschev wanted to capitalise on the propaganda. So Korolev was told to launch a second satellite within one month and in time for the fortieth Anniversary of the October Revolution. A vehicle was designed from scratch and this time it would have a pilot: a dog called Laika, the first living creature to reach space. Sputnik 2 was launched on November 3, 1957.

The story of Laika is bizarre, and I suggested to Stanislav that we go to a cafe in the park for lunch and to discuss it further. Even though the Black Sea is depleted of fish, a visit to Odesa is a rare chance to eat fresh seafood. We settled down at a table under the dappled shade of a plane tree to a meal of green borscht, grilled fish, and a bottle of Crimean red wine. The etiquette of white wine with fish means nothing in Ukraine.

It was never intended for Laika to return to earth, and the capsule was not designed for re-entry into the earth's atmosphere. But the real story of Laika's death has surfaced only recently. For more than forty years the Soviets maintained that the dog had died painlessly in space about a week after takeoff, and that she showed that space travel was safe for humans. Just recently, however, it was revealed that she died from overheating and panic about five hours after takeoff,[2] a distressing fact that would not have been overlooked by Yuri Gargarin as he prepared for his own flight.

More has been written about Laika than about most of the Soviet cosmonauts who died during the early missions. Probably because she is the first creature knowingly sent into space to die and her death sparked animal right's debates across the planet. Her coffin circled the earth 2,570 times before burning up in the earth's atmosphere.

"What do you make of the news about how Laika died," I quizzed, as Stanislav brushed the napkin across his precious beard.

"We were jubilant about Laika. It sent the message, 'next will be a man,' and though Soviets were prisoners on earth, we knew someone would soon escape." He paused. "But you have to realise we knew nothing of what was going on in the outside world. The authorities lied to us about the way the dog died, but we had no way to check the facts. Believing falsehoods was part of our life."

"So, perhaps it didn't really happen. I'm sure you know the stories of space travel and the moon landings being faked," I challenged.

As a fork full of fish moved towards Stanislav's mouth, a broad smile appeared. "Nonsense," he responded somewhat playfully, "If they'd told us it was a male dog, then it would have been a lie."

The comment was lost on me; though I smiled at his rely, taking my cue from his expression. Only later did I learn that a female dog was chosen because of the limitations of the suit design: female dogs do not have to stand and lift a leg to urinate.

He continued. "Shortly after Sputnik 2 a cigarette manufacturer sold the 'Laika' brand. Every time I lit one, I envisaged the capsule burning up on re-entry. The Soviet Union was full of distasteful things which we often overcame with humour."

The Space Race

After the Soviet Union had put a dog in space, it was clear that they were leading up to a manned programme and that they were going to carry it out as soon as they could. Now that the Soviets had cured their inferiority complex and the Americans had lost their superiority complex, there was an opportunity for both of them to find common ground in order to avoid mutually assured self-destruction.

I mentioned to Stanislav that the Nobel Committee had wanted to award a prize to the Sputnik's Chief Designer. According to Khrushchev's son,[3] it was not the secrecy surrounding Korolev's name that was the problem but the rivalry between the competing Soviet developers. Khruschev believed that if Korolev won the prize, Glushko and Chelomei, who were working on rival projects, would refuse to work with him. As they saw it, putting a man into space was not going to defend the motherland from attack. Khrushchev replied to the Nobel committee that all the Soviet people had distinguished themselves and the prize should be awarded to the Soviet Union, but in the end the prize went elsewhere.

By 1960, Korolev's Luna 2 had impacted the surface of the moon, Luna 3 had sent to earth the first ever photographs of the far side of the moon, and the Soviets had sent the first probes to Mars and to Venus.

The midday sun was encouraging more and more people to seek the shade of the cafe's awning. We ordered coffee — usually served strong and black in Odesa — and Stanislav took up the story of Yuri Gagarin.

"The main objective was to put a man in space and preparations were underway. We started using dummies instead of astronauts, and it was agreed that when two successful launches and landings had been achieved, a man would be used. Korolev was adamant that the flight should be automatic with no astronaut intervention whatsoever. He was insistent that the flight manual for the pilot would only say, 'Put on suit, check communications, and observe functioning of the spacecraft.'"

We both smiled. How times have changed.

"On April 12, 1961, Yuri Gagarin, one of six astronauts that had been trained, sat on top of a modified missile ready for launch from Baikonur Cosmodrome. In his pocket was a sealed envelope containing the combination code in case he needed to assume control of the ship; otherwise everything would be automatic. Three press releases were prepared, one for success and two for failures. Gagarin circled the earth once, and after re-entry he ejected at seven kilometres and descended using his own parachute."

According to some reports, Gagarin landed in a field near the village of Smelovaka in Russia. Wearing a bright orange suit, he was seen descending by two farm workers who were convinced Gagarin had arrived from outer space.[4]

"It may be true," Stanislav said. "There was jubilation across the Soviet Union. The streets were filled with people, on balconies, on rooftops, and there were flags everywhere. We joked that it was easier to become a cosmonaut and to visit the stars than to become a tourist and to leave the Soviet Union."

"The US Congress was up in arms," he continued, "They realised there was only one space race left — to put a man on the moon — and so Korolev capitalised on the Americans' determination to obtain even greater funds for his work."

According to what I had read, this served only to increase tension with the military. Khruschev summoned the Soviet leadership to his private dacha for a decision on whether to fund a moon programme at the expense of the military programme. But the generals could offer nothing to match the glory that Korolev's space program had already achieved for Communism, and a lunar program was approved. As it turned out, Gagarin's flight was, perhaps, the last great achievement of the Soviet Union.

From American scientific journals, Korolev knew that the American programme to put a man on the moon had won decisive backing in Congress, and that they now faced the full might of America's military industrial complex. Before landing on the moon they needed first to perfect the technology of the space walk, and Korolev designed an airlock and set about testing it with the astronauts. Alexei Leonov, who was eventually chosen to make the first walk in space, remembered that Korolev referred to the trainees as his "Little Eagles," and recalled Korolev's instruction to him that "A sailor on a ship must be able to swim, and so a cosmonaut aboard a spacecraft must be able to swim in space."

On this most dangerous mission to date, Korolev wished Leonov "a fair solar wind," and the Voskhod 2 was launched in March 1965, and Leonov performed the world's first space walk.

Stanislav provided some little known details. "The return was dogged by problems. After ten minutes outside the spacecraft, Leonov found he could not reenter the airlock due to the stiffness of the spacesuit, and he had to bleed air from the suit in order to get into the airlock. On re-entry, a rocket failed to fire, the service module failed to separate properly from the rocket, and the module landed in snow in a heavy forest. It was two days before soldiers cut a clearing for a helicopter, and Leonov had to ski to the clearing!"

It very nearly ended in disaster and, according to Stanislav, Korolev probably now realised that the space race was lost, if he had not thought so sooner.

Rivalry with the military was causing delays and risking lives and the pressure he faced was huge. His job responsibilities, if you were to equate them to US comparators, included five major aerospace companies, several NASA centres, and all the university research centres.

Information sources disagree on when and why Korolev entered hospital, but according to Stanislav, he entered for a routine operation some time during the second week of January 1960. He was diagnosed with a more serious ailment thought to be a cancerous tumour in his gut. The Minister of Health performed Korolev's surgery personally, even though this was not his speciality, but Korolev died after five hours on the operating table. (Glushko — Korolev's rival for the post of Chief Designer — reported that Korolev actually died due to a poorly performed operation for haemorrhoids.)

The day after his death, Korolev's name was declassified, and despite the appalling winter weather, thousands of people came to his funeral and to see his burial in the Kremlin wall. In a twist of fate, only after his death did he receive the recognition he'd craved, and Khruschev, though no longer in power, spoke kindly of him by saying, "Columbus opened the new world to everybody, and though Spain declined as a superpower and nobody remembers the Spanish kings, everyone still remembers Columbus."

Stanislav looked pensively at me and raised his eyes. "The Kremlin was always prepared. Within two days of Korolev's death they published his life biography."

As if shamed into action, the Kremlin now demanded an accelerated launch plan, but without Korolev's coordination ability the programme was ill prepared. During the next test flight the cosmonaut died, and then the N-1 rocket that would go to the moon exploded during a practice takeoff. Seventeen days later, in July 1969, Neil Armstrong stepped onto the moon and planted the American flag.

One Last Effort

Replete with good fresh food, we left the park and followed the grid-like boulevard to the famous Potemkin Steps. Unlike other Ukrainian cities that predominantly exhibit muted colours and shuffling citizens, Odesa's streets are lively and boisterous in a way that conveys nonconformity and self-confidence. Beneath the peeling paint, the old multiethnic identity is beginning to reassert itself. Odesa is the non-Soviet city that other Soviets dreamt about.

The stairs were named after Grigori Potemkin, a lover of Catherine II and the leader of the Crimean military campaign who is perhaps best known for his attempts to fool others into believing that the sparsely populated lands of southern Ukraine where well populated. He did this by erecting facades of village buildings (so called "Potemkin villages"), which when viewed from a distance appeared as physical buildings.

En route, Stanislav drew Korolev's story to a close by describing the last big Soviet effort in the space race which came in the 1970s.

"The Soviet authorities knew that a space shuttle wasn't a cost effective idea and yet the Americans persevered with it." Giving me a quizzical look, he said, "It was only when the Kremlin realised that a US shuttle, launched from Vandenberg military airbase, overflew supposedly top-secret Soviet military sites just four minutes after launch, that they realised the US had multiple motives for the development."

I learned later that a submarine-launched cruise missile took ten minutes to reach the USSR and the extra minutes saved could prove crucial if events went "nuclear."

"So in the 1970s the Soviet Buran programme was devised as a counter-threat. The leader of the program was Gleb Lozino-Lozimsky, another of the Ukrainian scientists. Like Korolev, his name was also kept secret; this time until 1999."

"It sounds just like the James Bond movie, *Moonraker*, I commented, purposefully leading Stanislav towards a new conversation topic.

"Yes, in the film the American space shuttle is shown piggy-backing a Boeing 747 and, in an echo of that scene, the Soviet Buran was flown to the Paris Air Show sitting on top of an Antonov Mryia."

The films of James Bond, Ian Fleming's fictional British secret service spy, are very popular in the former Soviet Union, first beginning to appear during Perestroika. *Moonraker* was one of the first to be shown, and in the absence of official news about the cold war they have influenced the views of many Eastern Europeans.

"Perhaps you'll be surprised to learn that the inspiration for the character of Bond was a Ukrainian," I said. Stanislav was noticeably surprised, as evinced by multiple tugs of his beard. "Well it's true. He was an Odesan man called Georgi Rosenblum. Let me return an honour and tell you his story."

I'd spent the previous day trying to trace the Rosenblum's roots.

The Man Who Was James Bond

Whilst Fleming was an Intelligence Officer in the Royal Navy, he confided to some colleagues that he wanted to create a fictional spy character. The former diplomat, Robert Bruce Lockhart, had regaled Fleming with the real life stories of a British spy he had worked with during the Russian Civil War, and Fleming used this material to create the character of James Bond.[5]

Rosenblum was born in Odesa in 1874, and as a young man he had a talent for languages, eventually speaking seven languages fluently. Whilst still in his teens he was arrested for espionage and jailed, but on his release he learnt his mother had died, and his uncle told him that he was the result of an adulterous affair between his mother and a Jewish doctor. This was unwelcome news. The young Rosenblum had strong anti-Semitic beliefs so he left Ukraine in search of a new life.

He took a boat to Brazil, and through a fortuitous event he saved the lives of a group of people who were attacked by locals. Amongst them was a British spy who rewarded Rosenblum with help in obtaining a British passport. In England, Rosenblum took the name of Sidney Reilly (hence the phrase "the life of Reilly"), and he began a life of criminal activity, audacious scams, and serial bigamy. He killed the husband of the woman who would become his first wife and even impersonated the doctor who signed the woman's death certificate. Devious, ruthless, and self-serving, he was also known to be a charming and charismatic character, just like James Bond.

Although Reilly claimed to have worked for the British Secret Service from the mid-1890s, according to their records he became an "official" agent only in 1918 and he was dismissed three years later. Over these years his exploits are remarkable. They include passing Russian defence documents to the Japanese during the 1905 war, impersonating a German officer whilst attending a meeting of the German High Command, bluffing his way onto Rothschild's yacht disguised as a priest, and seducing the wife of a Russian Minister to find out about German weapons shipments.

His Russian contacts, in particular, made him valuable to the British Secret Service, which sent him to work undercover with Lockhart to kill Lenin and to destabilise the Bolsheviks. But the Bolsheviks' security force — The Cheka — infiltrated the plot and Reilly was forced to flee, disguised as a German art dealer. In his absence, he was sentenced to death and two of his mistresses were sent to Butyrka Prison in Moscow.

According to Andrew Cook, Reilly was tricked into returning to Moscow a few years later.[6] He was captured as he crossed the Finish border and taken to Lubyanka Prison for interrogation. Boris Godz, the Colonel who organised Reilly's capture, provided Cook with a firsthand account of Reilly's execution which was ordered by Stalin in November 1925. Reilly was taken to Sokolniki woods, ostensibly for exercise, and he was shot in the head with a pistol. British intelligence documents released recently confirm this.

Leaving Odesa

Following a gentle stroll along leafy boulevards and across fountain-splashed squares, Stanislav and I arrived at the top of the Potemkin Steps; obviously practical, but also an extravagance and an illusion. From the top, the pedestrian sees only the platforms that separate each grouping of steps, whereas from below he sees only the steps. At the bottom they are nearly twice as wide as at the top — playing with the perspective — making them much appear much longer when viewed from the bottom than from the top. There — at the top —

stands a statue of the Duc de Richelieu, looking like a Roman in a toga, greeting visitors or wishing them well on their departure.

"What do you think of the recent space program?" I asked, drawing our interesting conversation to a close.

"The moon has not been stepped on for twenty-six years," Stanislav lamented. "It has been shunned like a holiday destination that one abandons in place of somewhere more lively, and the US space shuttle is a lumbering bus that has stifled innovation. Chapter one — the Sputnik and the Shuttle — was about world domination, not science. But perhaps chapter two will be collaborative and science will come first, in much the way that Nikolai Fedorov envisaged."

PRESIDENTS AND THE PEOPLE

HUNDREDS OF THOUSANDS OF PEOPLE have died in the name of Ukrainian independence, but when liberation came it was with a whimper rather than a bang. The likes of Taras Shevchenko and Stepan Bandera, who called for revolution, were not heeded; there was no revolution, and there were no revolutionaries. In the end, Communism was lost by Communists.

Following the abortive coup by Communists in Moscow to reestablish control in August 1991, many of Ukraine's two million Communist Party members feared reprisals, and so they joined the nationalists in their call for independence. Many people in eastern Ukraine, who realised that for decades their resources of coal, iron ore, and other materials had been misappropriated by Moscow, also saw it as a way to end Russia's "free lunch." So, in the December referendum, 90 percent of Ukrainians voted for independence; a surprisingly high majority given that we now know just how fractious is the Ukrainian electorate. At the same time Leonid Kravchuk was elected Ukraine's first president.

Leonid Kravchuk, third in command in the Soviet Ukrainian leadership, waited until it was clear from events in Moscow that the old regime was history. Then he tore up his Communist Party membership card and made a bid for power.

The martyrs of Ukraine may well have turned in their graves. Neither Kravchuk nor his cohorts were heroes of the people, and none had demonstrated loyalty to the idea of Ukraine as a nation above that of their own personal enrichment or support of the Soviet ideals. Kravchuk's qualities were as a shrewd, cunning, and compromising character who sought to balance the reformists, led principally by the Rukh Party, the Communists, and conservatives. In short, it is hard to argue that Ukraine's leadership had the emergent nation's development as its top priority.

The rest of the world was also ill-prepared to understand this newly independent country on the eastern border of Europe. There were Sovietologists, Kremlinologists, and Imperial Russian specialists, but no Ukrainologists. Almost nobody supporting Western governments could speak the language. Major world libraries had sections for works from Eastern Europe, Russia, and the Soviet Union, but virtually none of them had a section dedicated for works concerning Ukraine.

Ignorance and misinformation were widespread, and to some extent continue to be so. During a visit to Kyiv in 1990, Margaret Thatcher told Ukrainians that she had no wish to see the disintegration of the Soviet Union, and that Ukraine was no more separate than the state of California.[1] The following year, US President George W. Bush cautioned Ukraine against "suicidal nationalism" in what came to be dubbed his "Chicken Kyiv" speech.[2] This was widely interpreted to mean that Ukraine should not separate from Russia.

Transition without Violence

To Ukraine's credit, the transition from Communism was managed without the violence that has been a characteristic of other former Soviet states. Numerous challenges could have provided the tinder for a conflagration, but the Ukrainian skills of compromise, dogged determination, and expedient inaction enabled them to muddle through. As examples, more than a million Soviet troops were stationed in Ukraine, but they were reassigned without major incident, and though Ukraine inherited the world's third largest nuclear arsenal of more than five thousand nuclear weapons, it became the first country in the world to give them up.

The greatest source of conflagration was Crimea, which is so central to Russian Imperial history and Soviet history. As the home to a majority of ethnic Russians and to the Black Sea fleet, citizens voted to break away from Ukraine in 1991, but rescinded the declaration of independence two weeks later. As well as quarrels over the division of the fleet of eight hundred ships, there was the important question of access to the deep water naval base at Sevastopol. Kravchuk laid the groundwork for the sharing agreement, which gave Russia the right to use the site until 2017, but it was left to his successor to sign the agreement.

One of the reasons behind the Russia-Georgian war in late 2008 may have been to gain access to Sukhumi, the Black Sea capital of the disputed territory of Abkhazia in Georgia. Though it is a far less ideal port than Sevastopol, it is clear that a resurgent Russia will have limited credibility without a Black Sea port to call its own.

Emblems of State and Institutions of Democracy

Kravchuk's other main preoccupation was the installation of the emblems of state and building the institutions of democracy. Throughout Soviet times it was forbidden to fly the yellow and blue national flag without it being accompanied by the flag of the Soviet Ukraine, but in April 1990 it flew alone in the city of Ternopil.

In pre-Christian times, the colours yellow and blue were considered symbolic of fire and water, respectively, and they were used by the cities and principalities of Kyivan Rus. The painting, *Reply of the Zaporozhian Cossacks* by Ilya Repin, which depicts an event in 1686, also shows the yellow and blue banding of a Cossack flag. In the mid-nineteenth century the colours were inverted so that the top band was blue and the bottom band was yellow. This was largely done for aesthetic reasons, but it has erroneously given rise to the view that the flag depicts yellow wheat growing beneath a blue sky.

As a faithful son of the communist system, it must have been difficult for Kravchuk to fully embrace the idea of a division of power between the executive, legislative, and judicial branches, or to the concept of elections. Why a powerful person would base his livelihood on the outcome of an unpredictable event, such as an election, is an anathema to many Ukrainians who have grown up in a system where having power means shaping the outcome of events to your advantage. But pushed by those in Ukraine who genuinely wanted a democratic system, and pulled by the lure of the European or American aid donations, Kravchuk did create the institutions of democracy. In reality, however, they had more form than function.

Quite reasonably, ordinary Ukrainians expected some sort of transition for the better during those early years of independence. But they mattered very little to the elite, and though there was transition, it was not for the better. The Chornobyl disaster weighed heavily on the national budget, and those large enterprises that struggled on were mostly military-orientated, energy-intensive, environmentally polluting juggernauts of a lost era. Price liberalization took its toll. Energy prices that had been artificially set at kopeks in Soviet times increased more than a hundred-fold, and food subsidies, which had accounted for more than one-fifth of the state budget of the Soviet Union, were removed. Most experts suggest the resulting inflation was unavoidable, but its magnitude was overwhelming. Ukraine's inflation rate recorded the world record high of 10,000 percent annually in 1993 (perhaps exceeded by Zimbabwe in 2008), and gross domestic product was 60 percent below the 1991 level. In this European country, three in four people lived below the poverty line.

Kravchuk had achieved much, but his failure to address the economic plight of the electorate (and the mounting evidence that he had his own hands in the till),[3] led to his being ousted in the elections of 1994 and replaced by Leonid Kuchma. The "Donbas Mafia" was now in decline, and the "Dnipropetrovsk Mafia" was in the ascendant.

A Currency and a Constitution

By most accounts Kuchma started off reasonably well. He brought into positions of influence some of his friends from Dnipropetrovsk, but others did not change, including Viktor Yushchenko, who was head of the National Bank. Having used the coinage of intruders for a millennium — the grosh of Poland and Lithuania, the thalers, ducats, and florins of their western neighbours, and since the eighteenth century, the Russian rouble — it was his responsibility to reintroduce the currency of Kyivan Rus, the hryvnia (pronounced grivna).

As it happened, all the former Soviet states introduced a new national currency much sooner than Ukraine, where a lack of local expertise combined with the obfuscation of politicians caused significant delay. With inflation raging, but without the power to print roubles (which was the prerogative of Moscow), Ukraine was forced to adopt a transition currency called the coupon-karbovanets, a sort of monopoly money that bore the brunt of the budget deficit, hyperinflation, and currency devaluation. By the mid-1990s when one million coupon-karbovanets was worth approximately four dollars, Ukraine could rightly say that every citizen was a millionaire.

"I knew I was rich," remarked one friend. "I would reach across to the gas stove, light a coupon and use it to light my cigarette."

In 1996, the same year the hryvnia was introduced, Kuchma pushed through a new constitution that defined the parliamentary democracy and delineated the powers of the executive and legislative branches of government. As with the currency issue, Ukraine was the last former Soviet state to introduce a constitution, but the result did not reflect long wait; it was a dog's breakfast. Epoch making, perhaps, but the ambiguities contained in it continue to plague Ukrainian politics today. No doubt many welcomed it, however. An ambiguous constitution, combined with laws which overlap, duplicate, or fail to address important issues, allowed the new class to continue to take possession of the public wealth.

Kuchma and Lazarenko

Before long, Kuchma was corrupted by power. Having initially resisted privatization (because the elite thought it would mean the end of government subsidies), Kuchma and the oligarchs came to embrace it when they realised that therein lay the path to even greater riches. By defining property rights and the concept of ownership (as distinct from control), the new Constitution opened up the gamut of property and credit-related scams.

The most conspicuous "innovation" has been the foreign currency bank loan, whereby just about anyone has been able to go to a bank with either real or falsified documents and take out a loan denominated in US Dollars, Swiss Francs, or Euros. But borrowers now face a "double whammy" in that the global recession has devalued the hryvnia, making it more expensive to pay the interest, or repay the loan. In addition, the asset guaranteeing the loan, such as a business, house, or salary, has fallen substantially in value. Ukrainians are belatedly coming to understand foreign exchange risks.

One of the people who helped me to understand the politics of recent years was Konstantin, who worked at a Jewish NGO and was also a part-time journalist. He was a rotund, flabby-faced man whose thick, circular spectacles gave him the appearance of an owl. I met him through his wife, who had a second job selling catalogue products door-to-door. Items such as Avon products (cosmetics), Tupperware (kitchen items), homeopathic remedies, and book clubs nowadays enjoy the high popularity that they did forty years ago in Western Europe and America.

They lived in a single room of a large apartment, and shared the kitchen and bathroom facilities with three other families. Such "Kommunalkas" (as they are known) were a common living arrangement during Soviet times and served to remove the "bourgeoisie" from their large apartments. Coincidentally, they were an ideal solution to accommodate the rapidly growing urban population and supplied the authorities with an enormous network of informants who were motivated by envy, distrust, or simple dislike for their close neighbours. Needless to say, they were saving hard to buy their own apartment.

"I guess the Rockefellers and Carnegies were no angels, but Kuchma reached the height of cronyism," Konstantin reflected. We sat at a wooden table adjacent to the window in their room. His bulk seemingly blocked out much of the light and the flower-patterned wallpaper made the room seem oppressively small.

"Give me some examples," I prompted him.

"The most scandalous was probably the Pavlo Lazarenko affair. As Kuchma's Prime Minister, he orchestrated numerous scams including the award of natural gas contracts to a company called United Energy Systems, which was headed at the time by Yulia Tymoshenko." He paused before filling me in on the details of the complex company structure. "The company used public money to pay for low-priced gas from the Russian gas giant, Gazprom that was then sold either in Ukraine or internationally at higher prices. The sales receipts never found their way back to the public purse, but were siphoned off by Lazarenko and his coterie. Incidentally," he added as an after thought, "if you think that gas disputes between Ukraine and Russia are new, it's not true. The squabbles are at least fifteen years old."

In 2006, Lazarenko was sentenced to nine years in prison by a court in the USA on charges of laundering at least US$114 million of his illegally obtained fortune, estimated at more than one billion dollars, through banks in the United States.[4] He had been apprehended while entering the USA on a false Panamanian passport, en route to a California mansion he had bought from film star, Eddie Murphy.

"Kuchma stopped supporting Lazarenko, the relationship soured, and mutual recriminations followed," Konstantin continued. "Lazarenko was accused of hiring two contract killers, both of whom died mysteriously. Not long after, taped evidence dubbed 'Kuchmagate' emerged, which linked Kuchma and his Minister of Internal Affairs, Yurii Kravchenko, to the beheading of a popular journalist, Georgiy Gongadze. Later Kravchenko was found dead at his summer house with two gunshots to the head, and a brief suicide note was found next to his body."

"How did he shoot himself twice in the head, at close range?" I asked, showing an incredulous expression.

"Didn't you know? It's something Ukrainians excel at." He hardly paused. "Ukrainian politics had become a political circus. Kuchma put self preservation above everything else. When the Military accidentally shot down a civilian airliner carrying eighty passengers, he initially called claims of Ukrainian involvement as 'groundless,' and later had the gall to say, 'We should not make a tragedy out of matters if it was a mistake. Bigger mistakes have been made.'"

Konstantin feigned exasperation and laughed, beseeching his wife, "Where did I leave my gun?" Over the next few hours, he explained the politics of the last decade.

With the position of prime minister vacant, Kuchma offered the post to Viktor Yushchenko, and asked Yulia Tymoshenko to be his deputy. The partnership was effective, but short lived. By reforming taxes, making the privatizations more transparent, and by reforming the energy space, they improved Ukraine's economy and paid all the salary and pension arrears. Though these changes heralded eight years of economic growth and proved popular with citizens, the duo was ousted within two years by disgruntled oligarchs who objected to their anti-corruption efforts. According to Konstantin, the Orange Revolution of late-2004 was probably the most politically significant event in Eastern Europe since the fall of the Berlin Wall, and it was all made possible by these dismissals.

The Orange Revolution

In opposition, Yushchenko and Tymoshenko proved far more destructive to Kuchma than in alliance. Though as personalities they were like chalk and cheese — Yushchenko, the articulate diplomat willing to compromise, and Tymoshenko, the determined, passionate popularist — they found sufficient common ground on which to work together.

Incidentally, the colour orange has no particular significance for Ukraine, and why it was chosen is not completely clear. In fact, many had expected the uprising to be called "The Chestnut Revolution" after the predominance of chestnut trees on Kyiv's leafy streets, and following the theme established by Georgia's "Rose Revolution" in 2003.

People realised that the presidential election of 2004 might, for the first time, offer a credible reformist opposition, and Kuchma (who could not stand for election) was forced to seek support from Moscow for Viktor Yanukovych, his preferred candidate and favourite of the increasingly powerful Donetsk clan. But it was an odd and a miscalculated choice. Odd in that Yanukovych appeared totally out of place next to the cultured Yushchenko. (Indeed Yanukovych made numerous simple grammatical and spelling mistakes on his application as a presidential candidate.) Miscalculated in that Yanukovych's unredeemable qualities and stance of continuity with the past meant that his mostly-Russian spin doctors could not promote him in a positive light, and had to run a dirty tricks campaign.

My discussion with Konstantin was in full swing when the telephone rang. He eased his bulk out of the chair and went to the corridor to answer it. The families also share a single phone; a source of inconvenience.

"He's out," Konstantin barked before putting down the receiver. His wife was watching a small TV on the other side of the room. In the last few years, Latin American soap operas featuring smouldering Latinos have been replaced by Ukrainian or Russian soap operas featuring cool and duplicitous Kyiv or Moscow housewives.

"All the usual tricks were employed," Konstantin continued, moving nimbly back towards his chair. "NGO offices were raided, and drugs or explosives were planted as a reason to close them down. Media outlets were closed and the others were sent 'temnyk.'"

A "temnyk" is an unsigned communication, sent each day to editors instructing them how to report the day's news; to be ignored at their peril.

"But the dirtiest trick of all was saved for Yushchenko, wasn't it?"

"Yes; his poisoning. After that he must have realised that the authorities would never allow him to win."

Systemic mistakes of power by Kuchma and his cronies, dirty election tricks, plus an organized opposition worth voting for, all contributed to the mass protest. But almost no one thought the Ukrainians had the commitment to democratic values, or the stamina and willingness to defy the state in mass protest. On the contrary, almost everyone thought that civil society was too weak and a Prague 1989 scenario was impossible.

The presidential election results of October 31, 2004 showed Yushchenko to have won by a tiny margin, but because neither candidate achieved 50 percent of the vote, a runoff election was planned for three weeks later. As information emerged that the Yanukovych team had orchestrated a number of significant violations of voting procedure, people — often students from a youth movement called "PORA" (It's Time!) — took to the streets and formed a "tent city." Little by little the protest grew, and by the eve of the second-round election, thousands of peaceful protestors occupied Kyiv's main street and square. The early signs were ominous. Exit polls showed Yushchenko with a clear lead, but early results of actual ballot counts put Yanukovych ahead.

Knowing that it has long been a simple truth in Ukraine that getting the most votes doesn't mean you've won, I asked, "What was the tipping point that brought people to the streets? The poisoning of Yushchenko, seeing President Putin walk down Khreshchatyk like an old Soviet-style leader, or something else?"

"I think each person had a slightly different reason. 'No more,' was my thought. All values, outside the family, had become debauched."

I visited Ukraine in December 2004, and as I walked among the crowd, huddled and stamping feet to keep warm while listening to the politicians and rock bands on the concert stage in Maidan Nezalezhnosti (Independence Square), I had gained a sense of what he meant. There was no obvious intimidation, no anger was expressed, all generations were seemed to be represented, and I heard both Russian and Ukrainian being spoken. Those taking part had made an effort to show that they cared about their country, and that they were individuals, united with each other in their expectation for a better future. Perhaps this is why xenophobic Russia continually tries to undermine the credibility of the Orange Revolution: if it can happen in Kyiv it could happen in Moscow.

Konstantin had the rare gift of making a ballot sound exciting as he recalled the events of that chilly winter's day. With the votes counted, the Electoral Commission wasted no time in announcing Viktor Yanukovych as the winner of the second-round election and the third President of Ukraine. Congratulations were conveyed swiftly by Moscow, but the rest of the international community held back. Behind the scenes they had worked towards a fair election. The USA adopted visa bans and asset freezes on those impeding a fair electoral process and embassy staff provided food to demonstrators. Kuchma had been warned against an "engineered" communications blackout on election night, and diplomats had used their bodies (and diplomatic immunity) to prevent security forces from entering newspaper offices.

Within a few days, information leaked out that showed fraud on a massive scale. In Luhansk district in eastern Ukraine, the voter turnout was above 100 percent, and perhaps most audaciously of all, the Yanukovych team was found to be running a parallel computer server to collate the election results, to change them, and to substitute them.

Such revelations served to swell the numbers gathering daily in Maidan, which by many estimates regularly exceeded half a million people. The crowds were the revolution's biggest asset, ultimately forcing the authorities to back down, but it was skilful manoeuvring by Yushchenko and others who ensured there was no bloodshed.

With PORA preventing Kuchma from entering Parliament, he was forced to retreat to his villa outside Kyiv, where he cut a deal giving himself diplomatic immunity. In an atypical gesture, the Supreme Court reversed the pro-Yanukovych verdict and decreed a repeat runoff for December 26.

Only now did some of the major media operators switch over to supporting Yushchenko, as did some of the Kuchma elite who held controlling positions in the institutions of state. What followed at the end of December was one of the most invigilated elections in history, overseen by twelve thousand foreign observers and three hundred thousand local observers. Yushchenko won by a narrow margin and he was sworn in as President of Ukraine a month later.

"We certainly celebrated that day," announced Konstantin, casting a glance towards his wife, who was totally absorbed in the shenanigans of the soap opera. "A wrong had been righted. Democracy was the winner and expectations ran high. Very high."

An Opportunity Lost

What many outsiders chose to overlook was that fully 48 percent of the electorate voted for Viktor Yanukovych, a man whom they knew to be a convicted criminal who had orchestrated massive electoral fraud. The opposition had lost, but they had certainly not been crushed. And, in what many now regard as a strategic mistake, President Yushchenko initiated an immediate tour of major capitals. In Washington, members of Congress cheered and chanted his name as he stood to deliver a speech to announce that Ukraine was open for reform and for business. In doing so, he left Kyiv in hands of the renegades.

"Margaret Thatcher once wisely said," President Yushchenko later commented in an interview with *Welcome to Ukraine Magazine*, "and I like to repeat her words quite often: 'In order for a society to have a future, two things must be done, — social justice established and strong currency introduced.' This still holds true."[5]

Social justice was a fundamental expectation of the Orange Revolution — that people should be equal before the law — but Yushchenko seemed to forget this promise rather quickly. Though the Supreme Court ruled that there had been massive electoral fraud, no senior figures were charged; in fact, they were promoted. His commitment to punish the killer and those who ordered the killing of the beheaded journalist, Georgiy Gongadze, came to nought; in part, because he allowed Kuchma's Prosecutor General to remain in his post. Perhaps most incredulous of all is that Yushchenko's would-be assassin remains free, and is suspected to be living a comfortable life in Moscow. I asked Konstantin what went wrong.

"My father used to tell me," he recalled, "that when faced with a wily opponent, I should change the game. Play chess instead of chequers. That way you force him to walk away, or adapt to the new rules. Yushchenko's mistake was that he didn't change the rules when he had the chance, but he got caught in the same old game."

I was well aware of the events that followed. Just nine months after his inauguration, he defended a close ally against corruption charges. (In fact, Yushchenko is godfather to the man's daughters.) The matter got so out of hand that he sacked the entire cabinet of ministers, and created a rift with his Prime Minister, Tymoshenko. Yushchenko then granted Yanukovych amnesty from prosecution for his role in rigging the elections, and invited him to be his Prime Minister. Soon afterwards, Tymoshenko was accused of selling parliamentary seats for US$7 million each, but that didn't stop Yushchenko from reappointing her as Prime Minster yet again. The circus, it seemed, was back in town.

Nowadays, few articles about Ukraine appear in the international press. The political twists and turns and the allegiances and treacheries render the whole situation just too complicated to sustain reporting.

"So," I wondered, "if the President's biggest failure has been to establish consistency in governance and to make everyone feel equal in law, what is parliament's biggest failure?" They also have a significant responsibility; some would say an even bigger one given that they pass the laws.

"Well, to borrow Bill Clinton's phrase, 'it's the economy, stupid,'" snapped Konstantin. "Just look outside the window. The street scene hasn't changed in five years. Museum-piece trams ply the heavily potholed hill, Babushkas stand on cardboard and sell fruit and vegetables, new PVC windows reveal that a few are undertaking renovation, and new apartment blocks stand half-finished."

Most would seem to agree with him. A recent Pew Global Attitudes Survey indicated that when confronted with a choice between a good democracy and a strong economy, 80 percent of poor or middle-class Ukrainians choose a strong economy.[6] Sadly they have neither.

The Idea of Ukraine as a Nation

"Can we at least give the current political elite credit for rejuvenating the idea of Ukraine as a nation?" I proffered, knowing that in the Yushchenko administration the average age is forty-eight years, compared with sixty-eight for the previous administration. This difference of a generation gave impetus to the idea that a fresh image of Ukraine might emerge.

"Not really," lamented Konstantin, who looked increasingly like a man who could do with a drink. "Yushchenko, in particular, has looked to Ukraine's past — to our defeats and subjugation — for events to celebrate. It's an odd strategy given that different parts of the country have such different histories. It has been divisive and negative."

Pro-Yushchenko TV channels regularly commemorate the Ukrainian defeats at the Battle of Kruty, the Battle of Berestechko, and Ivan Mazepa's defeat at the Battle of Baturin. The most sombre event, of course, is the commemoration of Holodomor victims in late November. Amidst all the fugue and threnody, a cynic might suspect it is a government ploy to distract attention from the fact that they are incapable of solving the basic problems of society.

"You're not being cynical," responded Konstantin on hearing the idea. "That's realistic. Look at Italy, where corruption is rife. Billions have been invested in East Germany and look at the problems. Cyprus is a haven of white-collar money laundering, and Spain has an unemployment level not seen in my lifetime. No, no, Ukraine's problems will take decades to overcome."

He added, "If we're going to wallow here for long, we'll need a glass of vodka to see us through."

"Oh, no you don't, Kostya," snapped his wife, who had started packaging cosmetics for delivery. I noticed the sagging lower eyelids and hollowness in her cheeks.

"Well, in a few weeks time, we'll welcome a new President, so what does the future hold?" I questioned. Ignoring his wife's command, Konstantin brushed aside some pink sponge hair curlers and filled the shot glasses.

"Ukraine hasn't gained sufficient velocity to escape the pull of Russia and, perhaps, the very idea of Ukraine is just not sufficiently cohesive," he replied. "At best, we will muddle through, playing off Europe against Russia. At worst, we'll find we've exhausted the Europeans' patience, and our Russian brother's outstretched hand will greet us once again."

"You remind me of your melancholy national anthem!" I scolded him.

Concomitant with the fall of the Soviet Union, people began to sing the words of the anthem of the 1917 Ukrainian People's Republic, which was banned in Soviet times. When it was adopted by Ukraine as its national anthem, it created a stir because of its stolid title, *Ukraine Has Not Perished*. Whilst attesting to the long struggle and indomitable spirit of Ukrainians, the anthem also evokes images of a country struggling to assert itself.

He raised his glass and proposed a toast.

Just over a month later, on the day after the first round of the presidential election in January 2010, I strolled across Maidan in Kyiv. The ballot count was complete and it was clear that Yulia Tymoshenko and Viktor Yanukovych were the two candidates to go forward to the second round. The square was clean and showed none of the detritus — discarded leaflets, deflated balloons, bottles and cigarette stubs — that had accompanied the large crowds that gathered there during the 2005 presidential election.

On the previous evening a small group had gathered but apathy and a temperature of −16° Celsius had kept many people away. The 18 candidates' campaigns hadn't helped; they were much of a muchness, eastward leaning, and bearing the hallmarks of Soviet nostalgia. Talk of joining NATO was no longer fashionable.

As I walked across the empty square I was both alone and lonely. Unexpectedly, Konstantin had died just before New Year; of tiredness, if his wife was to be believed. I wondered whether he had sold his vote in his final days. In our last conversation he told me that he had sold it three times, to different candidates, during the 2005 campaign. (It is common for canvassers, working from door to door, to offer money in return for a pledge to vote for their candidate.) It was not so much for the money, he said, though the US$65 helped, but the satisfaction of clawing something back from candidates he viewed as thieves. He considered the direct election of a president as a farce in which only the rich could win and that the spending of US$1 billion — the estimated cost of the 2010 presidential election — was intolerable. Fairer, he thought, would be for parliament to elect the head of state.

In a widely predicted embarrassment, outgoing President Viktor Yushchenko polled just over five percent of the vote. During an interview he gave just prior to the voting he said that he had not wanted to be a politician and had never loved it. He expressed the wish to be remembered as a statesman rather than a politician. But whether history will be so kind to him remains to be seen.

The surprise of the first round of voting was the third place position of the little-known billionaire businessman Sergey Tigipka. Some people voted for him, they told me, because he was a fresh face in politics, others because of his good looks. Both criteria — a fresh face and good looks — appear to be sensible ways to judge candidates if you subscribe to the view, as Ukrainians do, that election promises never turn into reality.

By the time you read this you will know the outcome of the second round, and barring unforeseen circumstances the final round, of voting. Ukraine will have a new president; the fifth since independence.

As I stood beneath the statue of Bereynia I recalled Konstantin's toast the last time we met. His head was bowed low with his neck brimming over his collar. It was his signature pose that I will remember for as long as I remember him. He flicked his eyes towards me and said, "There is no politician who can unite the nation. We have the politicians we deserve. We must live with free hearts and look after ourselves, our family, and friends. That is the Cossack way, the Ukrainian way. We may be second among equals, but we are the indefatigable people of Ukraine."

CHRONOLOGY

BC

8000 BC	Neolithic tribes live in the Dnipro and Dniester valleys
800–100 BC	Organised society of Scythians and "Amazon" warriors
100 BC–600	Succession of tribes: Eastern Goths, Visigoths, Huns, and Avars

AD

400–500	Kyiv was founded
839	Kyivan Rus mentioned in the Bertynsky Chronicles
980–1015	Reign of Vladimir I (also known as Vladimir the Great)
988	Kyivan Rus accepts Christianity
1019–1054	Reign of Yaroslav the Wise
1113–1125	Reign of Vladimir II Monomakh
1147	Moscow was founded
1187	"Ukraine" first used to describe Kyiv and Galician lands
1234–1264	Reign of Danylo of Halych
1240	Mongol army captures and destroys Kyiv
1256	Lviv was founded
1362	Lithuania controls Kyiv
1387–1772	Poland controls Galicia
1475–1774	Turkey controls Crimea
1490	Earliest reference to the Cossacks
1550	Zaporizhska Sich (Cossack Fortress) was established
1569	Union of Lublin creates the Polish-Lithuanian Commonwealth
1596	Union of Brest creates the Uniate church
1648–1657	Bohdan Khmelnytsky rules as a Cossack hetman

1654	Treaty of Pereiaslav brings Cossacks under Muscovite rule
1657–1686	Russia, Poland, Turks and Cossacks fight for control of Ukraine
1686	Kyiv and lands east of the Dnipr controlled by Russia
1687–1708	Ivan Mazepa rules as a Cossack hetman
1710	Pylyp Orlyk rules as a Cossack hetman
1772	Habsburg Empire controls Galicia
1775	Catherine II destroys the Zaporizhska Sich
1783	Russia controls Crimea
1820	Sugar refineries established on Ukrainian territory
1840	Taras Shevchenko's publishes "The Kobza Player"
1848	Supreme Ruthenian Council established in Lviv
1861	Railroad built on Ukrainian territory (Peremyshl–Lviv)
1863	Russia prohibits Ukrainian language and literature
1870s	Industrialisation of the Donbas
1876	Edict of Ems bans Ukrainian language publishing and teaching
1890	First Ukrainian politial party formed in Lviv
1898	Mykhailo Hrushevsky publishes history of Ukraine-Rus
1900	First Ukrainian political party in the Russian Empire
1917	Nicholas II abdicates; Central Rada formed in Kyiv
1918	Establishment of the independent Ukrainian People's Republic
1918–1919	Ukrainian People's Republic declared in Lviv
1920	The Bolsheviks establish control over eastern Ukraine
1923	Allies recognise Polish sovereignty in Galicia
1929	Organisation of Ukrainian Nationalists (OUN) established
1932–1933	The Ukrainian famine
1937–1939	Purge sweeps Soviet Ukraine
1938–1949	Nikita Khrushchev is Communist Party leader in Ukraine
1939	Soviet Union controls Galicia

1941–1944	Nazi occupation of Ukraine
1942	Ukrainian Insurgent Army (UPA) established
1944	Crimean Tartars deported
1950s	Dissident organizations and illegal literature begins to appear
1954	Khrushchev gives Crimea to Soviet Ukraine
1963–1972	Petro Shelest is Communist Party leader in Ukraine
1972–1989	Volodymyr Shcherbytsky is Communist Party leader in Ukraine
1980s	Movement for the liberation of Ukraine is formed (Rukh Party)
1986	Chornobyl explodes
1988	One thousand years of Christianity celebrated
1990	Mass demonstrations and hunger strikes in Kyiv
1991	Ukraine declares independence
1991–1994	Presidency of Leonid Kravchuk
1992	Coupons replace rouble as new currency
1994	First Olympic gold medal for independent Ukraine
1994–2004	Presidency of Leonid Kuchma
1996	Ukrainian Constitution and new currency are adopted
1998	1933 famine is given official recognition
2004	The Orange Revolution
2004–2010	Presidency of Viktor Yushchenko
2010, February	Yulia Tymoshenko and Viktor Yanukovych compete to be President of Ukraine

NOTES

Pondering Ukraine's Controversial History

1   Hrushevsky, Mykhailo. Illustrated History of Ukraine. 1913. This was the first synthesis of Ukrainian history. Printed as ten volumes, it covered the period from pre-history to the 1660s. Hrushevsky died in suspicious circumstances in 1934. His daughter Kateryna and his nephew died in the gulags and his brother died whilst in exile in Kazakhstan. All of them were historians.

Cossacks and Vikings

1   Snowyd, D. *Sprit of Ukraine – The Ukrainian Contribution to World Culture.* United Nations, New York, 1935.
2   Härke, Heinrich. "Archaeologists and Migrations: A Problem of Attitude?" *Current Anthropology* (No.39, 1998) 19-45.
3   Permanent Representative of Ukraine to the Council of Europe. Available online www.mfa.gov.ua/coe/en/publication/content/804.html
4   Unknown author. "Fortieth Anniversary of the V.I. Lenin Dnipr Hydroelectric Station." *Gidrotekhnicheskoe Stroitel'stvo* (No. 12 December, 1972).
5   Durcheva, V.N., Kazachenko, A. N., Puchkova S. M. "Concrete Dam of the V.I. Lenin Dnipr Hydroelectric Station." *Gidrotekhnicheskoe Stroitel'stvo* (No. 7, July, 1986)
6   Michalonis Litvani. *De moribus Tartarorum Fragmina*, X. Basilliae, 1615.
7   Snowyd, D. *Sprit of Ukraine – The Ukrainian Contribution to World Culture.* United Nations, New York, 1935.

Steamy Business

1   Drucker, Peter. "Schumpeter and Keynes" *Forbes* (May 23, 1983).
2   *Great Soviet Encyclopedia.* State Publisher, 1926.
3   Simis, Constantine. *USSR: The Corrupt Society.* Simon and Schuster, 1982.
4   *Dictionary of Foreign Words.* 1987.

A Medal at any Cost

1   Available online: http://sports.jrank.org/pages/694/Bubka-Sergei--Bubka-Does-Jump-He-Flies.html
2   "Report of Ukraine on compliance with the European Sports Charter" *Council of Europe* (2006).
3   Edelman, Robert. "A Small Way of Saying 'No': Moscow Working Men, Spartak Soccer, and the Communist Party, 1900–1945" *American Historical Review* (Vol 107, No. 5, December 2002).

4   Romanov, Nikolai. "The First Step Towards the Olympics" *Olympic Panorama* (No:1, 1981).
5   Keys, Barbara. *The Soviet Union, Global Culture and the 1956 Melbourne Olympic Games.* California State University, Sacramento, 2005.
6   "Foreign News: The Costs of Temptation" *TIME* (October 22, 1956).
7   Vlasov, Yuri. "Ya Pravdu Rasskazhu Tebe Takuyu" (translated as "I'll Tell You this Truth") *Sovetsky Sport* (October 31, 1991)
8   Vlasov, Yuri. "Drugs and Cruelty" *Moscow News* (No 32, 1988).
9   Ter-Ovanesyan, Igor. "I declare war on Anabolics" *Moscow News* (No. 50, 1988).
10 Maraniss, David. *Rome 1960: The Olympics that Changed the World.* Simon and Schuster, 2008.
11 Maslachenko, Vladimir. "Ya Po-Prezhnemu V Igre" (translated as "I'm Still in the Game") *Sobesedni,* (No. 46, 1990).
12 Riordan, James. *Sport in Soviet Society.* Cambridge University Press, 1977.
13 Riordan, James. "The Rise and Fall of Soviet Olympic Champions" *Olympica* (Vol. II, 1993).

Feast or Famine

1   Sheeter, Laura. BBC News, Kiev. November 24, 2007. Available online: http://news.bbc.co.uk/2/hi/europe/7111296.stm
2   Muggeridge, Malcolm. "The Soviet and the Peasantry: an Observer's Notes" *Manchester Guardian* (March 27, 1933).
3   Jones, Gareth. "Famine in Russia, an Englishman's Story: What He Saw on a Walking Tour" *Manchester Guardian* (March 30, 1933).
4   Duranty, Walter. "Russian Hungry but not Starving" *New York Times* (March 31, 1933).
5   Lyons, Eugene. *Assignment in Utopia.* Greenwood Press Reprint, 1937.
6   Chernomyrdin, Viktor. "Russia won't apologize for Great Famine" *Kyiv Post* (August 6, 2003).

Politicians and Partisans

1   Golovanov, Vassily. *Literary Gazette.* (February 8, 1989).
2   Neufeld, Dietrich. *A Russian Dance of Death.* Hyperion Press, 1977.
3   "Petlura Trial" *TIME* (November 7, 1927).
4   Trotsky, Leon. *My Life.* Charles Schribner, 1930
5   Duke, David. *Jewish Supremacism—My awakening on the Jewish Question.* Free Speech Press, 2003.
6   Churchill, Winston. "Zionism versus Bolshevism: A Struggle for the Soul of the Jewish People" *Illustrated Sunday Herald* (February 8, 1920).
7   Kuromiya, Hiroaki. "The Political Leaders of Ukraine, 1938-1989: The Burden of History" *The National Council for Eurasian and East European Research* (October 25, 2004).
8   Unknown author. *Murdered by Moscow.* Ukrainian Publishers Limited, 1962.

9   Investigations include: the 1945-46 Nuremburg Trials; an International Commission in The Hague in 1959; and a study by legal historian Alfred-Maurice de Zayas in 1975.
10 proUA.com. Available online http://ua.proua.com/news/2007/11/15/092742.html November 15, 2007
11 Kuromiya, Hiroaki. "The Political Leaders of Ukraine, 1938-1989: The Burden of History" *The National Council for Eurasian and East European Research* (October 25, 2004).

In Shevchenko Land

1   Unknown author. *Shevchenko Land.* Kiev Mistetsvo, 1989.
2   Shevchenko, Taras. *Shevchenko, Taras. Selected Works:Poetry and Prose.* Compiled by the Ukrainian Shevchenko Jubilee Committee. Edited by John Weir. Progress Publishers, 1964.
3   Valuev, Pyotr. *Valuev Circular.* (July 18, 1863).
4   Snowyd, D. *Sprit of Ukraine – The Ukrainian Contribution to World Culture.* United Nations, New York, 1935.
5   *Selected Poems.* Translated from the Ukrainian by Gladys Evans. Dnipro Publishers 1975.
6   Wilson, Andrew. *The Ukrainians: Unexpected Nation.* Yale University Press, 2000. (Cited in chapter 5, footnote 49, p. 88).
7   Kunitz, Stanley and Hayward, Max. *Poems of Akhmatova.* Mariner Books, 1973.
8   Drutt, Matthew. *Exhibition Catalogue, Solomon R. Guggenheim Museum.* New York, 2003.
9   Luckyj, George Stephen Nestor. *Literary Politics in the Soviet Ukraine, 1917-1934.* Books for Libraries Press,1971.
10 Ehrenburg, Ilya. *The Thaw.* Harvill, 1955.

Taking the Medicine

1   Arnaudova, Albena. "Health Questions about the New EU Neighbours" *World Health Organisation, Regional Office for Europe* (2005).
2   Lerner V., Margolin J., Witztum E. "Vladimir Bekhterev: His Life, His Work and the Mystery of his Death" *History of Psychiatry* (Vol. 16, No. 2, 2005) 217-227.
3   Krull, Marianne. *Freud and his Father.* W. W. Norton, 1986.
4   National Museum of Medicine. Available online http://www.histomed.kiev.ua/agapit/agp00.html
5   Mistiaen, Veronique. "Time and the Great Healer" *The Guardian* (November 2, 2002). See also Waksman, Selman Abraham. *My Life with The Microbes.* Simon and Schuster, 1954.

Religious Wars

1   Snowyd, D. *Sprit of Ukraine – The Ukrainian Contribution to World Culture.* United Nations, New York, 1935.

2   "In the Service of the Cult" *Izvestia* (March 10, 1953).
3   Merridale, Catherine. *Night of Stone: Death and Memory in Twentieth Century Russia.* Viking Penguin, 2001.
4   Zbarsky, Ilya. *Lenin's Embalmers.* Harvill Press, 1999.
5   Soviet Extraordinary State Commission. Nuremburg Document USSR-006
6   Yakunin, Gleb. Vice Chairman of the parliamentary commission studying the role of the social structures in Russia. *Woodstock Report* (Woodstock Theological Center, October 1992).
7   Armes, Keith. "Chekists in Cassocks: The Orthodox Church and the KGB" *Institute for the Study of Conflict, Ideology and Policy, Boston University.* Citing the press conference of the Russian Federation Supreme Soviet Commission to Investigate the Causes and Circumstances of the Putsch (the Ponomarev Commission). Foreign Broadcast Information Service, December 26, 1991.
8   Armes, Keith. "Chekists in Cassocks: The Orthodox Church and the KGB" *Institute for the Study of Conflict, Ideology and Policy, Boston University*

Sex and the Soviets

1   Batkis, Grigorii. *The Sexual Revolution in Russia.* Moscow Institute of Soviet Hygiene, 1923.
2   Goscilo, Helena. *Dehexing Sex: Russian Womanhood During and After Glasnost* University of Michigan Press, 1996. Citing Koppel,Ted. "Sex in the Soviet Union" (60 Minutes. January 1991)
3   Cortemiglia, Vittoria Luda di. "Trafficking in Minors for Commercial Sexual Exploitation, Ukraine" *United Nations Interregional Crime and Justice Research Institute.* (2005)..
4   "Sociological Survey of 636 Women in 11 Cities" *Ukrainian Institute for Social Research*, Report UISR01 (September 2000).
5   "The Socio-Economic Impact of HIV/AIDS in Ukraine" *International Labour Organisation* (2005).
6   Kuprin, Alexandre. *Yama,* John Hamilton Limited, 1930.
7   *Selected Writings of Alexandra Kollontai* Allison and Busby, 1977.
8   Healey, Dan. *Homosexual Desire in Revolutionary Russia: The Regulation of Sexual and Gender Dissent.* University of Chicago Press, 2001.
9   Gutman, Carol. *The Legacy of Dr. Lamaze: The Story of the Man who Changed Childbirth.* St. Martin's Press, 2001.
10 I. Velvovsky, K. Platonov, V. Ploticher, and E. Shugom. *Painless Childbirth Through Psychoprophylaxis, Obstetrics and Gynecology.* Leningrad, 1954.
11 Murray, Nora. *I Spied for Stalin.* Wilfred Funk Inc., 1951.
12 Murray, John. *A Spy Called Swallow: The True Story of Nora, the Russian Agent.* W.H. Allen, 1978.

At the Coal Face

1   Krawchenko, Bohdan. *Social Change and National Consciousness in Twentieth Century Ukraine.* Canadian Institute of Ukrainian Studies, 1985.

2   Lenin, V.I. (1958-1965). Complete Works. 5th Edition, Volume 45. State Publishing House of Political Literature.

3   Resolution of the plenum of the 1st All-Union Stakhanovite Conference in The Kremlin, December 1935.

4   "Heroes of Labor" *TIME* (December 16, 1935). 26-27

5   White, Stephen. *Russia's New Politics — The Management of a Postcommunist Society.* Cambridge University Press, 2000.

6   Fitzpatrick, Sheila. *In the Shadow of Revolution.* Princeton University Press, 2000.

7   Fitzpatrick, Sheila. *In the Shadow of Revolution.* Princeton University Press, 2000.

8   Chekaliuk, Emmanuil B. Paper presented at All-Union Conference on Petroleum and Petroleum Geology, Moscow, 1968.

9   Krayushkin, Vladilen. Paper presented at 7th International Symposium on the Observation of the Continental Crust through Drilling, New Mexico, 1994.

Bits, Bytes, Trits, and Trytes

1   Gogol, Nikolai V. *On the Architecture of the Present Day.* Vol. 6. Moscow, 1959.

2   Malinovsky, Boris.N. *Pioneers of Soviet Computing.* Translated edition Anne Fitzpatrick, 2007.

3   Ware, Willis H. (Editor). "Soviet Computer Technology, 1959" Report of the USA-USSR Cross Cultural Exchange.

4   Malinovsky, Boris N. *Pioneers of Soviet Computing.* Translated edition Anne Fitzpatrick, 2007.

5   Swade, Doron. "A museum curator suggests Russia's BESM supercomputer may have been superior to ours during the Cold War" *INC Magazine* (June 1996).

6   Goroshko, Ludmila. "Ukraine: Hackers School" *Computer Crime Research Center* (April 26, 2004).

7   Zemanek, Heinz. "Eulogy: Viktor Mikhailovich Glushkov, 1923—1982" *Annals of the History of Computing* (Vol. 4, No 2, 1982).

8   "Father of the Cell Phone" *Economist* (Technology Quarterly, June 4, 2009).

9   Mertz, Richard, "Interview with Jacob Rabinow" *Archives Center,* Smithsonian National Museum of American History (November 23, 1970).

10 Balanced Ternary is different from numerical ternary that uses 0, 1 and 2.

Touring Crimea

1   Otto Pohl, J. *Ethnic Cleansing in the USSR, 1937-1949.* Greenwood Publishing Group, 1999. Citing Bugai, Nikolai F. "They Must be Deported"

2   Russian State Archive of Social-Political History (fond 17, opis 44, delo.759, l.103).

3   Tolstoy, Leo. *The Sevastopol Sketches.* Penguin Classics, 2007.

4   Clarke, Edward Daniel. *Travels in Various Countries of Europe, Asia and Africa.* Vol. 2. 1816.

5   Twain, Mark. *Innocents Abroad.* Signet Classics, 1966.

Whirlybirds and Witches

1   *Odessa News* (February 14, 1918) 2.
2   *Bor'ba.* The newspaper of Odesa's Socialist Revolutionary Party (July 10, 1918).
3   *Air Pictorial Magazine,* 1958
4   For an excellent account read Pennington, Reina and John Ericksey. *Wings, Women and War: Soviet Women in World War II Combat.* University of Kansas Press, 2002.
5   Hauptmann Johannes Steinhoff, Commander of II./JG 52.

Zoos, Scientists, and Evolution

1   Limonov, Eduard. *The Young Scoundrel.* Translation by John Dolan. University of Otago, Department of English, 1997.
2   Joravsky, David. *The Lysenko Affair.* University of Chicago Press, 1986. Citing Mitin, M.B. (1939).
3   Birstein, Vadim. *The Perversion of Knowledge: The True Story of Soviet Science.* Basic Books, 2001.

The Chief Designer

1   *Encyclopaedia Britanica* 10th Edition (1902).
2   Malashenkov, Dmitri. Institute for Biological Problems in Moscow. Report presented at the World Space Congress in Houston, Texas, October 2002.
3   Khrushchev, Sergei N. *My Father, Nikita Khrushchev.* Rhode Island, 1957.
4   Various versions of this story are available online.
5   Lockhart, Robin Bruce. *Reilly: Ace of Spies.* Hippocrene Books, 1986.
6   Cook, Andrew. *Ace of Spies: The True Story of Sidney Reilly.* Tempus Publishing, 2002.

Presidents and the People

1   Nahaylo, Bohdan. *The Ukrainian Resurgence.* University of Toronto Press,1999.
2   "Bush Sr. Clarifies 'Chicken Kiev' Speech" *The Washington Times* (May 23, 2004).
3   Various versions of this story are available online.
4   For legal aspects of the trial see: Nichols, Philip M. "United States versus Lazarenko: Filling in Gaps in Support and Regulation of Transnational Relationships" The Wharton School of the University of Pennsylvania.
5   "Interview with Viktor Yushchenko" *Welcome to Ukraine* (No.1, 2000).
6   Pew Research Center "End of Communism Cheered but Now with More Reservations — The Pulse of Europe 2009: 20 Years After the Fall of the Berlin Wall" *Global Attitudes Project.* (February 11, 2009).

INDEX

Breinigsville, PA USA
11 May 2010
237827BV00004B/12/P

9 780956 512901